AF540504

Challenges for a Mega City

The Author

U.S. Jolly was Principal Commissioner in the Delhi Development Authority. He was invited twice, in 1980, to the University of Birmingham, United Kingdom under the Colombo Plan for Professional Studies on Management of Urban Development and Management of Urban Renewal. He has wide experience of more than 35 years in Urban Development and as Head of the Department of Lands and Housing. Large scale acquisition of land in major project areas of Dwarka, Rohini and Narela was done during his tenure. He was associated with large scale Urban Renewal Programme in Delhi involving Resettlement of 2.4 lakh families.

He has contributed a good number of papers in professional journals and magazines on urban development, housing, slum upgradation, environment and development, urban sustainability, traffic and transportation and values in administration. Also he has participated in various national and international conferences and seminars on urban development, human settlement and administrative values. Presently he is associated with AMDA as adviser (Capacity Building).

Challenges for a Mega City

(Delhi—A Planned City with Unplanned Growth)

U.S. JOLLY

Former Principal Commissioner
Delhi Development Authority

CONCEPT PUBLISHING COMPANY, PVT. LTD.
NEW DELHI-110059

ISBN-13-978-81-8069-666-4 **ISBN-10-81-8069-666-9**

First Published 2010

Published and Printed by

Concept Publishing Company Pvt. Ltd.
Regd. Office:
A/15-16, Commercial Block, Mohan Garden
New Delhi-110059 (India)
Phones : 25351460, 25351794, *Fax* : 091-11-25357109
Email : publishing@conceptpub.com,
Website: www.conceptpub.com

Editorial Office:
H-13, Bali Nagar, New Delhi-110 015, India.

Cataloging in Publication Data-- *Courtesy:* D.K. Agencies (P) Ltd. <docinfo@dkagencies.com>

Jolly, U. S.
Challenges for a mega city : Delhi, a planned city with unplanned growth / U.S. Jolly.
p. cm.
Includes index.
ISBN 13: 9788180696664 ISBN 10: 8180696669

1. Urbanization--India--Delhi--History. 2. City planning--India--Delhi. I. Title.

DDC 711.4095456 22

Dedicated
to

My Respected Mother

Ram Rakhi

To Whom I Owe Everything
In My Life

PREFACE

To me, Delhi is more than a city. I have seen it growing step by step. I have grown with the city and city has grown with me. I can still see before my eyes the various facets of the city down the years – a city with a very thin population; a city with personal relations where no one was unknown in the neighbourhood; a city with a friendly character and a city close to nature. Even the heat of summer and cold of winter were different from those today. Everyone in the neighbourhood was a friend. Life was simple. There was no hassle on roads, no heavy traffic, no accidents. Distances were covered by walking or cycling or on public transport. Most of the houses around the neighbourhood consisted of a single storey – half built or fully built. There were no mansions. Instead of competition we lived through cooperation. Travelling from Lajpat Nagar to Tilak Nagar even on cycle would take forty-five minutes to one hour. This was all in sixties. No pressure was felt on physical infrastructure like roads etc. The required social infrastructure in the form of hospitals, schools and dispensaries available readily matched with the population requirement. It was a harmonious city.

Then in the early seventies I started to see the changes all around. The real process of urbanization had started. More people were seen on roads and market places. Construction activity was also picking up. The Delhi Development Authority was also seen as an agency contributing to Delhi's development. Its residential schemes were a relief to those who needed houses. Its development was primarily in South and West Delhi. Land development work had also started in areas like Shalimar Bagh along the Ring Road. By 1971 Delhi's population was about forty lakhs — more than double during the last twenty years. Work in areas like Nehru Place District Centre had started. A number on unauthorized colonies had also come up in East, South and West Delhi that were regularized in 1977. Massive Resettlement Programmes were undertaken by the DDA and 2,40,000 plots of 25 sq. yds. each were developed and allotted in twenty seven Resettlement Colonies. An area around Bela Road, which was cleared in late sixties, was developed in beautiful greens. Large unauthorized settlements beyond Kalkaji and Hauz Khas had come up. Extensive planning was conducted for the Trans-Yamuna area and a large number of cooperative group housing societies were allotted land. This was an important landmark for the Trans- Yamuna area where development in a large tract of land was to come up in planned and regulated manner. Areas like Dilshad Garden and Mayur Vihar gained popularity through the Delhi Development Authority's schemes. From Wazirabad to Dilshad Garden on the northern side of G.T. Shahdara Road one could see extensive development. The work was going on as per the Plan but one could see the deviations also in the form of unplanned growth.

Then came another phase of 1980's when the city had actually grown. One could see the pressure on land and urban infrastructure. The personal relations between the neighbours of sixties disappeared because of mobility of population. People had added additional storeys to their houses. New neighbours had arrived in the form of tenants. A feeling started to pervade that Delhi had become a city of strangers. The Delhi Development Authority had launched a major Rohini Residential Scheme and also started working on implementation of its largest Residential Registration Scheme for flats known as the New Pattern Scheme of 1979. Though more land was acquired the acquisition and development process was slow. Existing areas were getting over-densified including special areas like Karol Bagh, Paharganj and the walled city. Many more *jhuggi-jhampri* clusters had come up all over the city. Some flyovers in South Delhi and Bridge on Yamuna River were constructed in view of the Asiad 1982 Games. In view of this important event Jawaharlal Nehru Stadium, Indira Gandhi Indoor Stadium, the Asiad

Games Village Complex and the shooting range etc. were constructed. But this was the time when population pressure was building up as more and more people came to the city for jobs.

Then in nineties it became a city of Total Cosmopolitan Character. It was a mixed city of planned and un-planned pattern. Government Economics Liberalization Policy gave opportunities to the Young Educated Youth and there was pressure on the city infrastructure. That was the time when one could see the unauthorized construction in the existing areas in the form of additional coverage or extra floor. More than one thousand Unauthorized Colonies had come up and by the late nineties their number increased to fifteen hundred or more. Similarly slum clusters had grown up in many parts of the city and existing slum clusters were getting densified. Unauthorized Colonies were growing so fast that no green buffer land was left between Delhi-Haryana and Delhi-U.P. border in South and East Delhi. In Trans-Yamuna and West Delhi a number of residential areas had been Unauthorizedly converted to industrial areas. Residences were converted into shops. Government lands were encroached. Land acquisition and development having slowed down it further led to unauthorized colonization. In the late nineties the seriousness of the situation was realized by the authorities but the urban forces were more strong than the planning process. In 2001 the city population had reached 1,37,00,000 and inspite of Master Plan 2001 the city had grown in an unauthorized manner because of population pressure and failure of enforcement.

Thereafter one could see the large population living in unauthorized colonies, slum clusters, *jhuggi-jhompri* clusters, unauthorized industrial area, unauthorized commercial areas, unauthorized dairies and urban settlements beyond Lal Doras of Village Abadi. Their number was more than 50 per cent of Delhi's Population. That is why I call it **Delhi a Planned City With Unplanned Growth** . I am witness to all these stages of the Development of the City, phases through which it has passed, efforts made by the Government and bureaucratic policies, role of political framework and also unconcerned attitude of Delhites who are also responsible for the present condition of the city.

Though we see the effort of the Government in improving the infrastructure in the form of road network, construction of flyovers, constructing new bridges over the Yamuna River, putting up new improved street lights, beautification of city through green developments but the fact remains that Delhi instead of growing on planning norms has grown in an unauthorized manner. The unauthorized growth has been regularized through regulatory mechanism. This has been the case for unauthorized colonies, *jhuggi-jhompri* clusters, encroachment on public land, unauthorized development, unauthorized construction in the flats, unauthorized additional floors in the existing areas, unauthorized development in urban villages and the periphery of such villages, unauthorized dairies, unapproved industrial areas and unapproved commercial activity. It has become a practice over the years to regularize the unauthorized activities rather than regulating the growth as per planning norms. I had started this book in 2003. The conditions in the city are changing so fast whether these are relating to unauthorized residential areas converted into commercial use, orders of the Government to regularize unauthorized colonies, orders of the Court to seal the misused properties and orders of the Government to regularize unapproved industrial areas. Even in terms of infrastructures, population and pressure of vehicles on Delhi Roads, the situation changes daily. I had to update my information so that it speaks for the condition of Delhi as on today. There are some repetitions about population figure and also about Relocation of Squatters but this repetition was essential for the convenience and clear understanding of the facts and sequence by the readers. This was essential to explain the relevance of events.

Since the urban forces in Delhi are more powerful than the planning process, we see the present situation where Delhi has grown Unauthorizedly inspite of the fact that it had plans since

1911 when the Britishers shifted the capital from Calcutta to Delhi. We had Delhi Improvement Trust, Delhi Development Authority, Master Plan for Delhi –1962 and also Master Plan for Delhi for 2001 and 2021. Inspite of these plans major population of the city forms part of unauthorized growth. It needs strong conviction, commitment on the part of the authorities and sincerity and restraint on the part of citizens to make Delhi a respectable, livable and harmonious city. We should endeavour to make Delhi a city of hope, a city of aspiration, a city of fulfillment and a city that smiles.

I owe special thanks to my daughter Dr. Kanwar Sonali, who herself has four books to her credit, for giving valuable suggestions on the formation of chapters, the process of writing down my personal experiences, guidance on the placement of content and constant exhortion to bring out a book that would be different from others. She wanted my vast field experience to be shared with others. Time that she should have ideally dedicated to her little son Amitoj was given to this book. Rather, I should say thanks to little Amitoj who allowed her to work on the book. My daughter Dr. Kanwar Supreet also deserves special thanks — she constantly kept me reminding while herself studying in the United States, to give sufficient time to the book, which she wanted to be launched this year. My son Prabhnoor not only gave valuable suggestions but also edited certain chapters. He believes in quality and perfection. His working schedule with a multinational company was quite constricting but he still took out time for some detailed editing work. My wife Dr. S.K. Jolly always wanted me to write about my experiences while I was associated with the City's development. She is a source of strength and it gives me great pleasure to acknowledge her support. Ekta, who helped with the typing in order to make edits and also add more content, deserves special thanks.

25 May, 2009 **U.S.Jolly**
New Delhi

CONTENTS

List of Colour Photos

List of Tables

1 THE HISTORY OF DELHI

The history of a city is not only the history of its rulers or those who were ruled over but it is also the history of the evolution of human settlements. Human settlements, many of which have now assumed the shapes of large towns, cities, metropolises or mega metropolises, have grown with time through the various phases of urban development. However, it is not necessary that each small settlement will grow into a large city. For example, a place like Khajurao, though of religious, historic and architectural significance, has not grown significantly. Similar is the case of Kurukshetra and many other settlements. More often than not, major cities have grown near rivers or other sources of water. In general, the growth of urban settlements depends on their location and connectivity. Delhi was almost in the center of undivided India and also on the banks of the Yamuna River. Even the ruins of smaller settlements, which came up around Delhi and were marginalized in history, have contributed in one way or the other in the development of present day Delhi. For instance, the setting up of Shahjahanabad was also important for the development of modern-day Delhi since Sher Garh and Ferozabad, which we now call Ferozshah Kotla, were quite close to the place where Shahjahanabad was established. Even the Britishers had the locational advantage of Delhi in mind when they shifted their capital from Calcutta to Delhi. Once a city is specialized either in terms of its administrative advantage or religious sanctity, like the holy cities of Haridwar and Varanasi, or business potential like Bombay, it develops very fast. In essence, the growth of Delhi is in no small part due to its geographical location and unique position as the seat of administration and the capital of India. The city has, therefore, inherited rich historical, geographical and administrative advantages. The first chapter, The History of Delhi, is a reflecti , on these urban trends.

Delhi possesses a long cultural, social and economic history. It has lived through centuries. It has encountered and assimilated various cultures. It represents great architectural design and planning concepts. It has a very glorious history of communal tolerance, and no neighbourhood in Delhi better exemplifies this than Chandni Chowk, where we see a temple, a mosque and historic gurudwara all in co-existing in close proximity.

The city has passed through various stages of development and decay and is thus often referred to as a city of Several Cities. The Qutub Minar and the area built around it speak of an era of architectural richness and communal harmony. This city was known as Lal Kot, the name given by Raja Angad of the Tomar Dynasty. It later evolved into Quilla Rai Pithora, named after Prithvi Raj Chauhan. During the 12th Century the city was invaded by Mohammed Ghauri who defeated Prithvi Raj Chauhan. Ghauri left his new kingdom in the hands of Alla-ud-din-Khilji who kept Lal Kot as its capital till 1303. After defeating the Rajputs, Alla-ud-din-Khilji built another city at Siri (what we call as Siri Fort today). The third city of Delhi, which we today call Tughlaqabad, was built by Ghias-ud-din-Tughlaq. Delhi continued to remain a place of attraction for new rulers around the region. Next in line was Mohammed-bin-Tughlaq who constructed the fourth city known as Jahanpanah. The gradual process of change continued with the passage of time and this time it was Feroz-shah-Tughlaq who founded the Ferozabad, called the fifth city. Following the Tughlaqs Delhi entered the glorious era of the Mughals who left rich archeological reminiscences of their unique architecture, culture and way of living.

Delhi has lived through centuries and has a long and glorious history. It's history is one of courage, dedication, an urge to live, a spirit to achieve and passion. The various ruins of past civilizations present in modern-day Delhi, whether they be in the form of pottery pieces, big and small stones, mortar, monuments or art, can trace its evolution from its first settlement till its present-day status as the capital of modern-day India. If we delve into further details of the individual historical kingdoms. as reflected by the historians and archeologists, we can identify more than 7 "kingdoms" or "Delhis", which prospered and perished with the passage of time. The evolution of Delhi over the annals of history is reflected in table 1.1.

Table 1.1 : Chronological History of Delhi's Development

Order	*Sl.No.*	*Date*	*Name of the Settlement*	*Founders*	*Present Probable Site*
I	1.	900 B.C.	Indraprastha	Yodhistra	Purana Quilla
	2.	1020 A.D.	Suraj Kund	Anang Pal	Suraj Kund
	3.	1052	Lal Kot	Prithviraj Chauhan	Near Qutab Site
	4.	1180	Quilla Rai Pithora	Prithviraj Chauhan	Near Qutub Site
II	5.	1301	Siri	Alla-ud-din-Khilji (1295–1315)	Near Hauz Khas
III	6.	1321-1323	Tughlaqabad	Gayasudin Tughlaq (1321–1325)	Tughlaqabad
	7.	1325	Adilabad	Mohammad Tughlaq (1325–1351)	Near Tughlaqabad
IV	8.	1327	Jahanpanah	Mohammad Tughlaq	Between Siri and Raipithora
V	9.	1354	Ferozabad	Feroz-Shah Tughlaq (1351–1388)	Near Feroz Shah Kotla Stadium
VI	10.	1530 (1533?)	Dinpanah and Sher Garh	Humayun (1530, 1538;1555-1556) Left incomplete; Completed by Sher Shah Suri (1538-1545)	Purana Quilla
VII	11.	1638	Shahjahanabad (1638-1649)	Shahjahan (1628-1658)	Old Delhi (Walled City)
	12.	1912 (1911)	Delhi	British Capital	North of walled city Shahjahanbad; Old (Civil lines) Secretariat etc.
	13.	1931 (opened)	New Delhi	British Capital (designed by Lutian and Baker)	New Delhi around Rashtrapati Bhawan and Coannuaght Place Area
	14.	Aug. 15 1947–Date	New Delhi	Capital of free India (subsequently designed by T.P.O, T.C.P.O. and DDA)	Present Day New Delhi.

An important phase in Delhi's history started when the Mughals came to power. The great emperor Humayun chose the erstwhile Indraparastha to craft Delhi's sixth city. It was subsequently refortified by Sher Shah Suri and renamed Sher Garh. Finally it was Shahjahan, who was known for his artistic and creative taste, who founded the walled city, which we even today call Shahjahanabad. This era gave Delhi a wonderful heritage and a unique character of architecture in the form of imposing structures such as the Jama Masjid and the Red Fort. The architectural remains of that era still remind us of the gloriousness of those times. Cities, which were built from Ferozabad till Tughlaqabad, were all on the southern side of the Shahjahanabad, with Qutub Minar, or the Pithora Garh, being the extreme South. The massiveness of Tughlaqabad Fort, the historical monuments of the Mahrauli area, Pithora Garh wall, Purana Quilla and Siri Fort Area all speak of the indelible uniqueness and urban development concepts of that period.

Shahjahanabad, which extends about 4 km. along the right bank of Yamuna was the major urban settlement of that time. The city is divided into two somewhat equal portions by the Chandni Chowk, which runs for just over 1.6 km. from the Lahori Gate of the city to the Lahori Gate of the Red Fort. These were at that time called as Lahore Gate as the present Kashmiri Gate and Ajmeri Gate were called as Kashmir Gate and Ajmer Gate. Lahori Gate, Kashmiri Gate, Delhi Gate, Turkman Gate and Ajmeri Gate were the entry points for Shahjahanabad. Hauz Kazi, Lal Quan, Chawri Bazar and Jama Masjid etc. speak of rich architectural cultural heritage of that period. The settlements were in Katras, which are still seen as symbols of homogeneous community living. Chawri Bazar, Dariba and Nai Sarak still have a commercial attraction for Delhites from other parts of modern-day Delhi and outsiders. Shahjahanabad was a unique blend of urban planning and cultural assimilation. It continued in the same fashion even in the beginning of 20th century as is reflected from the fact that in 1901 of the total population of 2,08,000, 88,000 were

Mohammedans, 1,14,000 were Hindus, 2,000 were Christians and 4,000 were of other religions (Figure as per Census of 1901).

Shahjahanabad was originally planned for a population of 60,000. Now with the passage of time and an increase in commerce and trade activity about 10 lakh people are reported to be living in the area. Some localities like Dariba reflect the highest congestion rate in the world with a density of about 900 persons per acre in certain parts. About 66 per cent of the households in Shahjahanabad have only one living room. Nearly 38 per cent of its residents live below the poverty line and 34 per cent have a marginal subsistence level. Only about 6 per cent of its residents are considered to be well off. In most of the streets there is retail shopping on the ground floors and residences on the upper floors. The settlements are called Katras. These are mostly in a dilapidated condition on account of their age and poor maintenance. Consequently, rentals are very low. The walled city has a total area of 570 hectare which is sub-divided into various zones and sub-zones, most being of mixed land use character. The area lacks social infrastructure, even though it is surrounded by Lutiens' Delhi on its south side, Civil Lines on the north, Karol Bagh on the west and the Yamuna on the east. Since the population in the walled city is at a saturation point and there is no proper infrastructure available, many residents have opted to move out from the walled city. The trend of population in the walled city is reflected in table 1.2.

Table 1.2 : Population Trend in the Walled City

Census Year	*Population*	*Rate (Persons per year)*
1951	3,81,800	
1961	4,20,000	+3820
1971	4,09,000	-1100
1981	3,99,915	- 909
1991	3,50,159	-4976
1998	2,80,000	-7016

Similarly, there has been a drastic change in the land use

pattern over the years. In 1971 residential use was 34.6 per cent of the total, which came down to 24 per cent in 1991. Similarly commercial-use area, which was only 8.7 per cent area in 1971, increased to 24 per cent in 1991. Though the 1991 census shows that 17 per cent of the area was under parks and playgrounds if one does not take into account the open space with the Jama Masjid and Gandhi Ground then the remaining open space is only 6.6 per cent. These statistics show that more and more people are moving out of the walled city for better lifestyles elsewhere.

The two monumental structures in the Walled City are the Red Fort and the Jama Masjid. The Red Fort was built on the banks of the Yamuna River adjacent to Slim Garh Fort. The Chandani Chowk connects the Red Fort (seat of the Emperor) on its east and Fateh Puri Masjid (seat of the God) on its west. The whole walled city development is a combination of slum Katras, *Mohallas*, Bazars, *Phataks*, *Kuchas*, *Sarais* and *Galis*. A number of houses with a common gate constitute a Katra. In some cases even a big house with an enclosed courtyard and a gate is treated as a Slum Katra. A *Mohalla* is defined as an area of residential and commercial activity fronting on a spine street. At times, a *Mohalla* is identified with the socio-economic group of its residents. A few Katras can also be part of a large *Mohalla*. The market place is called the Bazar, and we see many examples of Bazars in the Walled City — Chawri Bazar, Sita Ram Bazar Kanari Bazar etc. The gate, or entry point, for a settlement is generally called a Phatak. Similarly, we have *Kuchas* in the walled city. It is a Persian term which means a small lane or alley. In reality we sometimes encounter *Kuchas* as large as a *Mohalla* or a *Phatak*. A *Kucha* also represents a specific community. During the Mughal period the *Kuchas* were probably exclusive residential areas for Hindus and Muslims. Another Persian term commonly used while describing the walled city's layout is the *Sarai*, which literally means a lodging house or inn, especially for Muslim pilgrims or travellers. The large numbers of narrow lanes in the walled city, called *Galis*, have houses and small shops on either sides. The *Gali* is the main approach of each house. In the early days of the walled city, living there implied having a friendly neighbourhood and general social cohesiveness. With the limited needs of its citizens and minimum hassles involved in living there the walled city was complete by itself.

Then arrived the British: this was the end of the Mughal era and beginning of a new one: of a new civilization, new tastes and preferences, and a new administrative set up. In 1911 the British decided to shift their capital from Calcutta to Delhi. Two prominent British architects of that time, Sir Edwin Lutyens and Herbert Baker, were assigned the job to create a new capital for the Empire. They envisaged the capital as a Garden City with wide avenues. The planners wanted the city to reflect the prestige and splendor of the British Raj. Their vision eventually bore fruit and New Delhi was born as the new capital of India. The design of New Delhi, with its wide roads, spacious bungalows, the magnificent President House at Raisina Hills and the Parliament House Building speak of the magnificent architectural vision of its creators — Lutyens and Baker.

Initially the Secretariat was built what is known today as Old Secretariat near the University Campus. Soon they decided to build the capital at Raisina Hills. This is where we have the President House, Parliament House, Government Offices and Bungalows for Senior Officers. The basic character and architecture of this area is still preserved.

In 1922 a small office called the Nazul Office was set up with 10-12 officers to review the development of New Delhi. In 1937 the Nazul Office was upgraded and the Delhi Improvement Trust was set up, and development outside the walled city in areas like Karol Bagh, which is called western extension area, and Kamla Nagar etc. was started.

Prior to September 17, 1912, the territory of Delhi was known as the "Imperial Delhi Estate" and was included within the province of Punjab. After it was decided in 1911 to shift the capital of India from Calcutta to Delhi, proceedings for the acquisition of land were started by the Collector of Delhi District pursuant to the notification of Punjab. When the capital was shifted from Calcutta to Delhi, the Governor-General–in Council by his proclamation dated 17th September 1912 took under his immediate authority and management the territory of Delhi with the sanction of the Secretary of State for India. The Delhi Laws Act, 1912 came into force with effect from 18th September 1912, and provided for the administration of the territory of Delhi by a Chief Commissioner as a separate province to be known as the province of Delhi. Under section 58 of the Government of India Act, 1919 and under Section 94 of the Government of India Act, 1935 Delhi remained administered as a Chief Commissioner's province.

Thus Delhi has had a long history, evolving starting from Indraparastha in 900 B.C. to the present day capital of modern India. It's a history of civilization, of culture and architecture, of a struggle against the odds, of survival as well as progress. All the settlements that contributed to the making of present-day Delhi were situated within an area covering about 10-20 kilometers. A Chronological sequence of the development of these settlements/kingdoms is given in Table 1.3.

Table 1.3 : Delhi through History

Sl. No.	*Settlement*	*Period*	*Location*
1.	Indraparastha	900 B.C.	Purana Quilla
2.	Siri	1301 A.D.	Near Hauz Khas
3.	Tughlaqabad	1321	Tughlaqabad
4.	Jahanpanah	1327	Between Siri and Raipithora
5.	Ferozabad	1354	Ferozshah Kotla
6.	Sher Garh	1530	Purana Quilla
7.	Shahjahanabad	1638	Walled City
8.	Delhi	1911	Old Secretariat – Civil Lines
9.	New Delhi	1931	Present New Delhi – the Capital

The historical perspective of the development of these settlements reveals the richness of planning concepts, architecture and cultural heritage present at those times. Historical monuments that are available right from Mehrauli area uptill Ferozshah Kotla, including those at Tughlaq Road, in Lodhi

Gardens and Sher Shah Suri Gate and Purana Quilla, bear testimony to the Delhi's rich heritage.

With arrival of the India's Independence conditions had changed and the needs of Delhi's citizens had changed. The city had to reflect this change in its character. The city not only had to function as an administrative seat but also generate employment for not thousands but lakhs of people. Newly independent India was a democratic set-up where everyone was aware of his/her rights and expected more and more from the Government. It was a free India and therefore a new urban scenario was required to meet the needs of the common man and to give a ray of hope to each citizen alongwith an assurance of security, safety, respectful living and dignity. This was the genesis of the new urban set-up in Delhi, with a new planning concept and a dawn of new hope to Delhites.

The Government always felt that Delhi should be developed as a Planned City. Shahjahanabad had its own urban form. It was an entity in itself and a self-sufficient city. There were residential and commercial spaces available in Shahjahanabad besides large common green areas for community gathering in front of the Red Fort, behind the Delhi Public Library near Old Delhi Railway Station and at the Ramlila Maidan at Ajmeri Gate. Similarly, the New Delhi set-up by the British was an administrative seat, which provided residential accommodation in the form of bungalows and commercial space at Connaught Place. The population of the city was growing and therefore the plan was to be drawn to accommodate a larger population outside the walled city. Therefore, in 1936 Mr. A.P. Hume, ICS, was placed on special duty by the Government of India to study the housing problem in Delhi and to suggest measures for the resolution of the same. Hume came up with twofold suggestions, viz. congestion of people in houses and of houses on the roads. In his report he also indicated an immediate access population of 1,00,000 for whom accommodation was necessary. He also identified slum areas and unsanitary conditions, which were a threat to public health and finally suggested a number of schemes to be deployed. As a result, a statutory body known as the Delhi Improvement Trust (DIT) was set-up in 1937 for the execution of these schemes.

The schemes were to be implemented on Government land and acquired land. The United Province Town Improvement Act, 1919 was made applicable for the formation of the Delhi Improvement Trust. The Trust carried out development work in Delhi and disposed of plots on a leasehold basis in areas such as W.E.A. Karol Bagh, Scheme opposite Ganga Ram Hospital, Pusa Road, Original Road, Paharganj, G.B. Road and Daryaganj. The Delhi Improvement Trust also acquired its own land and sold out plots on a freehold basis in areas like Shakti Nagar and Roop Nagar etc.

In 1947, after the partition of the country, a large influx of refugees came to Delhi from West Pakistan. The population of Delhi, which was about 7 lakhs till then, increased to 17 lakhs by 1951. The Government had to make arrangements at various places to accommodate the refugees. The refugees themselves had also occupied spaces wherever they could find them. This was the stage when Delhi first started developing in a disorderly manner. A massive rehabilitation programme was taken up by the Government of India under which thousands of houses were constructed in areas like Lajpat Nagar, Kalkaji, Malviya Nagar, Patel Nagar, Moti Nagar, Ramesh Nagar and Tilak Nagar etc. Simple one room with verandah houses on plots of 100 sq.yards each, with plenty of open spaces in the neighbourhoods, were constructed in these areas. Basic facilities like bathroom, toilet and drinking water was provided. These houses were made of asbestos sheets. The houses were "expandable" and as and when resources permitted the allotees could build more and create more space. With the passage of time the occupants have built three to four storey tall houses and these areas no longer look like refugee colonies. The hardworking Punjabi community has really changed its fortune since the Partition, which can be seen from the economic and residential developments in these areas.

As there was an enormous growth of population in Delhi due to the influx of refugees from West Pakistan, it resulted in a haphazard growth of colonies, scarcity of accommodation and slum-like conditions in many parts of the city. A committee, known as Delhi Improvement Trust Inquiry Committee, was set-up under the chairmanship of Shri. G.D. Birla in April 1950 to review the working of the DIT and suggest changes, if any, required to be made in constitution of the DIT. The Committee submitted its report in 1951 and came to the following main conclusions:

1. Several agencies in Delhi were entrusted with the development of the city and there was neither coordination of effort nor overall supervision and planning of the activities of these agencies.
2. The work of the Trust has been handicapped to some extent on account of the fact that the agency responsible for the execution of its works was the C.P.W.D., an authority independent of the Trust.
3. The Trust had not been able to produce either a Civil Survey or a Master Plan with the result that the growth of Delhi has been proceeding in a haphazard way, with little foresight and imagination and without any coordination.
4. There had been no proper zoning, and all the essential requirements of a community have not been provided for in the layouts of the Trust.
5. The policy followed by the Trust in selling land to the highest bidder or tenderer regardless of the consideration whether the buyer was a genuine builder or only a speculator in land had prevented even a partial solution of the housing problem in Delhi.

The Committee also gave a number of recommendations, the main of which were as follows:

1. There should be a single planning and controlling Authority for all the urban areas of Delhi. It should be an independent authority with a non-official majority.

2. The Authority should be given extensive planning powers.
3. The Authority should be a financially autonomous organization.

As a follow-up to the Birla Committee Report and to check the trend of haphazard growth, a Town Planning Organization (TPO) was set-up in 1955 and the Delhi (Control of Building Operation) Act, 1955 was passed. The Town Planning Organization prepared an Interim General Plan (IGP), as a preclude to the Master Plan. The Delhi Development Authority (Provisional Authority) was set-up to implement the plan. The Delhi Development Act, 1957 was notified on 30th December, 1957. With this, all the officers and the employees of the DIT or Delhi Development Authority (Provisional Authority) became employees of the Delhi Development Authority. The United Provinces Town Improvement Act, 1919 ceased to have effect in the UT of Delhi and the Delhi (Control of Building Operation) Act, 1955 was repealed. The newly formed Delhi Development Authority had its first office in the Regal Building with a very small staff strength.

Now at a stage when we have the third Master Plan for Delhi upto 2021 for remarkable change in the city since the Delhi Development Authority was constituted in 1957 and we had the first Master Plan in 1962 for a span of 20 years upto 1982. Except the geographic area of the city, which is 1483 km. everythingelse has changed. The city is totally different from what was conceived at the times of the first and second Master Plans. The economic liberalization policy of the Government of India has helped in bringing about rapid transformation in the economic and social fields. It has created so many new employment opportunities that people not only from the neighbouring states but also the farflung areas of the country have been coming to Delhi for their livelihoods. Now the multinationals and corporate world have given even more opportunities of employment at all skill levels attracting young talent and promising professionals. Though there are still large numbers of people who live in unauthorized settlements, *jhuggi-jhompri* clusters, and unauthorized colonies a larger number of people have been able to afford their own shelters and many of them have moved out to the NCR areas for housing and employment.

After the Delhi Development Authority was set-up all the aspects of Delhi's development were reviewed. In view of the prevailing conditions of unorderly development in city areas, it was felt that there was a need to have a plan and to make a new beginning. This is when the idea of the First Master Plan in Delhi was initially thought of. The First Master Plan was prepared for a span of 20 years keeping in view the perspective upto 1981. Thereafter the Second Master Plan was prepared for the development of Delhi till 2001 and the latest and the Third Master Plan upto 2021 is a continuation of the efforts to ensure an overall planned development of the city.

The First Master Plan of 1962, which was prepared keeping in mind the development of Delhi for next 20 years, had some special features:

I. It was estimated that the population of Delhi would be 53 lakhs by 1981.
II. For the first time all the four ring towns, *i.e.* Narela, Gurgaon, Ghaziabad and Faridabad were considered for necessary development.
III. Separate land-use was determined for residential, commercial, institutional and industrial activities.
IV. The concepts of district centres, community centres and local shopping centres were perceived.
V. Planning was done for an area making a 50,000 strong population as the base.
VI. Planning and construction of a ring road and a rail route were also part of the First Master Plan. The planners also envisioned creating a Green Belt around the city.

Though the Master Plan had projected the city's population as 53 lakhs by 1981 the actual population by then was 15 lakhs more. Furthermore, inspite of the separate land-use arrangements made in the plan commercial activity was occurring everywhere in the residential areas. The density of population was also increasing. Because of the unpredicted increase in population and density pressure the available urban infrastructure started crumbling. The proposal of shifting of the industries to other areas was also not implemented.

The next Master Plan upto 2001 was for a period of 20 years *i.e.* from 1981 to 2001. This Master Plan was finalized and approved only on August 1990. Half of the plan period was lost merely in the preparation of the plan. The year 1990 should have been the period of interim review for the Master Plan of 2001. Unfortunately this got severely delayed. As there was little accountability many of the people involved found ready excuses for the delay. The important features of the Second Master Plan were:

I. In view of the changed scenario material changes were made from the First Master Plan – 1962.
II. It was estimated that the population of Delhi would be 1 crore 28 lakhs by 2001.
III. In view of the increasing population emphasis was laid on the NCR's development.
IV. 18,000 to 24,000 hectare of land were identified for urban development.
V. A framework was drawn for the development of Rohini, Narela and Dwarka sub-cities.
VI. The walled City area and Karol Bagh area were declared as special areas.
VII. Coordination of MRTS, Ring Rail and Road Transport under the public transport system was envisioned.
VIII. Mix land-use, and preservation of environment and historical monuments were given due consideration.

The Delhi Development Authority, which had acquired about 74,000 acres of land, has also provided a lot of accommodation in the form of plotted housing, cooperative house building societies, cooperative group housing societies, DDA flats for self-financing, MIG, LIG, and Janta category flats. All those houses that used to be single storey in the 70's have now become 3-4 storeys tall. DDA alone has constructed more than 3 lakh flats of various categories. It had also developed 2,40,000 plots in various re-settlement colonies which were allotted to squatters upon their removal from *jhuggi* clusters. At one point of time in 1977 Delhi was almost free of *jhuggi* clusters. This was the result of a major one-time campaign, that only an agency like DDA could have undertaken. DDA's efforts at the time can be attributed in a large way to the spirit and effort of Sh. Jagmohan, the then Vice-Chairman of Delhi Development Authority who later became the Lt. Governor of Delhi and then Union Minister for Urban Development. It was his vision that squatters should be rehabilitated rather than simply removed from public land. In addition to relocating squatters, dairies were also shifted from the city area to Planned Dairy Complexes in areas like Madan Pur Khadar, Masud Pur and Ghazipur.

In the field of social upliftment, the city has attained new heights during this period. Most of the educational facilities available in the city are of international standards, whether they be Government or private institutes. In addition, hospital administration has been strengthened. The medical facilities available in Delhi are par excellence, so much so that many of the large private hospitals receive patients from foreign countries too. The city has also become culturally rich over the years with various events and institutions being established to make the citizens more culturally aware.

With the increase in economic prosperity the purchasing power of Delhites has improved considerably. Instead of having only one major business district center (Connaught Place), we now have a number of district centers in areas like Nehru Place, Bhikaji Kama Place, Rajindra Place, Janak Place and Netaji

Subhash Place at Pitam Pura. The culture of Malls is not new to Delhi either. A number of new Malls have come up especially in west Delhi in the Rajouri Garden area. The city is also full of large multinational and Indian Stores. These kinds of business centers were not thought of when First Master Plan was conceived.

Today there are 56 lakhs vehicles on Delhi's roads. This figure alone is enough to demonstrate the prosperity and upward growth of the city. Though Delhi has a long history behind it we have recorded unprecedented growth during last 40 years. If we look towards the series of events involved in the development of Delhi from Indraparastha to the establishment of Shahjahanabad, the city had always grown with increasingly more cultural and Architectural Heritage. However, after 1911 when the British shifted their capital to New Delhi till 2008, the trend of development has been one of greater economic prosperity, which includes a good sense of living, through administrative, economic and social institutions.

Furthermore, the green areas and sports facilities that exist in the city are unparallel in terms of quality. Delhi is one of the few cities where an urban city forest was created (known as the Jahanpanah Forest.) Two Bio-diversity parks in North and South Delhi at Bhalswa and Vasant Kunj are present day landmarks of environmental protection. These also have educational significance for children besides giving Delhiites the chance to stay close to nature; an opportunity afforded by few cities to its citizens.

Though the city has progressed impressively a lot still needs to be done, which the Master Plan 2021 has to take care of. About one-third of the city's population is living in unauthorized areas and unauthorized regularized areas. A shortage of commercial space has led to misuse of residential premises. People have constructed more than the permissible limits thus adding to congestion in existing areas. Besides applying increasingly more pressure on the city's physical infrastructure it has also created social problems. With the growing population of the city the crime rate has increased leading to more Court cases. Similarly, due to the large number of vehicles on the roads the traffic accidents have increased. All this leads to economic depression and social tension — in families in particular and in society in general.

It was disheartening to note in the Master Plan 2001 that zonal development plans for all the zones had still not been finalized. Against an estimated population of 1 crore 28 lakhs, the population went upto 1 crore 37 lakhs. Houses could not be provided by the Delhi Development Authority to all registrants. Even those who got registered in 1979 for allotment of flats and those who got registered in 1981 for allotment of plots in Rohini were still waiting in 2001. However, with respect to green development and the creation of sports complexes a lot of work was done and this is generally appreciated by users.

The Third Master Plan for Delhi was finalized in 2007. The focal points of the Master Plan 2021 are :

I. *Land Policy*

The land policy would be based on the optimum utilization of available resources, both, public and private in land assembly, development and housing.

II. *Public Participation and Plan Implementation*

- Decentralized local area planning by participatory approach.
- Performance oriented planning and development, with focus on implementation and monitoring.

III. *Re-development*

Incentivised re-development with additional FAR has been envisaged as a major element of city development covering all the areas.

1. *Planned Areas:* Influence Zone along MRTS and Major Transport Corridor; underutilized/low

density areas; Special Area; shopping/commercial centers; Industrial Area/cluster and re-settlement colonies.

2. *Unplanned Area*: Villages; Unauthorized Colonies and JJ Clusters.

IV. *Shelter*

- Shift from plotted housing to group housing for optimal utilization of land.
- Private sector participation for development/re-development of housing.
- Removing unnecessary controls (like height) for optimum utilization of land and to facilitate creation of signature projects.
- Enhancement of ground coverage, FAR and height for all categories of residential plots.

V. *Housing Poor*

- In-situ slum rehabilitation, including using land as a resource for private sector participation.
- In order to prevent growth of slums, mandatory provision of EWS housing/slum rehabilitation in all group housing to the extent of 15 per cent of permissible FAR or 35 per cent of dwelling units on the plot, whichever is higher.
- Housing for urban poor to the extent of 50-55 per cent of total;
- Recategorisation of housing types, development control norms and differential densities to make EWS/LIG housing viable and economical.

VI. *Environment*

- Special emphasis on conservation of the ridge.
- Rejuvenation of River Yamuna through a number of measures including ensuring adequate flow in river by

release of water by riparian state, refurbishment of trunk sewers, treatment of drains, sewering of unsewerd areas, treatment of industrial affluent, recycling of treated effluent and removal of coliforms at STPs.

- Provision of lung spaces/recreational areas and green belt to the extent of15 to 20 per cent of land-use.
- Multipurpose Grounds: A special category for marriages/public functions.

VII. *Unauthorized Colonies*

Unauthorized colonies, which are to be regularized as per Government policy, should be effectively incorporated in the mainstream of urban development. This requires provision of infrastructure development, services and facilities for which differential norms and procedures have been devised.

VIII. *Mixed-Use*

- To meet the growing demand of commercial activities and overcome the shortfall of available commercial space, a liberalized provision of Mixed-Use in residential areas has been adopted adhering to the requisites of the environment, while achieving better synergy between workplace, residence and transportation.
- 2183 streets have been notified by the GNCTD *vide* notification dated 1.09.06 for local commercial and mixed-use activities.
- Small shops of daily needs have been permitted on ground floor, in residential areas.

IX. *Trade and Commerce*

- District and Community Centers are proposed to be developed as facility corridors along major transport networks to prevent unintended and unplanned ribbon development and for better synergy between public transport and work centers.

- Development of Integral Freight Complexes/wholesale markets at the urban periphery.
- Mandatory provisions for service and repair activities.
- Informal shops, weekly markets, handicrafts bazars, used books/furniture/building materials bazars to be developed.
- Enhancement of FAR.

X. *Informal Sector*

- The informal and organized sector is a major source of employment in the economic fabric of the city for which the following approach is proposed.
- Earmarking the 'Hawking' and 'No Hawking' Zones at neighbourhood and cluster levels.
- The weekly markets to be identified and planned/ developed.
- New areas for informal trade to be developed and integrated with housing, commercial, institutional and industrial areas.
- Provision of common basic services like toilets, water points etc.
- Institutionalizing designs of stalls, push-carts and mobile vans.
- Involvement of NGOs envisaged.

XI. *Industry*

- Environment as a major concern and listing of prohibited industries.
- Modernization/up-gradation of existing industries including non-conforming industrial centers.
- Special provisions for service and repair centers.
- Inclusion of new activities like IT industry etc.
- Enhancement of FAR.

XII. *Conservation of Heritage*

- Identification of heritage zones and archeological parks.
- Development of special conservation plans for listed buildings and precincts.

XIII. *Transportation*

The proposals include the following:—

- Unified Metro Transport Authority.
- Synergy between land-use and transport.
- A new parking policy including private sector development of parking facilities, increase in norms for parking space, multi-level parking and underground parking.
- Integrated multi-mode public transport system to reduce dependence on personalized vehicles.
- Road and rail-based mass transport system to be a major mode of public transport, optimal use of existing and network and development of missing links.
- Restricting of existing network through express ways, elevated roads, arterial roads, distributor roads and relief roads.
- Provision for introducing cycle tracks, pedestrian and disabled friendly features in arterial and sub-arterial roads.

XIV. *Health Infrastructure*

- Health facilities proposed to achieve norms of 5 beds/ 1000 population.
- Enhancement of FAR for hospitals and other health facilities.
- Nursing Homes, clinics etc. also allowed under relaxed Mixed-Used norms.

XV. *Educational Facilities*

- Rationalization of planning norms with enhanced floor area.
- Locating new school sites adjacent to parks/ playgrounds.
- Provision for vocational and other educational facilities.
- Schools and training centers for mentally/physically challenged with differential development norms.

XVI. *Disaster Management*

- Disaster Management center provided in each administrative zone.
- Building regulations for safety of structures as per seismic zone.
- Land-use zoning as per microzonation.

XVII. *Provision of Sport Facilities*

- Provision for sports infrastructure for local, national and international events.
- Incentives provided for sports facilities and swimming pools in schools, clubs and group housing.

XVIII. *Focus on Infrastructure Development*

- Perspective plans for water, power, drainage and solid waste management of service agencies part of MPD-2021. Alternative sources of energy and new technology. The plan emphasis on energy conservation, efficiency and exploring alternative sources of energy.
- Realistic standards of water supply for equitable distribution."

The Master Plan is only a guideline. The actual shape of the city will assume during the process of implementation of the Third Master Plan and at the time of its completion in 2021 will depend on the administrators who are responsible for executing various schemes, the political machinery which has to support the planning concepts and the public in general which must adhere to the planning norms and policies laid down under the Master Plan, be these for the use of the land, building norms, unauthorized encroachment and construction, industrial regulations etc. Even if we cannot generate more, we can at-least avoid wastage of our precious resources for tomorrow's happiness. We must collectively ensure that each one contributes to city development and harmonious living. This will help in both providing satisfaction to the individual citizen and in bringing prosperity to the community at large. Each citizen of Delhi must contribute him/herself instead of blaming the planning or the administrative machinery, even if these may be at blame at certain times.

Source: Master Plan for Delhi-2021.

2 DELHI - AN OVER-CROWDED CITY

A city is a living organism which has its own developmental pattern. It breathes through green areas and through open spaces. Cities need proper care through planning, execution of schemes and sincere law enforcement. The infrastructure of a city, such as roads, which are its lifeline, needs to be properly maintained and looked after. Every city has its boundaries and is a geographical entity within itself. However, it has its own manageable limits. Therefore, you cannot expect a city to provide everything for everybody. Like a train compartment, if it is over crowded, you cannot sit comfortably, you cannot move easily, you cannot breathe and rest properly. Thus, an over-crowded city cannot satisfy its inhabitants entirely. Over-crowding in the city causes problems for everybody. These include problems of education, health, employment and shelter. If city is over crowded its citizens will have to struggle for survival, peace of mind and co-existence. However, if a city is governed properly with a manageable population for which it has been planned, it can provide good health, entertainment, educational and social avenues, employment opportunities and above all a healthy and purposeful living. This chapter deals with Social, Economic and Developmental consequencies of overcrowded city.

Delhi was a manageable small city at the beginning of the previous century *i.e.* in 1911 when its population was only 4,05,000. By 1941, its population was 9,17,939. Thereafter in 1947, as a result of the partition of the country, a large influx of refugees came to the city and the next Census of 1951 recorded a decadal population growth of 90 per cent. In 1951, the population of the city was 17,44,072. Thereafter from 1961 to 1991, it registered a decadal increase of a little more than 50 per cent as is reflected in table 2.1.

Table 2.1 : Population Growth -1941– 2001

Year	*PopulatioPn*	*Decadal Growth (percentage)*	*Annual Growth (percentage)*
1941	9,17,939	—	—
1951	17,44,072	90.0	6.54
1961	26,58,612	52.4	4.31
1971	40,65,698	52.9	4.34
1981	62,20,406	53.0	4.36
1991	94,20,644	51.5	4.24
2001	137,82,976	46.31	3.81

The rate of growth of population during 1991-2001 was 5.19 per cent less than the population growth registered during 1981-91, when it was 51.5 per cent. It is early to draw any conclusion at this stage, for this lower growth rate. There can be numerous explanations like a decrease in flow of migrants to the city or the role of Ring towns such as Gurgaon, Faridabad, Noida, Ghaziabad, etc. This would need further study before any conclusive analysis can be drawn.

The demographic features brought out by the 2001 Census will not help in establishing a linkage between population on the one hand and physical and social infrastructure available in the city on the other. This is more so because besides its registered population, thousands of people come to the city daily for service, business and other activities from areas as far as Meerut, Aligarh, Palwal, Rohtak, Sonipat and Panipat. Similarly, in terms of direct pressure on the road network and transportation system, a large number of vehicles from other states come to the city or pass through it daily. This migratory and transitory population puts additional burden on the city's physical and social infrastructure. Frequently held political rallies where lakhs of people come to the city also add to its existing problems. They contribute to insanitation, traffic jams, shortage of water supply, insecurity and crime etc.

New Delhi, the capital city, was conceived as a planned city, hence, the capital was shifted from Calcutta to New Delhi in 1911. In 1937, the Delhi Improvement Trust was formed to organize and regulate its future planned development. In 1957 when the need for an organized body dedicated to developmental projects in the city arose, the Delhi Development Authority was created by an Act of Parliament. It was created as a body to ensure planned development of the city.

Immediately after the partition of the country in 1947, there was a large influx of refugees into the city. These refugees squatted anywhere and everywhere in areas such as parks, on roadsides and even in monuments like the Purana Quilla (Old Fort). In order to accommodate this large influx, the Government undertook a massive project and created a large housing stock in a number of rehabilitation colonies like Lajpat Nagar, Kalkaji, Malviya Nagar, Rajinder Nagar, Patel Nagar, Ramesh Nagar, Moti Nagar and Tilak Nagar etc. These refugees, mainly Punjabis, are a very hardworking community and, therefore, in a very short time, they created jobs for themselves, explored opportunities, ventured into new areas, and became self-sufficient and were settled in their new locations.

It was in the 1960s that shanty settlements in the form of *jhuggi-jhompri* clusters came up in several parts of the city. A survey of these clusters was entrusted to the Bharat Sevak Samaj. It was a social organization engaged in the activities of child welfare, women welfare, youth welfare and helping the needy poor. The organization was functioning on Government Grants with its office located opposite the Regal Building, Connaught Place. The survey of squatters was enterested to the Bharat Sevak Samaj to find out the type and extent of encroachments on public land with a view to propose a Re-settlement Scheme for such squatters.

The Government formulated a scheme in 1960 known as *Jhuggi-Jhompri Removal Scheme*. Under this scheme, alternative plots of 80 sq.yards were allotted to these squatters in areas such as Raghubir Nagar and Moti Bagh. Soon the Government realized that the number of squatters was increasing so fast that it would be difficult to offer plots of 80 sq.yds. to every squatting family. Therefore, the scheme was revised and the plot size was reduced to 25 sq.yards. However, even at this reduced size, the number of plots available was not sufficient enough to meet the need of the growing number of squatters, therefore, a cut-off date was decided by the Government. This implied that only those who were squatting on Government land upto the cut off date were to be allotted alternative plots of 25 sq.yds. in colonies like Mandangir, Raghubir Nagar, Madipur and Seelam Pur etc. Those who were squatting on public land after the cut off date were also to be removed in order to clear the public land but were treated as ineligible squatters. However, these ineligible squatters were also re-settled in the Re-settlement Colonies, which were developed at distant places such as Hastsal, Nangloi and Seema Puri etc. It was also decided that to discourage further squatting on public land, ineligible squatters should be shifted to far-flung areas and were to be provided with a lower level of physical infrastructure facilities such as public hydrants, public toilets and public washing spaces.

Population increase in Delhi is noticed everywhere. Shahjahanabad, which was built for a small population of about 60,000 in 1638, is now severely over-crowded. Although during the last 10-15 years residential population has decreased because of an increase in commercial activity the over-all population in terms of residential, commercial and workers has not come down. Due in part to this we find a large homeless population in Delhi, which is why the Slum Department has had to construct night shelters. The highest density in the area itself is an indicator that the walled city is over-crowded. If we go by the statistics it will appear that the population in the walled city has gone down after 1971 but in real terms these statistics cover residential population only. Thus, a statistical decrease in population in the walled city does not mean a reduction in over-crowding and congestion. It is on account of the fact that vacated houses are being converted to commercial use that congestion and over-crowding are on the rise there. There is no doubt that the walled city is high-density area. The gross density varies from 2,068 persons per hectare to 340 persons per hectare. The highest density was found in Kucha Patiram and Suiwalan area, where there were 2,068 persons per hectare. The lowest density of 340 persons per hectare was found in Daryaganj. Another reason for the migration of residential population from the walled city is that 75 per cent of the structures are more than 50 years old. Although 90 per cent of the structures are of *pucca* nature their age requires major repairs and rebuilding, which is leading to the residential population moving out and commercial activities moving into the area.

The over-crowded conditions are also noticed in areas like Paharganj, Sadar Bazar and Karol Bagh etc. In these areas, especially in Paharganj and Sadar Bazar, it is difficult to walk on the roads and the streets during day time because of over commercialization and over-crowding. Two storey buildings have been converted into 4-5 storey ones; small budget hotels in Paharganj area leading to over congestion. These were the areas, which were in existence prior to setting up of Delhi Development Authority.

The demography of Delhi has changed considerably after 1947 as the Census of 1951 noted a decadal increase of 90 per cent. It is the same city where the decadal increase in 1911 was recorded as low as 2 per cent. The increase in 1951 Census reflects the influx of refugees who came from West Pakistan due to the partition of the country. This was all homeless population. They had lost everything — men and money in West Pakistan. They narrowly escaped and came over to New Delhi. This was the time when the Government had to face a great challenge in ensuring rehabilitation of refugees. The population of Delhi, which was 9,17,939 in 1941, went upto 17,44,072 in 1951. The major increase was in the urban population of Delhi which increased by 106.6 per cent from 1941 to 1951. The urban population of Delhi which was 6,95,646 in 1941 became 14,37,134 in 1951. Thereafter the decadal increase for Delhi urban population was 64.2 per cent, 54.6 per cent and 58.2 per cent for 1961, 1971 and 1981 periods respectively. However, the decadal increase during next two decades *i.e.* during 1991 and 2001 was 44.30 and 42.2 per cent respectively. By 2001 the population of Delhi had reached 138 lakhs.

Now the population increase was visible in all directions of the city. All the urban villages had been over-densified. A large number of *jhuggi* clusters have come up in Delhi, where there are about 25 lakhs slum dwellers. Similarly besides the regularization of 567 unauthorized colonies in 1977 about 1500 more such colonies are awaiting regularization now where there are reported to be 40-50 lakhs residents. The existing residential areas have been further densified, primarily by adding additional floors to existing buildings. All this has made the city more crowded. Efforts made by the Government to provide housing through the Delhi Development Authority are not sufficient. Through 42 residential schemes DDA has allotted more than 3 lakh flats besides permitting additional FAR in the existing colonies. DDA has also facilitated housing by providing land to the Co-operative House Building Societies and allotting 2,40,000 plots of 25 sq. yds. in the Re-settlement Colonies. In addition the Slum Department has also allotted about 70,000 plots of 18 and 12.5 sq. meters under Relocation of Squatters Programme.

This alone is not enough because the city has to provide jobs and employment opportunities to such a large population as well. It has also to provide space for the informal sector. Shops and shop plots have been provided through District Centers, Community Centers, Local Shopping Centers and Convenient Shopping Centers. The employment opportunities and level of infrastructure in Delhi has also attracted migrants adding to the city's population and making it yet more crowded. The city's population increased through migration at the rate of 44.2 per cent in 1981, 40.8 per cent in 1991 and 39.82 per cent in 2001. Another factor which has contributed to the over-crowding of the city is the growth of unauthorized industrial areas. Lakhs of workers find source of livelihood in these industrial areas. The Government's decision to regularize areas where more than 70 per cent of the houses are used for industrial purpose has also added to population pressure and over-crowding of the city. There were 1,29,000 industrial units in

Delhi in 1998 as against 85,050 in 1991. The number of employees in these units went up from 5,68,910 to 7,30,950 in 1991 and 14,40,000 by 1998.

Infrastructural facilities in terms of sewer, water and electricity are also needed in the same higher proportion. Similarly, a lot of institutional services such as schools, hospitals, post offices, police stations, play-fields and parks etc. are required to meet the growing needs of the urban population. Even the norms have had to be reduced for allotment of land to these institutions because of the shortage of land.

Go anywhere in the city, *e.g.* the walled city, Paharganj, Sadar, Karol Bagh, Sarojini Nagar Market, Central Market Lajpat Nagar, Greater Kailash Market, Kalkaji, and you will find places packed of crowds. All areas, including Old City Zone which is the smallest in terms of physical jurisdiction and South and West Zone which have largest area in terms of physical jurisdiction, are overflowing with people. The railway stations, the airport and inter-state bus terminals are always bursting at the seams with crowds. Since the area of the city is just 1483 sq. km. the rural area is getting reduced by the conversion of more and more of it into urban extension areas. Though there are norms earmarking sites for institutional use but these norms are being revised and reduced for all facilities including schools and school play-grounds. The magnitude of the problem can be judged from the fact that Government had to spend an astonishingly huge amount in providing sewer lines in 567 regularized Unauthorized Colonies, 44 Re-settlement Colonies and 135 Urban Villages. Similar is the case with water and electricity. There is obviously a physical limit for the civic administration as far as meeting physical and social infrastructure needs besides housing and housing environment are concerned. The city has certainly over-grown. Even the NCR, though it has picked up in its growth during last 10-15 years, has not been able to fully reduce the population pressure from Delhi.

Besides over-crowding some areas were over-densified as well. These are basically *jhuggi-jhompri* clusters where on a small piece of land hundreds of *jhuggies* come up without any infrastructural support. They live in an unhealthy and unsafe environment. The DDA had also cleared large areas of squatter settlements to improve the environmental conditions in the city. The projects had dual purpose; firstly to rehabilitate the affected families and secondly to improve the environmental conditions on the squatted sites.

During 1975-77, about 2,40,000 squatters were shifted to 27 newly developed Re-settlement Colonies in areas like Trilok Puri, Kalyan Puri, Dakshin Puri, Sultan Puri and Mangol Puri etc. Besides providing physical infrastructures like wide roads, street lights, drinking water and common toilets etc. a network of institutional services in the form of dispensaries, community centers and television clubs etc. were also provided in these Re-settlement Colonies. However, despite these major rehabilitation and re-settlement programmes, the problem of squatters was not over. By 1994, again about 4,80,000 new *jhuggies* had come up and the number further increased over the years.

Another major problem related to squatters, faced by the city is that of Unauthorized Colonies. Although 567 Unauthorized Colonies were regularized by the Government in 1977, by 1993 about 1071 more Unauthorized Colonies had come up and this number has further increased since then.

Besides housing shortage or lack of quality housing, Delhi also faces a problem of power and water shortage. Traffic congestion on roads and law and order problems have further added to its plight. Land encroachment, unauthorized construction, electricity theft, wastage of drinking water, pollution of river Yamuna, unhygienic dairies and stray cattle on the roads, road accidents and general insecurity amongst the people are real problems that Delhiites are facing daily.

Roads, which are a lifeline for any city, are much abused and over-used in Delhi, where traffic on roads has increased manifold. The number has gone upto 56 lakhs vehicles. Delhi is one city where the number of registered vehicles is more than the number of families. The number of vehicles in Delhi alone is more than the number of vehicles in Bombay, Calcutta and

Chennai put together. About 600 new vehicles are added in Delhi everyday. Thousands of vehicles come to the city from neighbouring states either to deliver goods or to pass through the city. Commuting time required to go from one place to another in 1971 was half of what it is today.

A number of new unauthorized industrial areas have come up, thus adding to the existing pollution. The Supreme Court had ordered the closure of polluting industries. There are areas, which were not industrial as per land-use plan but efforts are being made to declare them as industrial areas. In fact, these are certain areas where 70 per cent houses are under industrial use. Unfortunately, the remaining 30 per cent law abiding citizens who have not violated the rules and are using the premises for residence purposes alone are silent sufferers.

Another major task faced by City Developers is that of garbage disposal as about 6000-6,500 metric tonnes of solid waste is generated in the city everyday. 471 gm. solid waste is generated per person in a day in Delhi. There are at present three landfill sites at Ghazipur, Bhalswa and Okhla. All three sites are saturated. The Municipal Corporation of Delhi is planning to develop new sites at Jaitpur, Narela-Bawana Road. There is a limit to finding land-fill sites for garbage dumping, hence alternative uses and methods for disposal of garbage will have to be explored.

The root cause of all these problems is over-population. As against 92 lakhs in 1991, we were 1crore and 37 lakhs people in Delhi by 2001 — an increase of more than 45 lakhs. No Government agency, howsoever, efficient, dynamic and resourceful it may be, can provide physical and social infrastructure for such a large population, especially when the beneficiaries are not willing to contribute. We must find out ways to divert the population to other cities and towns. The National Capital Region Board has not fully succeeded in developing magnetic Ring Towns.

A similar situation was handled effectively in U.K. in seventies when new towns like Miltonkeynes were developed between London and Birmingham. Although, it took some time eventually people recognized the convenience of commuting from Miltonkeynes to London rather than getting stuck in traffic jams in London. Large commercial centers and office space besides residential infrastructure was created in Miltonkeynes. It became a very attractive proposition for those who were living in London and helped to ease the over-crowding and congestion of the city. Miltonkeynes also provided employment opportunities to the youth through its large commercial and business centers. Other new towns similar to Miltonkeynes developed around the same time also attracted people from other over-crowded cities. Thus, the experiment proved successful in decongesting the over-crowded cities.

Thus, we realize that the planning and development of Delhi cannot be perceived in isolation. Though Delhi's area is limited it is still expanding through the transformation of agricultural land for urban use. In turn, its growth is acting as a magnet for people from all-over the country. Planning for Delhi, therefore, has to be done keeping in mind the larger context — keeping in view its catchment area in the Nation Capital Region. If planning is limited to Delhi alone it cannot be in totality. Delhi, with the growth of Ghaziabad, Noida, Faridabad and Gurgaon, has literally become a boundary-less city in terms of planning and economic development. If you fly from Agra to Delhi at night and see expanse of light below you, you will be seeing the whole NCR and will not be able to identify Delhi as a separate city. There is no green buffer left between Delhi and the neighbouring states except some agricultural land in North and West Delhi. With the unauthorized settlements that have come up in Khera colony in Noida the physical boundary between Delhi and Noida has disappeared. So is the case between Badarpur and Faridabad near Suraj Kund. Similarly on National Highway number 8, except through the police check post, it is difficult to demarcate the boundary between Delhi and Gurgaon.

Though New Delhi is the capital of the country it is not an island by itself. Today, it is an integral part of the National Capital

Region. All sorts of development works including economic upwardness and its employment generation potential have a direct bearing on the NCR towns. Similarly, developmental activities in the form of housing in the NCR towns have a direct relation with Delhi in terms of problems and solutions. In the early seventies there was an emphasis on the development of ring towns like Gurgaon, Faridabad, Ghaziabad and Noida. However by the late seventies and early eighties the emphasis shifted to the development of the NCR area to ease the pressure on Delhi since the population of Delhi had crossed much beyond the projected population by 1981. The NCR could not develop at that time because of the low priority attached to it and a lack of funds.

Now, over the years there has been tremendous development in Gurgaon and Noida. In addition, other important towns like Sonipat, Panipat, Manesar, Kundali, Bahadurgarh and Greater Noida have come up very fast. However, we have to keep in mind the fact that it is not the housing stock but the infrastructure, which is more required in the NCR area.

If we look at the four important towns of the NCR, *i.e.* Noida, Gurgaon, Ghaziabad and Faridabad, we can see that there has been a lot of change and developmental activities have been occurring all-over. Gurgaon and Noida have grown at a faster pace than the other towns. Besides creating a large housing stock for all categories of people, they have attracted multi-nationals by developing office and commercial spaces. Gurgaon has taken further lead in proving quality housing. Builders have introduced a new concept of luxury housing by constructing apartments for the upper and upper middle class. Delhi Development Authority could not construct apartments for upper and upper middle class except for some self-financing category flats for the higher income group. In Delhi the rich have to make their own arrangements if they want to build/live in an apartment/house of more than 3 bedrooms. On the other hand, Gurgaon and Noida have come out with schemes through private builders even for non-resident Indians for world-class luxury flats. Ghaziabad has also come up as fast growing city.

Faridabad has lagged behind the other NCR towns because of connectivity problems. There has long been talk of the construction of a flyover at Badarpur Border but the promises haven't materialized yet. Unless a proper traffic approach and internal transport system is provided to Faridabad it cannot pick up the development pace. Though Faridabad started as an industrial town with lots of potential it has not progressed as fast as it could have. Once the flyover at Badarpur Border is constructed to give an easy approach to commuters the developmental activities in Faridabad, and beyond upto Palwal, will pick up. Similarly though Ghaziabad has grown very fast it has not attained the level of prosperity of Gurgaon since it needs more infrastructure and improved communication links. Just like people have to wait in the traffic jam at Badarpur Border while going to Faridabad they have to face a similar situation at Anand Vihar in Delhi while going to Ghaziabad. Similarly people find it difficult to go from Noida to Ghaziabad and Noida to Faridabad because of the non-availability of a fast, straight and smooth transportation link.

On the other hand, Gurgaon and Noida have steadily attained new heights in the real estate sector. They have set-up new standards in urban living. The quality of building materials used and facilities created in the interior as well as exterior of residential complex area have given a new dimension to urban living. The housing sector created in high tower buildings is in class by itself. After making extensive investments in Gurgaon builders have now shifted their attention to Noida, Faridabad and Ghaziabad. While Ghaziabad had started creating lot of residential space and a number of shopping malls Faridabad has yet to pick up. Its main activity now is likely to be in the Nehar Par area, which can also have connectivity from Noida and Greater Noida. Gurgaon has developed as a prime corporate and industrial hub of the country. Gurgaon's position will further improve when it gets connected with Delhi through the Metro. It is going to be a busy route providing a comfortable and convenient commuting option to the masses.

Of the total NCR area of 30,242 km 5 per cent is in Delhi, 44 per cent is in Haryana sub-region (Faridabad, Gurgaon, Rohtak, Panipat, Sonipat and Riwari etc.), 15 per cent in Rajasthan sub-region (Alwar and Ramgarh etc.) and 36 per cent is in Uttar Pradesh sub-region (Meerut, Ghaziabad, Buland Shehar etc.) In the Master Plan of Delhi 1962 it was emphasized that special attention be payed to the ring towns like Faridabad and Gurgaon. Besides this the plan also contained provisions to improve infrastructure to create employment possibilities in these towns. The Delhi Master Plan 2001 had mentioned the setting up of 17 ring towns around Delhi. And more currently, the Master Plan 2021 has laid emphasis on the provision of a Rapid Transport System, a Regional Rapid Transport System and express-ways besides bye pass approaches.

As per the new plan the National Express Way in the National Capital Region will extend from Kundli-Manesar-Palwal. It is also planned to connect to Bahadurgarh (NH-10) and Ghaziabad (NH-24). After the construction of Eastern Peripheral way the Noida-Dadri Express way will be connected with Palwal. Thus, the express-way network will give tremendous relief from traffic jams. Moreover, after the Faridabad-Noida-Ghaziabad corridor is constructed it will be quite convenient for people to commute between these towns and Delhi. And upon completion of the proposed eastern peripheral express-way Ghaziabad, Noida and Greater Noida will get connected in such a way that people will be relieved of traffic jams at Kalindi Kunj, Badarpur, Faridabad and Ballabhgarh. Also, Noida and Faridabad will get closer in terms of time.

The Government is also trying to link Delhi with other towns through the rapid rail system. The Central Government has also released Rs. 2239 crore under the integrated rail-bus transit system in the NCR. The improved rail and road transport system in the NCR will help boost further development in the region.

The basic policy of the regional plan — 2021 is aimed at accelerated development of the urban and rural areas. For this to happen infrastructure has to be substantially up-graded at the local and regional levels (both by the State and Central Government) in order to induce growth in these areas, specifically in identified settlements/Metro Centers. This will make them more attractive for locating economic and allied activities and for attracting private sector investment. Delhi has a limited area of 1483 sq. km, out of which about half of the area is already utilized. For the remaining areas, optimum utilization of land is required so that while providing for the urbanization requirements natural features like the ridge and other major green areas, water bodies and places of ecological importance are preserved. The details of available land in Delhi for 2021 as proposed in the NCR Plan–2021 are given in Table 2.2.

Table 2.2 : Land Position in Delhi– 2021

Sl. No.	*Land Use*	*Area (Ha)*	*Percentage of Total Area*
1.	Total Geographical Area-NCT Delhi	148300	100
2.	Built-up area (as per IRS ICLISS III Satellite data 1999)	70162	47.31
3.	Natural Features (Forest, Wild Life Sanctuary, Ridge, River Yamuna and other water Bodies/drains)	19509.10	13.16
4.	Sub-total (build up+natural features)	89671.10	60.47
5.	Balanced land available in NCT Delhi (1-4)	58628.90	39.53
6.	Land to be kept reserved for:		
	(i) Disposal of solid waste generated up to 2051 sanitary land-fill and statutory green belts.	10000	6.74
	(ii) Metro services/utilities *e.g.* power plant, grid station water and sewage treatment plant etc.	10000	6.74
	(iii) Agricultural zone in NCT Delhi including dairy farming, horticulture, green belts etc.	11000	7.42
7.	Sub-total–6	31000	20.90
8.	Proposed/Actual Land available for urbanization (5-7)	27628.90*	18.63
9.	Total urbanization area 2021 (including built-up area 1999) (2+8)	97790.90	65.94
10.	Population which can be accommodate in 97790.90 ha @ 225 PPH = 220 lakh		

*This included unplanned and built-up area.
Source : NCR Plan 2021.

One has to learn from these experiments and experiences. Though initially these will require heavy investment from the Central and the State Governments in the long-run they will certainly help ease the pressure off Delhi, allowing it to breathe, grow and finally to provide a healthy living environment for its citizens. It is high time for us to make laws or create conditions to check the unending population growth in Delhi. We must develop new towns. Let Delhi be a city of hope and aspiration, a city of joy and opportunities rather than a city of plight and despair. New towns around Delhi can help to shape it in that form. All this must be done before 2021, when the city's population is projected to be around 2.3 crores.

3 UNPLANNED GROWTH OF THE CITY

Cities and towns have different characteristics, which are reflected in their growth patterns. These differences are evident in the pace of development, population growth, migration pattern, effort for planned development and social–economic institutions, which have emerged and played a specific role in a dynamic society. Though urban land is a very valuable resource, in order to be used to its maximum advantages, it needs to be properly regulated. Similarly there is a limit for every city to accommodate its growing population, migrants who come to the city as unemployed youth and sometimes as landless labourers with their families. Generally they squat on public land or stay in rented *jhuggies* provided by the local Pradhan (Headman) of the *jhuggi* cluster or alternatively they find a place in some unauthorized colony where there are no infrastructural facilities. This sets a trend for unplanned growth of the city. At an early stage, the migrants need help in the form of shelter, help in the form of hope, help in the form of healthcare and help in the form of employment to survive in a new unfriendly atmosphere in the new settings. Over the years, Delhi has been receiving 4-5 lakh migrants every year. These people need shelter, a somewhat secure living environment and a sympathetic approach till they are settled. They also need a proper network of institutional services – both physical and social, such as roads, parks, schools, hospitals, water and electricity etc. Urban resources are limited. Even if more resources were available they would have to be regulated and planned properly. Over the years, the pressure of population on Delhi has changed its very basic character as a planned city. That is why about 50 per cent of its population is living in *jhuggi clusters*, unauthorized colonies and other slum areas. Thousands of people have performed unauthorized construction in the DDA flats and also flats allotted to cooperative group housing societies. Similarly thousands of plot owners have performed unauthorized construction in their plots in the form of creating an additional floor or covering more area than permitted under the building bye-laws. Thousands of unauthorized industries have come up. Large scale unauthorized construction is noticed in and around the Lal Dora Area of villages. The majority of the city's population has performed unauthorized construction in one way or the other. In this chapter, an attempt has been made to elaborate on the various reasons and issues that are responsible for unplanned growth of the city.

Urbanization is not simply a process of rural-urban migration. Besides its demographic features, it has multifarious social dimensions. Migration is not always a progressive phenomenon. Sometimes it is a painful experience for the families moving from villages to cities. Urban population has grown at a much faster pace than was visualized by the urban planners. It is more so in the metropolises and mega cities. This has been established by the Census Reports of 1981, 1991 and 2001.

Had there been sufficient employment opportunities, in rural areas, the pace of migration to the cities would have not picked up so steadily. The Gandhian school of thought, which wanted every village to be self-sufficient, was not made a motto by our Planners. Five-Year Plans did not provide incentives and opportunities in rural areas. Thus, migration from villages to cities continued. We cannot expect our people to remain hungry and still live in villages. Even if they wanted to work, there were no jobs available for them. Community work and construction of village roads could hardly provide enough jobs. Similarly, the food for work programme has also not succeeded. People are forced to leave their homes not in search of employment but in search of basic needs *i.e.* food and their fight against hunger.

This phenomenon has disturbed the social equilibrium in Delhi as well. Delhi, which was a small manageable city during the Mughal Period and also thereafter during the British Rule, had never seen such a population explosion as the one that was witnessed in 1947 during the partition of the country. It was during this period that the population of this city almost doubled. Most available areas such as roadsides, parks, tombs and even monuments like the Purana Quilla (Old Fort) became refugee camps. Rehabilitation of these people was a tremendous task before the Government. These refugees could not comprehend or accept the meaning of independence because they had just left their native villages in West Pakistan and had lost everything, both human life and material wealth.

The first rehabilitation programme for these refugees was launched in the 1950s when the Government developed colonies in far-flung areas like Lajpat Nagar, Malviya Nagar, Patel Nagar, Rajinder Nagar, Ramesh Nagar, Moti Nagar and Tilak Nagar etc. Small one-room houses, with verandahs covered with asbestos sheets were constructed. There was no provision for individual toilets and lavatories. Neither were there any individual water connections.

Today, there being second and third generation refugee residents living in these localities, the condition of these areas has undergone significant change. Prosperity through hard work is visible. Today one will hardly find a house with asbestos sheets and most of these residents have constructed two-three storeyed houses with individual water and electricity connection.

Following the Partition, the next wave of migration to Delhi came in the form of rural to urban migration. Thus the second phase of re-settlement was visualized in the 1960s when the then Prime Minister Pt. Jawahar Lal Nehru thought of rehabilitating *jhuggi jhompri* dwellers. The survey of these areas was entrusted to the Bharat Sevak Samaj. A plan was drawn to re-settle these squatters on plots of 80 sq. yards each. This was in some areas of West and East Delhi including Moti Bagh where there exists an up-scale locality adjacent to Anand Niketan. However, immediately thereafter, it was realized that it would be neither possible nor feasible to allot plots of 80 sq.yards to the squatters. Therefore, when the job was entrusted to the Delhi Development Authority in 1968-69, it was decided that instead of the previously agreed upon 80 sq.yards, plots of only 25 sq. yards should be allotted to the squatters. To discourage the tendency of encroachment in future, it was also decided that eligible squatters should be re-settled in the nearby areas like Madan Gir, Seelampur, Madipur, etc, whereas ineligible squatters should be re-located at distant places like Seemapuri, Tigri, Nangloi and Hastsal etc. Even the yardstick of infrastructure to be provided in these colonies was a lower one. Facilities to the eligible squatters' colonies were of a higher order than those available to the ineligible squatters' colonies. Norms were laid-down to provide hand-pumps, latrines and other facilities for re-settlement colonies.

From 1975 to 1977, a massive re-location drive was launched by the Delhi Development Authority and about 2,40,000 families were re-settled in 27 Re-settlement Colonies (in some records of the Department the figure is 44 Re-settlement Colonies - the explanation being that instead of counting the colonies they counted some blocks of a colony as a colony by itself) such as Trilok Puri, Himmat Puri, Sultan Puri, Mangol Puri, Khan Pur, Kalyanpuri, Seemapuri, Nangloi, Jawalapuri and Dakshinpuri to name a few (the number is also taken as 44 if some large areas are divided in smaller sizes).

The problem of squatters, however, was not over. Another problem, of unauthorized colonies, was raising its ugly head. Although under the policy of large-scale acquisition development and disposal of land, the Government had notified for acquisition vast areas of land for planned development and also for the implementation of the First Master Plan of Delhi-1962. However, at the same time, a number of Unauthorized Colonies, specially, in the trans-Yamuna areas had come up. About 564 colonies were in existence by 1975 where thousands of families were living. Regularization of these colonies was also a major problem before the Government. In these matters, it is not the

Planner alone who decides since the decision becomes part of a political process. A decision was taken to regularize these colonies at the time of general elections.

There are certain conditions for regularization of unauthorized colonies. The affected families or plot-holders are supposed to contribute a certain amount towards the infrastructure to be provided over there. However, this remains a mere paper exercise. People are interested only in the notification to be issued for regularization of these colonies. They are however, not willing to contribute towards the infrastructure in the form of roads, water, electricity and storm water drains etc. Moreover, they feel that these can also be managed by political pressure. The process helps the land mafia and land speculators to encash their investments. Even vacant plots, boundary walls, *kuccha* and semi-*pucca* structures get included in the unauthorized colonies and notification about their regularization helps them secure their title deeds.

As a result of this approach no vacant land could be acquired/ taken over by the Government in these so called unauthorized-regularized colonies for parks, play fields, hospitals, dispensaries, fire stations, milk booths, police stations, schools, mother dairy outlets and other such institutional needs. So much so that the land could not be acquired even for widening roads in order to allow fire tenders to pass through in emergencies. Today these colonies have been regularized without any such facilities. The same story is going to be repeated now when about 1539 unauthorized colonies are being considered for regularization.

Shortage of houses in Delhi in the planned areas is also a reason for unplanned urban growth in the form of unauthorized colonies. Delhi Development Authority has not been able to provide sufficient housing for the masses. Instead of constructing flats for, LIG and MIG category it has switched over to self-financing schemes for those who could afford them. It was only DDA which was supposed to provide flats to middle income and lower income groups people. Failure on the part of DDA has partly contributed to unauthorized colonization. People have no option but to go for a plot or house in unauthorized colonies inspite of the fact these were not well planned and lacked basic infrastructure.

Housing Shortage

The shortage of housing in Delhi is also a reason for its unplanned growth. The city's population increased very fast but provision of housing and shelter by the agency responsible could not be made adequately enough. In 1971, the population of Delhi was 40,44,338. In the 1981 Census population increased was recorded at 55.80 per cent. Again in 1991 the growth rate was recorded as 59.21 per cent and most recently in 2001 the growth rate was 60.80 per cent. Table 3.1 indicates the population in Delhi and its increase from 1981 to 2001 and projected increase by 2011 and 2021.

Table 3.1 : Population Growth in Delhi-1981-2021 (2021 projected)

Year	*Addition by Natural Growth*	*Increase by Migration*	*Net Increase (In lakhs)*
1981	12.02 (55.8 per cent)	9.52 (44.2 per cent)	21.54 (100 per cent)
1991	18.9 (59.2 per cent)	13.05 (40.8 per cent)	32.0 (100 per cent)
2001	26.6 (60.18 per cent)	17.64 (39.82 per cent)	44.30 (100 per cent)
2011	24.2 (54.8 per cent)	20.0 (45.2 per cent)	44.2 (100 per cent)
2021	24.0 (50 per cent)	24.0 (50 per cent)	48.0 (100 per cent)

Note: Figures (in bracket indicate percentage to total net increase.
Source: Census of India and projecting by DDA Sub-Group (MPD-2021).

The projected population of Delhi as per Master Plan 2021 is 220-230 lakhs. The progressive increase from 2001 onwards as brought out in the Master Plan 2021 is as follows:

Table 3.2 : Five Yearly Estimates of Projected Population

Year	*Population (in Lakhs)*
2001	138.0
2006	162.0
2011	182.0
2016	199.0
2021	230.0

Source: Census of India and projecting by DDA Sub-Group (MPD-2021).

Since 1968 when DDA started constructing flats it has so far allotted 3,67,991 flats of various categories through 42 different schemes launched from time-to-time. These flats were constructed all over Delhi. The types of flats range from one room Janta flats to 3 bedroom ones. It also includes flats constructed under self-financing schemes. Car garages and scooter garages were also contructed with some flats. DDA introduced various kinds of designs to suit the utility and financial requirement of the allottees.

DDA, being the sole agency responsible for planning and providing different forms of housing for various categories of the masses has not entirely measured upto the expectations of the public. Through various housing schemes launched since 1968 DDA has allotted only 3,67,991 flats. Scheme-wise details of these flats are given in Table 3.3

The Delhi Development Authority has on an average constructed 9,435 flats every year. It's a very small number compared to the size of the DDA, the resources at its disposal and the monopoly it enjoyed. Of the total flats constructed, about one-third are of the Janta and Economically Weaker Sections category. These are very small one-room tenements. If in place of these, regular two-three bedroom flats were to be constructed the number of flats constructed by the DDA would have been even lesser. Even the construction of flats over the years was not uniform. During 1970-71 and 2007-08 the number of flats constructed by the Delhi Development Authority was less than 1,000 flats each year. Similarly in 15 separate years

Table 3. 3 : Scheme-wise Details of Flats Allotted by the DDA

Name of the Scheme	*Total Allotments Made*
Housing General Scheme	65,590
New Pattern Registration Scheme-1979	1,67,310
Self-Financing Scheme/VVAY	53,938
Ambedkar Awas Yojna-1989	17,465
Expandable Housing Scheme, 1995-96/NHS/ Sharmik Avas Yojna, etc.	22,352
Janta Housing Registration Scheme-1996/Punjab and Kashmiri Migrant/Motia Khan	20,942
Retiring Govt. Servants/JK Migrant. (RPS)	1,015
Miscellaneous	440
HIG	3,337
Government Organization	4,670
Jasola Janta Tenements–2003	2,252
TBRHS (MIG) 2004	2,356
Festival Housing Scheme-2004 (HIG–1287 + MIG-862 + EHS-357)	2,506
New Housing Scheme-2006 (HIG-1504 + MIG-2018 + EHS-296)	3,818
Total	3,67,991

the number of flats constructed per year was less than 5000 – the majority of the flats being of Janta and Low Income Group category.

DDA has never prioritized its housing programme. It did not chalk-out a programmer for nearly 10 years. It mostly relied on year-to-year planning. With the change of each Vice Chairman as head of the organization, housing priorities were re-drawn and it became a personal agenda of those who mattered. Self-financing schemes for those who could afford them were taken up over looking the interests of poor registrants. Middle class and low-income group aspirants who got themselves registered for small houses and plots under new Patterns Registration Scheme-1979 and Rohini Registration Scheme-1981 were done grave injustice by not being given flats/ plots in time. Some of the registrants under these schemes who could afford small houses on installments are still waiting. It has been nearly 30 years since then — many of the registrants would have even passed away. Schemes which were taken after

New Pattern Registration Scheme 1979 and Rohini Registration Scheme 1981, stand completed to the satisfaction of Self-Financing Scheme registrants and members of the cooperative group housing society. Of the 1,71,272 registrants under New Pattern Registration Scheme – 1979, 1,043 registrants are still awaiting allotments. The category wise position of the registrants is given in Table 3.4.

Table 3.4 : Category-wise Position of DDA Registrants

Category	*No.of Registrants*	*No. of Flats Allotted*	*Backlog*
MIG	47,521	46,278	NIL
LIG	67,502	66,744	1,0403
Janta	56,249	54,288	NIL
Total	1,71,272	1,67,310	1,0403

Similarly, under the Ambedkar Awas Yojna 1989, which was launched 19 years ago, 449 registrants of LIG category are still awaiting allotment.

In all, DDA has constructed 306413 flats during last 42 years *i.e.* from 1966-67 to 2007-08. Of these 56662 were of self-financing category, 66389 of middle income group, 89241 of low-income group and 94121 of Janta/economically weaker section, community service personnel and servant quarters.

A report by the Engineering Department, which constructs the flats shows that 3,06,413 flats were constructed upto 2007-08 whereas as per housing department of the DDA it has allotted 3,67,991, flats. The discrepancy seems to be on account of cancellation and re-allotment of the same flat more than once and in some cases more than twice. Cancellation can be on account of non-acceptance by the registrants, or on the basis of default. In many cases cancellations is on account of non-receipt of the allotment letter because of a change in address or due to the DDA sending the letter to the wrong address. The fact remains that DDA has not been able to generate a sense of satisfaction among its registrants and allotees. However, the only satisfaction they have is that they own house worth its value, as it is difficult for a common man to build his own house or buy a flat from a private builder.

When we talk of a housing shortage we have also to examine the population holding capacity of Delhi. The Master Plan for Delhi projects Delhi's population to be 230 lakhs by 2021. Estimated holding capacity of existing urban areas as per Master Plan 2021 is 153 lakhs. Out of remaining 77–lakhs population 29 lakhs already exists in census towns, unauthorized colonies and JJ clusters in the present rural areas. The Master Plan therefore suggests that remaining 48-lakhs additional population be accommodated in the future urban extensions. The Master Plan has not clearly identified as to how much land and in which areas is available for future urban extensions. No such study seems to have been conducted to identify such land, which would accommodate the remaining 48 lakh-large population. If the Master Plan were implicitly referring to agricultural land it should have also come out with a plan of action for its acquisition. Unfortunately, this has not been done.

When we look towards development all-around Delhi, we notice that even the Delhi Development Authority has created different levels of development based on economic and bureaucratic priorities rather than planning norms. Most of the self-financing flats having been constructed in South Delhi (Vasant Kunj and Sarita Vihar). Planner and bureaucrats have purposely planned Janta and low-income group flats in areas other than South Delhi. This has been done to keep South Delhi a posh area. If confronted, the planners will retaliate with various kinds of arguments to support their planning concept but the ground reality lies clearly before the citizens of Delhi.

Although DDA has tremendous potential it is not utilized in a proper direction. There is no long-term planning. Piecemeal decisions are taken even on important matters like land development, construction of flats and creating commercial space.

Unplanned growth, noticed everywhere in the city, has added to pressure on services and given rise to mixed feeling of security and insecurity. This is reflected in the following kind of developments:

1. Walled City.
2. Slum Clusters.
3. Unauthorized Colonies.
4. Extra Coverage/construction.
5. Unauthorized Construction in DDA Flats.
6. Urban Villages.
7. Commercialization of Residential Areas.
8. Unauthorized Industrial Areas.
9. Dairies.

Walled City

The walled city was built for a population of 60,000 but its present population is 5-6 times more. Even the area has been commercialized and is not livable in from Urban Planning Standards. Workers' population has increased creating an imbalance in the demography. With the introduction of the Delhi Metro there is a possibility of commercial areas being further densified. The Metro has provided an easy and time-saving approach to the walled city. Areas like Chawri Bazar and Nai Sarak which are popular for specific trade attract thousands of persons daily from the city as-well as from outside Delhi. Similarly Kinari Bazar and Dariba etc. are still main attractions for shopping of specialized items.

Slum Clusters

Large areas in the form of small pockets all-Delhi have been occupied by slum dwellers. Construction labourers as well as migrants to the city squat on such publically encroached lands. This practice of encroachment started as early as the late 40's when refugees from West Pakistan, pushed out by the country's partition, came over to Delhi. But in essence, they were not squatters. They were middle class, upper middle and lower middle class families which had to flee from West Pakistan to save their lives. They had lost men and material in West Pakistan itself. Thus, they were refugees and not squatters. Therefore they were treated under a special rehabilitation programme. Tenements were constructed by the then Ministry of Housing and Rehabilitation was done in South and West Delhi in areas like Lajpat Nagar, Kalkaji, Malviya Nagar, Rajinder Nagar, Patel Nagar, Moti Nagar, Ramesh Nagar and Tilak Nagar etc.

The actual problem of encroachment of land by the squatters started in 50's when migrants started moving to Delhi. The number of squatters was low in the beginning but increased gradually until the problem became alarming by the late 60's. The number increased considerably from June 1975 to February 1977, 2,40,000 squatting families were shifted in Re-settlement Colonies. Even before that, from 1969 onwards a number of squatter families had been re-settled after shifting them from areas like Bela Road and Raigarh Pura in Dev Nagar. However, the problem kept on increasing. When large scale slum clearance was taken up during 1975-77 all the *jhuggies* from the city were removed and Delhi became a literally *jhuggi*- free city. However by 1981 98,709 new *jhuggies* came up. Again in January 1990 when Shri V.P. Singh the then Prime Minister visited Bhoomiheen Camp Govind Puri and stated that no *jhuggi* will be removed without providing alternative accommodation, the pace of encroachment a public land again picked up. As a result of these by 1994 there were 4,80,000 *jhuggies* in 1,080 *jhuggi* clusters. All these *jhuggies* and clusters came up after 1977. Even now there are about 5,00,000 *jhuggies* inspite of the fact that during these years about 70,000 squatters have been re-settled in the newly developed areas.

Another major area of unauthorized growth in the city is the development of Unauthorized Colonies. At some places *jhuggi* clusters have been converted into semi-*pucca* and *pucca* settlements. And at some other places colonizers have converted their agricultural land into unauthorized residences. A large number of Unauthorized Colonies came up in 60's in the Trans-Yamuna Area on land which was notified for acquisition. The residents of these areas were without infrastructural facilities and therefore were hoping to achieve regularization. They knew that regularization would provide them security and enhance their land's value. In February 1977, therefore, 567 out of 607 unauthorized Colonies were regularized.

By 1993 over 1,000 Unauthorized Colonies had again come up. When it was proposed that unauthorized colonies will be considered for regularization, it was found that there were 1,071 such colonies. The date for regularization was further extended and by now there 1,539 unauthorized colonies which are proposed to be regularized as per Government of Delhi. The regularization of these colonies will benefit a population of 40 lakhs–50 lakhs. Thus there are reported to be about 50 lakhs people in unauthorized colonies out of city's total population of 1 crore 60 lakhs. Condition in these colonies in terms of infrastructure and health standards is very poor. Many of the areas are not equipped with educational and health facilities. Roads and streets are yet to be laid down. Street lighting is also required for the safety and security of the population living in those areas.

Extra Coverage/Construction

Unauthorized construction in Delhi is noticed anywhere and everywhere.

In the walled city and in areas like Paharganj outside the walled city if a structure is demolished to rebuild a new one the new structure generally has more built-up area either in terms of additional storeys or in terms of more coverage from FAR point of view. This tendency of building more is prevalent all over Delhi. Everyone wants to construct more than the permissible area. Apparently no one is scared of the administration. Whether one owns a plot of 25 sq. yds, 100 sq. yds, 200 sq. yds. or 500 sq. yds. every one wants to build up more and more. In a plot of land of 100 sq. yds. where 75 per cent construction at ground floor was allowed the owners were permitted to construct upto 2 and half storeys. However, if you observe most of the colonies the occupants have not only made 100 per cent coverage, which is 900 sq. ft., but have also added balconies in front as well as the in the back of 3 ft. width having additional area of 180 sq. ft. Thus against a permitted area of 675 sq. ft. they have built 1080 sq. ft. on one floor. Again instead of 2½ storeys most of them have constructed upto four storeys. Thus, the total covered area becomes more than double of the permitted area. This is just to quote an example. When these same people extend their balconies by 3 ft. in the back lanes the actual width of the 10 ft. back lane is reduce to 4 ft. This kind of unauthorized construction to cover extra space and also to extra floor is common all over Delhi. It has not been possible for the municipal authorities to demolish the additional construction. Finally, the Government has decided to regularize such unauthorized construction by permitting 3rd floors on such small plots. This kind of relaxation in FAR for various sizes of plots by regularizing unauthorized and unlawful activity only adds to the congestion in the city. Admittedly, some relaxation was needed but the Government should have done long ago instead of keeping the people hanging in uncertainty for years altogether.

Unauthorized Construction in DDA/Cooperative Group Housing Society Flats

Allottees of DDA Flats have also resorted to large scale additions/alterations in their flats. In many cases these additions/alterations are of a minor nature but there are a large number of cases where they are pretty significant. Addition/alterations and unauthorized construction in DDA flats is so rampant that it has created lot of social tension between neighbours. A number of complaints are regularly received in DDA against such activities. Field functionaries also note such cases and issue notices. Large-scale demolition in these cases is not possible because a demolition at an upper floor will certainly have an impact on the neighbours' flats. During the public hearings conducted by Shri Jagmohan, the then Minister of Urban Development, in 1998 a large number of DDA flat owners used to come complaining against unauthorized construction in the adjacent flats, which caused social tension besides affecting sunlight and the privacy of the allottees. There was always a threat of damage to the adjoining flat. In many cases where two storeys flats were allotted by the DDA in areas like Kalkaji, people have added entire additional floors. The corner flat owners have added additional rooms thereby facilitating the upper floor allottees to construct them as well. In some cases Janta flats look like MIG flats where allottees have added additional rooms on the Government's land. Additions/alterations are also carried out by flat owners in cooperative group housing societies. Since the management of such societies often administers better control the number of such allottees violating the rules is not very large.

There was demand to permit addition and alterations in the DDA/Cooperative Group Housing Society flats which most of the residents had otherwise already done at their own. It was not possible for the DDA to issue notices in each case, pass demolition orders and after processing individual matters carry out individual demolitions. Demolition at upper floors is certainly difficult and can endanger the structural safety of the adjoining flats. The Ministry of Urban Development, Government of India thus constituted a committee on 19th September 2006 under the Chairmanship of Shri H.S. Dogra, Additional Director-General (Border), CPWD. The Committee, after having gone through the problem and considering various suggestions, made the following recommendations:

Recommendations

(i) "The Committee reviewed the present policy and procedure for permission and regularization of additions/alterations in DDA flats in the background of observations and suggestions received and also the input provided by the DDA and MCD. The Committee members expressed their serious concern about the gross additions/alterations that have taken place, especially in DDA Group Housing flats over the years. It was noted that some of these are not only dangerous to the structural stability of the flats, but are affecting the basis design, health parameters (light and ventilation) and aesthetics. In many cases, the facades and the elevations have changed completely. Although, the members in general were supportive of providing limited flexibility (without compromising the structural design and other basic parameters), it was unanimously felt that even the additions/alterations already allowed in DDA flats need to be rationalized. The flexibility of additions/alterations after rationalizations also needs to be extended to Co-operative Group Housing Society (CGHS) too.

(ii) In all such cases where owners/residents have undertaken additions/alterations in Group Housing flats which are within the permissible limits as per the guidelines, those be considered for regularization.

(iii) To deal with all the existing additions/alterations in DDA Group Housing the Committee recommends following guidelines:

(a) Wherein the owners have constructed a room or taken up other additions/alterations with prior permissions of DDA/MCD in accordance with the policy. There is no alternative except to treat them as regularized additions/alterations.

(b) In cases where the additions/alterations have been done by the owners in accordance with the policy laid down on the subject, but without prior permission of DDA/MCD, the Committee felt that a chance be given to all such owners to regularize the said unauthorized construction. For this a press notice giving three months time can be published in leading new papers requesting them to apply for regularization of such unauthorized constructions to the concerned authority such as DDA/MCD within three months failing which such additions/ alterations will be treated as unauthorized constructions and necessary actions for demolishing the same will be taken up by DDA/MCD. Such constructions will be regularized in accordance with the policy and subject to payment for additional covered area.

(c) Wherein the owners have taken up massive unauthorized construction such as addition of floor, changing the basic structure etc. will be treated as unauthorized additions. These additions/alterations are neither covered under the existing policy guidelines nor have owners obtained any prior permission from DDA/MCD.

It was decided by the Committee that a chance will be given to such owners by publishing a press notice giving three months time to remove such unauthorized construction at their own failing which the same will be removed by DDA/MCD at the cost of the owner. For this purpose RWA's can be declared as Nodal Agencies who will monitor and submit list of all flats who have carried out such unauthorized constructions.

(iv) Keeping in view of the fact that in many areas, the Group Housing flats built by DDA, other Government agencies, cooperative etc., have not utilized the permissible development norms in terms of FAR, density etc. and they also need major repair/ redevelopment on account of this, the redevelopment of such pockets with prevailing development control norms *i.e.* for ground coverage, FAR etc. not only amount to intense utilization of scarce urban land but would also encourage constructions of few housing stock as per the current socio-economic needs. The Committee recommends additional construction/ redevelopment of all such areas meeting the revised Ground Coverage/FAR norms for CGHS schemes subject to prior approval of all statutory authorities.

(v) The Committee was also supportive of the demand for provision of lifts keeping in view the requirements of physically challenged as well as growing elderly population.

(vi) The Committee was unanimous in not allowing additional floor in DDA Group Housing as well as in CGHS Scheme. The Committee was also not in favour of permitting/regularizing any encroachment on public land/common area. Both these are likely to compromise the laid down services and structural stability of the building.

(vii) After lot of discussion, following specific additions/ alterations were unanimously agreed upon in respect of both DDA Group Housing flats as well as CGHS.

(a) Grills and glazing in Verandah with proper fixing arrangements, subject to conformity with the fire safety norms.
(b) Raising height of front and rear courtyard wall up-to 7 feet (height) by putting up fencing.
(c) Providing door in courtyard, wherever not provided abutting road/service lane but not into the park. The door to open inside the property line.
(d) Providing sunshades on doors and windows wherever not provided with proper fixing arrangements, as per Building Bye-laws.
(e) Closing the door/doors.
(f) If the bathroom or EC are not having roof, these may be treated as open urinals and be allowed.
(g) Raising the wall of balcony/terrace parapet with grill or glazing upto 5 feet. height subject to conformity with the fire safety norms.

(h) Construction of open staircase (cat ladder) where no staircase has been provided for approach to the terrace (refer-condition about terrace right).

(i) To put/provide additional PVC water tank at ground floor area without disturbing the common passage.

(j) To provide an additional PVC water tank in the scooter/car garage at the surface level.

(k) To provide loft/shelf in the rooms without hole in the walls.

(l) To change the flooring with water proofing treatment

(m) To remove half (4 ½ inches) brick wall.

(n) To make a ramp at front gate without disturbing the common passage/storm water drain.

(o) To provide sunshades on the outer windows upto 2^1 wide projection.

(p) To provide false ceiling in rooms.

(q) To make an opening of maximum size of 2′6″ ′x 1′9″ for exhaust fan or air-conditioner in existing walls.

(r) Fixing of door in back and front courtyard, abutting roads/service lanes but not into the park. The door to open inside the property line.

(s) Converting of window into almirah subject to availability of light and ventilation as per building-bye-laws provided that no structural elements are disturbed and there is no projection extending beyond the external wall.

(t) Shifting of water storage tank/raising of parapet wall upto 5′ height and putting additional water storage tank. Wherever the existing water storage tank capacity is less than 500 liters in a flat, the existing water storage tank can either be replaced by a 500 liters tank or, if possible, the additional tank can be added so as to make the total storage capacity upto 550 liters. However, such replacement/provision of additional tank will be done only on the location specified for such tanks and the supporting beams will be required to be strengthened suitably. Parapet wall around terrace can be increased to a height of 5′.

(u) To shift the front glazing of windows upto those *chajjas* indicated in the original approved drawings.

(viii) Addition/alteration (s) permitted with prior intimation/ permission : Following addition(s)/alteration(s) can be carried out with prior intimation/permission of the concerned agency *i.e.* DDA/MCD as per the prescribed procedure:

(a) Inter-change the position of kitchen, bathroom and WC with proper connections subject to structure safety. To carryout this inter-change, all the allottees of one vertical stack will have to apply jointly to the concerned agency.

(b) Construction of bathroom and WC in the rear courtyard.

(c) Covering of open terrace with sloping roofs upto 9′ height with light weight material *e.g.* fiber glass/ AC sheets/ GI sheet with pipes and standards angle iron section etc. and enclosing with glazing.

(ix) *Additional Coverage Permitted with Prior Permission :*

(a) Covering of courtyard and floor level terraces is allowed subject to fulfillment of building bye-laws and structural safety.

(b) In three or four storeyed flats the owners at upper floor shall have the right to cover the area available as a result of coverage of courtyard of floor below. In such cases the residents of DDA flats in a vertical stack served by the same staircase should give their consent and jointly apply for permission.

(c) In two storeyed flats the allottee at first floor will have no right of construction above the courtyard built by ground floor allottee provided no construction was done earlier on the terrace.

(x) In CGHS colonies temporary fiber glass coverage in the set back area may be allowed for parking purposes. Similarly proposals of underground parking below green areas can be considered on case-to-case basis and subject to clearance by CFO.

(xi) In some DDA colonies, appurtenant land to the ground floor flat has been enclosed by residents with a compound wall. Such protection may be allowed on temporary basis subject to one time payment provided that the land is not used for additional coverage.

(xii) *General Conditions:* All the additions/ alterations and additional coverage will be governed by six basic principles:

- There is no encroachment on the public land.
- Structural stability of the building is ensured.
- Light and ventilations of the habitable rooms is ensured as per the building-bye-laws
- There is no infringement on other's right.
- The service elements such as manhole, rainwater fittings, sanitary fitting etc. are not disturbed and remain exposed for periodical inspection and maintenance.
- Terrace should be approachable to all the residents of that block and the terrace rights to vest with the society/R.W.A."

Urban Villages

Unauthorized construction was first noticed around urban villages when land was acquired there through notification of

1959 and 1961. As the village population expanded there was pressure on the villages to accommodate those who could not afford housing outside the village proper, which not only resulted in densification in the villages but also led to new developments. The Lal Dora of the villages was determined in 1908–1909; with the growth of population this should have been extended in order to accommodate the growing population. This was not done, resulting in unauthorized construction. At present, development in almost all the urbanized villages has grown much beyond the Lal Dora and the so-called extended Lal Dora. All these developments are unauthorized in nature and un-orderly from a planning and building norms viewpoint. There are repeated requests from the villagers, and their local representatives to extend the Lal Dora and to regularize their unauthorized developments.

Out of 358 villages in Delhi, 135 villages have been declared as urbanized villages. As mentioned above, unauthorized developments are noted around all these villages, where thousands of families are living in unhealthy and unplanned settlements. Thus, when land is acquired by the Delhi Development Authority it becomes difficult for it to take possession of areas where these settlements exist. These unauthorized settlements need to be properly regulated so that facilities necessary in terms of physical and social infrastructure are provided to them.

Commercialization of Residential Areas

Though we had prepared Master Plans in 1962, in 1981 and most recently in 2001 the pace of development and commercialization of residential areas occurred at a much faster pace than the provisions made for commercial areas by the authorities. The purchasing power of the people has expanded considerably and they are spending increasingly more on consumer goods. This calls for more commercial and manufacturing areas. The then planners had not visualized these facts while formulating the first and second Master Plans. Even the few provisions that had been made in the Plans were not properly executed. For example, the lands of District Centers have been steadily encroached due to the slow planning and non-execution of these projects. The planners also did not visualize that the city's increasingly affluent population would need more shopping areas. For the city's now 56 lakh vehicles, showrooms and workshops and motor markets were required. Eating habits have changed and more and more residential areas are now being converted into restaurants. It was, therefore, by compulsion that the authorities had to eventually declare more than 3,000 city roads as commercial roads, thus authorizing unauthorized use.

Unauthorized Industrial Areas

Like other unorganized activities, the industry has also grown in an unplanned manner. Enough industrial estates were not developed in the city. Since there were not employment opportunities provided by the Government small industrial units started functioning in residential areas in various parts of the city. The small-scale industries had grown very fast. In certain areas more than 70 per cent of the residential units were converted to industrial use. As per the 1998 economic census there were 1,29,363 small industrial units in Delhi employing 14,40,000 workers, whereas officially there are only 32 planned industrial areas in the city. Whenever there was a demand to take action against the unauthorized industries there was an equally strong voice supporting regularization of these industrial areas. The decision to regularize these areas meant implicitly condoning the other unauthorized growth in the city. In addition, even though these industries majorly pollute the environment they provide goods at competitive prices as well as employment to many Delhiites, thus being a necessary evil.

Dairies

There are many unauthorized dairies operating close to Delhi's village settlements. Even in the urbanized villages raising cows and buffaloes is a common practice. This large cattle population in and around Delhi has led to the prevalence of stray cattle on the city's streets and roads. There have been many cases of serious road accidents caused by these stray cattle, even in high-speed and traffic volume locations such as the Ring Road. The situation has grown so dire that the High Court itself has had to intervene and order the Municipal Authorities to check the menace of stray cattle. However, additional efforts need to be continuously made to ensure that atleast areas like the Ring Road be made safe of stray cattle. If we truly want to call Delhi a World Class City we must get rid of this blight on the city's roads.

The total population in these squatting settlements, unauthorized colonies, regularized unauthorized colonies, and residences with unauthorized construction is more than 50 per cent of the city's population. Similarly, the unauthorized industrial areas, which craved for regularization, represent a large section of population. Though Delhi had the Nazul Office, Delhi Improvement Trust and Delhi Development Authority to plan and regulate its development through three Master Plans the city has grown in a haphazard and, at times, illegal manner. Even though the authorities have resorted to regularizing the city's unplanned and unauthorized development the fact remains that they have been unable to stop, or atleast regulate, the unplanned growth of a supposedly planned city.

Thus, the casual attitude of the city's authorities and the lack of coordination between departments in the same organization or between the functional agencies of the Delhi Government and Delhi Development Authority have led to the city's current situation. One such example of the authorities' failure to execute plans is the proposed widening or alignment of Aurobindo Marg immediately after crossing the Qutub Golf Course. The Aurobindo Marg is supposed to connect with Andheria Mode Road at Phool Mandi Crossing. There is already quite a wide road, as provided under the plan, at the crossing of Mehrauli–Mahipal Pur Road and Lado Sarai Road, but this has not been connected with the same width to Aurobindo Marg at

Qutub Golf Course. Even the present Aurobindo Marg which connects Mehrauli-Mahipal Pur Crossing at Lado Sarai has a sharp left turn cut a little before Qutub Minar, which is very dangerous. There is a small structure near the turn which was renovated and a petrol pump of Bharat Petroleum, which was also upgraded recently. Some land South of the petrol pump has been acquired by DDA. If the land occupied by the small structure and the petrol pump site are acquired as well, atleast this part of the road can be smoothen and widened to avoid a sharp blind curve. Of course, alternative sites should be provided for the petrol pump and the small structure to compensate them. However the best course of action, which should be adhered to, would be to build a proper alignment of Aurobindo Marg from Qutub Golf Course till Mehrauli-Mahipal Pur Crossing at Lado Sarai. This example shows how the concerned authorities can constantly endeavour in many ways to take care of public interest.

The total population in these squatting settlements, unauthorized colonies, regularized unauthorized colonies, and those who have made unauthorized construction in the flats is more than 50 per cent of the city population. Thus those who have done unauthorized construction and resorted to unlawful construction are more than those who are part of the Planned Development of Delhi. Similarly, the unauthorized industrial areas, which craved for regularization, represent a large section of population and structures adding to the category of unplanned growth. Though Delhi had Nazul Office, Delhi Improvement Trust and Delhi Development Authority to plan and regulate its development through three Master Plans the city has grown unauthorizely. It is a different matter that the authorities resorted to regularize the unplanned growth and unauthorized construction by developing re-settlement colonies and regularizing the unauthorized colonies from time-to-time. The fact remains that it was unplanned growth of a planned city.

4 UNAUTHORIZED COLONIES

Unauthorized colonies in Delhi are not the result of an overnight growth, rather they have been part of a continuous process. Regularization of colonies in 1977 on the eve of the general elections until the recently proposed regularization of colonies in 2002 has been part of a regular system to woo the electorate, and clearly shows the way in which civic welfare is subordinated to vested political interests. Political patronage, weak enforcement, the unconcerned demeanor of the police, shortage of houses in Delhi and the general attitude of the people, who have very little respect for law, are major reasons for the mushrooming of unauthorized colonies and the encroachment of land. A strong will on the part of the enforcement agencies and political bosses including ground level political workers, can to some extent, certainly helping checking the emergence and growth of these unauthorized colonies. This chapter deals with the Process of the Emergence of Unauthorized Colonies and Reasons thereof including Non-Utilization of Vacant Land.

It is also interesting to note that in this context, the term 'colony' has also been misused. Colony is known to be a proper residential settlement with a certain percentage of houses constructed and occupied, besides a network of minimum institutional framework, in the form of commercial and other development. It must have minimum infrastructure consisting of roads, streets, drains and electricity etc. However it is clearly obvious that in the unauthorized colonies, which sprout in Delhi, these critical features are missing. A few structures, generally single rooms — some occupied and some unoccupied, few boundary walls showing speculation of land, in other instances, a few boundary walls and some small unoccupied rooms built with mud instead of cement and a few boards on some vacant plots to reflect sites for schools etc. (which are never meant seriously to be developed as institutions) are seen in these so called unauthorized colonies. In their true sense then, these are not colonies but only an attempt to get a certification from the Government so that these become residential or commercial areas, without proper change of land-use from agriculture, the originally intended land-use of these areas. This gives added value to the otherwise agricultural land. Colonizers, with the help of local political leaders and in collusion with civic officials including the police, try to make illegal fortunes in this manner. Normally, about 70 dwelling units are supposed to be constructed in one acre of planned area. It is seen that in these unauthorized colonies, which are proposed for regularization, there are pockets where the density is as low as 10 to 15 dwelling units per acre. However, once these colonies are regularized, the colonizers tend to plan the sale of each parcel of land. These colonizers do not believe in leaving land for wide roads, parks, schools, dispensaries, post offices and milk booths etc. There is no provision for physical and social infrastructure. Each square foot area is built up and after these are regularized, the density is as high as 90 to 100 dwelling units per acre.

No building norms are adhered to or enforced in unauthorized colonies as a result of which concerned structures come up on major roads, leading to congestion, over-crowding, insanitation and environmental hazards. As the sale of these plots on paper shows exchange of a nominal amount, the money, which is unaccounted for is invested on the construction of buildings ranging from three to four storeys including basements. A few examples of this nature would include areas like Sant Nagar near East of Kailash and a group of colonies in East Delhi in areas like Shakarpur and Laxmi Nagar.

The worst part of the whole scenario is that political parties blame each other in trying to get the support and votes of the people living in unauthorized colonies. They also want that besides regularization of these colonies (in many cases, which exist only in name's sake) proper services should also be provided to these areas. Nobody seriously talks about the nasty role played by the colonizers. Similarly, no party comes forward to suggest that land occupiers in the unauthorized colonies should pay and bear the cost of physical and social infrastructure. They all want Government agencies to carry out these infrastructural processes and undertake the accompanying huge financial implications.

Colonies which were regularized during 1977 have a very high density. Properties on the main road on Vikas Marg have tremendous commercial value. Although large show-rooms have come up in this area, no one has given thought to the fact that these beneficiaries should contribute, if not to the city's development, then atleast to the development of that area. Lanes and by-lanes of Shakarpur and Laxmi Nagar and most of the colonies in this vicinity lack of physical and social infrastructure. Roads are too narrow to take load of the traffic. Most of the inner roads have also been commercialized as a result of which regular traffic congestion is noticed here. There are no parks and open spaces in these colonies and so is the case with other such colonies.

One can see the amount of private capital investment, which has been undertaken in these colonies. However, nobody is willing to contribute for widening, repair and maintenance of roads, nobody is interested in uplifting the area. Everybody seems to be interested in raising residential and commercial mansions for themselves. Thus the concept of regularization of unauthorized colonies which initially starts on humanitarian grounds, leads to chaos, unplanned growth, congestion, crime, social tension and disturbs the whole social fabric. Similar conditions are witnessed in West Delhi areas where a similarly large number of unauthorized colonies were regularized.

While regularizing these unauthorized colonies in 1977, a pre-condition was laid down that wherever road widening or proper laying of roads was required, structures could be demolished. In practical reality, no structures are demolished and the road width remains as it is. While in the planned areas, planners propose roads, which are 30 meters to 60 meters, in these unauthorized colonies, the width of road is merely 3 to 6 meters. In 1993, when the whole matter of the regularization of unauthorized colonies was taken up by the Government, it was reported that there are 1071 colonies that needed to be regularized. Though, there were instructions that while these colonies were proposed to be regularized, no new colony should be allowed to come up. The latest estimate speaks about 1580 colonies. Thus, inspite of all kinds of instructions, neither the enforcement of this regulation has been possible nor the attitude of the people and the patronage of political parties has changed the scenario. Land occupiers and colonizers are thriving and there is always an attempt to look for unattended piece of land where these kinds of unplanned city vents can be created. No agency, which holds land in Delhi, like LandDO, DDA, MCD, PWD, CPWD, Flood and Irrigation and Railways etc. have been able to protect their lands. Vacant land under Delhi's prevailing real-estate scenario can be protected at the most for 2-3 years and not for 20-30 years. If lands remain unutilized, these are, in all probability, likely to be encroached upon first in the form of *jhuggi clusters* and then in their converted form of semi-*pucca* structures and classifying them as unauthorized colonies.

Another major reason for the sprawling unauthorized colonies situated on Government land is that even when demolition operations are planned by the land owning agencies, on the one hand, these are not allowed to be carried out freely and, on the other hand, there is lack of coordination between various agencies. If a demolition programme is planned by the Delhi Development Authority, it has to hook up in advance with the police. If on that particular day, police force is not available, then the demolition programme is postponed. Many a times even when police force is available, only a limited part of the structures is demolished. These partly demolished structures are quickly repaired and raised again by the encroachers. There are cases, where while demolitions are going on, local political leaders interfere and try to stop the demolition process. By the time, another demolition programme is fixed with police assistance after 4-5 weeks more unauthorized structures come up at the same site. Thus, inspite of fixing demolition programmes, the number of unauthorized structures come up, resulting in the expansion of such unauthorized colonies. It is a fact that demolitions are not carried out throughout the year. Sometimes police force is not available because of its law and order problem. Sometimes the local police is not able to help as outer force is not provided to supplement them. At other times, the police is busy and deployed on VIP routes. Similarly, during the rainy season and while the Parliament is in session, the process of demolition slows down. Demolitions are slowed down in March and April while school exams take place and in May and June because of extreme heat. All these excuses serve as reasons for a slow demolition process and the emergence of unauthorized colonies.

Non-utilization of land is also a major reason in land encroachment and development of unauthorized colonies. Sometimes, professionals like architects and engineers do not take up the project till the entire piece of land required for a project is made available. If a project is to come up on a 20 acre piece of land but part of it is encroached or is held up because of stay order from the Court, the project does not take off. The process of removing encroachment and effectively contesting Court case is quite lengthy. It is also noticed, sometimes that even while the matters are before the Court, unauthorized construction continues. By the time, order from the Court is given against the encroachers, the extent of unauthorized construction becomes so large that demolition becomes difficult if not impossible. Hence, the structures remain, land is lost and the development project is delayed or curtailed. Professionals have to be practical and realistic. If the entire project land is not available, even then the project should be initiated to save at-least the remaining land. There are large areas in places like

Shastri Park, Dilshad Garden, CBD Shahdara, Mayur Vihar etc. where there are large chunks of commercial land but these are all lying unutilized for years together. This gives temptation to land grabbers. Thus, timely utilization of Government lands is required. On the one hand, to execute the project in time, reduce the cost and, on the other hand to check the tendency of encroachment of Government land.

Unauthorized construction and unauthorized colonization is a regular feature. There are various factors for development of unauthorized colonies. These include a slow process of land acquisition, a long and tedious system of handing over possession of the acquired land by the Land Acquisition Collector to the Land and Building Department, Government of National Capital Territory of Delhi and then to the Delhi Development Authority, lack of coordination between various agencies and misuse of judicial process. Sometimes, the process of land acquisition takes ten to fifteen years. In Chilla-Dallupura near Noida border where land acquisition was undertaken sometime back in 1980-81, all the land ended up being built upon by the time litigation was over.

Initially, a few boundary walls scattered all over the area are constructed by unscrupulous elements. These people then wait and watch the action of the land owning authorities. The next stage is to construct one or two rooms. Even if the plot size is about 500 sq.yds. only one small brick room, generally, without plaster is constructed to show possession and also to have an entry in the revenue records proving that it is built up land. Sometimes chowkidars are also made to stay and their ration cards are prepared to prove that they are residents of the area. This is done to further establish that the site is built up and also occupied. These are all tactics to see that the structures are constructed with minimum investment. Possession is established through a full proof system of entry in the Revenue Record. During this period, more people try to buy land and construct one or two rooms and start living there. Initially, for a period of 4-5 years, density in these areas is very low. There are no laid down streets, roads, electricity, water pipes, the only source of water being through hand-pumps, needless to say there is no sewerage system either.

This kind of construction in such areas was carried out under the garb of a stay order from the Court. Land Owning Departments also are not very efficient. When they plan demolitions, they have to tie up with the Land and Building Department of Government of the National Capital Territory of Delhi and also with the police. It is very difficult to carry out a demolition of 100-150 structures. Thus, demolition is done in phases. When a few structures are demolished, *malba* remains over there and the occupants re-construct after a week or so. During this period, not only are the demolished houses re-constructed, but many more new ones are added. This is how the area gets densified. Local political leaders also interfere in demolitions. Those who sell the land have some sort of linkage with local leaders and the area police. Some people buy the land even when they know that the seller has no clear title to the land. Others buy even after knowing the risk involved. Today, the whole area of Chilla-Dallupura is built up.

As mentioned earlier, vacant land sites remain unutilized for long time. These are not fenced. Even if the Land Department wants to hand-over these vacant land (small pockets) to the User Department, these are not accepted by them on the ground that layout plans are not ready. Layout plans are prepared by the architects and Planning Department only when they get whole land parcel free of any encroachment or construction. This is a vicious process. In the whole process, land gets encroached, unauthorized colonization takes place and it is the city which suffers on the whole. Record also show that dozens of demolitions were planned but majority of them could not be carried out either because no police force was available or an insufficient number of the force was available. At times, it had to be postponed due to some other administrative reasons.

This is not the only story of its kind. It is in fact a common predicament in all areas characterized by unauthorized colonization. In the Mahipal Pur area near the Indira Gandhi

International Airport, land was acquired sometime back in 1986-87. The land-owners went to Court and got stay orders. These stay orders were vacated by 1997. During this period, the area got built unauthorizedly and thereafter whenever a demolition action was planned by the DDA, the local leaders interfered. This interference persists at all levels including that of the Cabinet Minister, who came at the site and stalled the demolition. This was the situation in an area where there were very few structures but demolition could not be carried to reclaim the whole land this was even more so the case when the land occupiers had lost their cases in the Court. In one year about a dozen demolition programmes were fixed to take over possession of acquired land by the Land Acquisition Collector for handing over to the Delhi Development Authority through the Land and Building Department, Government of the National Capital Territory of Delhi. This land lies in the vicinity of a defence area. This is a place where Delhi Development Authority has allotted land to Central Industrial Security Force (CISF). Nobody understands the security hazards being caused by these unauthorized settlements to our para-military and defence forces. Some politicians do not seem interested in national security. They are just interested in votes.

In river-bed area, instead of maintaining the sanctity of the river, people are recklessly involved in unauthorized colonization, Okhla and Batla House are examples where after filling the river area by carrying sand on donkeys, construction is being carried out day in and day out. In places where one expected that not a brick would be carried out to raise construction, three to four storey structures have been raised. The police should not have allowed the entry of building material in this locality. These are areas where civic administration has not acted boldly. One Junior Engineer of a department like DDA cannot check such rampant unauthorized construction. People are no longer afraid of the civic functionaries. They are afraid of uniform only, however, the police does not take a strong position either. Once these buildings have come up, demolition is not possible. Structures are numbered in hundreds and have congested the whole area. It is not possible to go with heavy machines to demolish these buildings with conventional methods as the lanes and by-lanes are very narrow. Even the *malba* cannot be removed after the demotion of these buildings. Moreover, since this is a minority community area, demolition can cause an even more serious threat than it normally does. It was suggested long back to construct a boundary wall towards the river-side to check further unauthorized colonization. If such a step had not been taken, these people would have gone on filling the river by carrying soil and dumping the *malba* to raise the ground level. This is what was happening as a matter of course each and every day. Ultimately, by the time the boundary wall was constructed, it was too late and hundreds of houses had already come up in the river itself. This had also affected the construction of a major road called NH-2, which was to link Maharani Bagh with Badarpur and ease the traffic congestion on the Mathura Road.

Even now when land has been earmarked for construction of roads, unauthorized construction by diverting the road alignment is still going on and not only have residential houses been constructed, but a *masjid* and a school were also attempted, knowing that it will be difficult for authorities to remove them. Nobody thinks of the city, which has to live for thousands of more years to come. Nobody thinks of the public convenience, or rather the lack of it, everyone is only thinking of themselves. Thousands of houses have been constructed in this area now, all are unauthorized, without any lay-out plan and without any sanction. It is a very sorry state of affairs for a supposedly planned city, that too the national capital to be growing in.

This story is true not only for this part of the city. It is the same everywhere and extends upto south and west Delhi as well. Unauthorized colonies start with a population density as low as 5-10 dwelling units in an acre but in areas like Batla House and Okhla, the density goes upto 90-100 units per acre. These areas do not have any provision for widening of roads, for the construction of lanes, for laying out parks, for building hospitals and other public infrastructure like police stations, milk booths and post offices etc. These are the areas where it will be difficult for Government agencies to provide water, electricity and sewerage services. Even for these services, they do not want to contribute anything. They just want to gain these services in lieu of their voting strength.

Some unauthorized colonies come up when *jhuggi jhompri* clusters are converted into such colonies. Initially, there are few *jhuggies*. Within the cluster, vacant land gets built up during the course of 2-3 years and gradually the entire area gets built up. Then the process of construction of rooms with bricks starts depending upon the individual's financial viabilities. Asbestos sheets are used for roofs. Electricity is tapped from the municipal electric polls, which are provided by the local authorities. Now, these are termed as unauthorized colonies. They want to have their right of regularization by calling upon and utilizing political mechanism. This trend, which has been set-up recently after the Government, announced in 1993 that colonies, which have come up unauthorizedly, will be regularized. Now even the cut-off date has been extended to cover unauthorized colonies, which came up even after 1993. Though *jhuggi-clusters* can be removed by providing alternative allotment but unauthorized colonies have to stay because these are to be regularized. This is known to all *jhuggi* dwellers and they want to take advantage of Government policy. There are many areas including areas in the river-bed itself where such settlements have come up and will be looking for regularization in the future, even though in principle the Government has decided not to regularize settlements in the river-bed and ridge area. It still remains to be seen whether the Government will be able to dismantle and remove such settlements in areas like Batla House and Okhla.

5 REGULARIZATION OF UNAUTHORIZED COLONIES

The emergence of unauthorized colonies in Delhi started soon after the partition of the country in 1947, when large number of refugees came from West Pakistan to Delhi. Most of them were accommodated in the rehabilitation colonies developed by the Government. Those who could not find accommodation started small unauthorized settlements, which were gradually converted into colonies. These lands were developed by private colonizers without any regard to community facilities. Between 1956 and 1961 the Government had issued a General Notification for the acquisition of 34,000 acres and 16,000 acres of land for the planned development of Delhi. But meanwhile, several colonies, especially in Trans-Yamuna Area, had come up on the notified land. Since it was not possible to demolish such a large number of such colonies it was therefore decided on 19th July 1961 to release them from the purview of acquisition and regularize them :

1. Those that were erected before the date of Preliminary Notification under section 4 of the Land Acquisition Act; and
2. Those that could be fitted into the sanctioned Regularization Plan.

Thus 110 colonies were regularized in 1961 — of which 34 were in West Delhi, 17 were in North Delhi, 45 were in East Delhi, 8 were in South Delhi, 5 were in Central Delhi and 1 was in the Rural Area. These colonies were declared to be regularized on a freehold basis.

In these colonies the built up areas had grown in a very haphazard manner and as a result it became difficult and in some cases almost impossible to provide municipal services, particularly roads and sewerage there. Similarly, there was not enough land in most of these colonies to satisfy basic amenities such as open spaces, institutional facilities like schools, hospitals and community centers etc. If such colonies were left to themselves the risk of slum conditions would have further developed and it would have become rather difficult to improve their condition if steps were not taken immediately after regularization to provide physical and social infrastructure. However, it was also not possible to deal with these colonies in accordance with the principles of town planning. Therefore developmental plans for them were prepared by adopting comparatively lower standards and by keeping the requirements to the minimum. Again, due to practical problems these standards varied according to prevailing conditions in the colonies, so that minimum inconvenience or dislocation was caused to residents. Although sites for community facilities like schools, dispensaries and parks etc. were shown in the plans of these colonies in reality very few such facilities could come up.

The pace of unauthorized construction did not slow down and new settlements came up very fast within and around these regularized colonies. Within the next five years another 101 unauthorized colonies came up. These colonies, which had come up between 1st September 1962 and 1st February 1967, were regularized in 1969. Out of these 101 colonies, 32 were in West Delhi, 43 were in East Delhi, 15 in North Delhi, 5 in South Delhi, 2 in Central Delhi and 5 in Rural Area. These colonies were regularized on the same principles which were prescribed for earlier regularization except that the land was to be provided to the occupants on a leasehold basis.

The trend of unauthorized colonization continues to this day with the constant increase in Delhi's population. From 1967 to 1974 another 260 unauthorized colonies came up. Thus on an average a little more than 3 unauthorized colonies came up every month. Population pressure was the major cause for such unauthorized development since authorized colonilization was proceeding at a very fast pace as well. The Government of India, therefore, appointed a Committee on 26th August 1974 under the Chairmanship of the Secretary Ministry of Works and Housing to study the situation. Surveys were conducted of all the unauthorized colonies with reference to the nature of structures use, physical and social infrastructure and structures affected under the land-use plan. About 39 per cent of structures in these colonies were of *pucca* nature. In all it was found in the survey that there were 1,42,000 structures existing in these unauthorized colonies proposed to be regularized. The structures were categorized as *pucca*, semi-*pucca* and temporary etc. The details about the condition of the structures and occupancy of the plots are given below :

Table 5.1 : "Condition of structures and occupancy of the plots"

Permanent Structures (37 per cent)	54,973
Semi-Permanent structures (28 per cent)	39,529
Temporary Structures (17 per cent)	24,432
Structures upto plinth level or Plots having boundary walls (7 per cent)	5,708
Fake Structures (5 per cent)	5,813
Vacant Plots (6 per cent)	7,545
Total	1,42,030

In terms of use it was noticed that 83 per cent of the properties were under residential use. Only 2 per cent were found to be in commercial use. Besides this, 7 per cent structures were used for residential-commercial use, 2 per cent for industrial–residential, 1 per cent industrial, 0.5 per cent religious and 5.5 per cent for miscellaneous uses. In terms of the infrastructure requirement it was noticed that services were available at a very low scale and that there was no land available in these colonies for providing physical and social infrastructure. The deficiency of services in terms of infrastructure can be noted from the fact that there was one higher secondary school per 26,000 persons and one medical dispensary per 40,000 persons in these colonies. Hand-pumps were the main source of drinking water in almost all the unauthorized colonies. Only 84 colonies had metalled roads with semi-metalled roads in another 82 colonies. 207 colonies had metalled and semi-metalled roads.

To remedy the deficiencies in physical and social infrastructure plots required for community facilities were to be acquired under the policy of large scale acquisition, development and disposal of land. However, this could not be done with the result that social infrastructure within these colonies could not be augmented.

On the basis of the report of the Secretary of Urban Development the Ministry of Works and Housing announced on 16th February 1977 a new policy for regularization of the remaining unauthorized colonies.

It also decided to approve the settlements around villages outside Lal Dora as unauthorized colonies. The policy covering the regularization had the following salient features:

(i) Both residential and commercial structures will be regularized.

(ii) Structures will be regularized after fitting them in a layout plan. After keeping clear space for roads and other community facilities in the immediate vicinity or neighbourhood such land should be utilized for these purposes.

(iii) Development charges as determined by DDA/MCD will be payable by the owners of the properties in such manner as may be laid down by these bodies.

(iv) The families which are displaced in the process of providing space for roads and other community facilities will be rehabilitated in the following manner:

  (a) Owners of the houses who or any of whose family members do not own a plot/house in Delhi will be provided alternate land/flat.

  (b) The tenants will be allowed alternate accommodation provided they, or any of their dependent member of family do not own house/plot in Delhi.

Thereafter, on 6th December 1978 the Ministry of Works and Housing of the Government of India communicated that regularization of unauthorized colonies conveyed by the Ministry *vide* its earlier letter dated 16th February 1977 will cover residential structures which had been constructed by 30th June 1977. However, this extension of date upto 30th June 1977 did not apply to commercial structures.

The tendency of unauthorized colonization and construction still continued inspite of Government efforts to prevent any such constructions. These settlements were still sprawling. Again by December 1983, colonies in the following manner had come up :

1. 155 in development areas of the DDA including some colonies in slum designated areas.
2. 66 extensions of urban villages concerning to the DDA.
3. 31 colonies falling in designated slum areas.
4. 452 in the jurisdiction of the MCD.
5. 30 extensions of villages falling in the jurisdiction of the MCD.

Unauthorized construction on Government land as well as on private land was ever-increasing since there was a heavy pressure of population in Delhi because of unemployment in the rural areas of some States. Migrants from those states who could not afford any sort of shelter squatted on public land and those could afford a little try to move to unauthorized colonies. DDA's flat was not in everybody's reach. Moreover, DDA could also not construct a sufficient number of flats to meet the housing needs of the population. Purchasing a DDA plot in the auction was nearly impossible. Thus, for an average lower middle class or middle class family there was no option but to move to some unauthorized colony where, even if there were no facilities, atleast the land was affordable. Even if the colony was at the periphery of the city with a long commuting time people were still attracted towards these colonies for their affordability.

The number of such colonies had again crossed one thousand by 1993.

Again, a proposal recommending regularization of unauthorized colonies as existed on 31st March 1993 was made by the Government. However, in the meanwhile, a civil writ was also filed by Common Cause (Registered) Society *vs*. UOI and others. seeking order from the Court restraining the Government from regularization of any unauthorized colonies. Pursuant to the order of the Honourable High Court, a Committee was constituted consisting of the following members to examine the problems of unauthorized colonies and suggest ways and means to deal with it :

1.	Shri N.P.Singh, Secretary(UD) M/o Urban Affairs and Emp.;	Chairman
2.	Shri P.V.Jayakrishnan, Chief Secretary, Govt. of NCT of Delhi;	Member
3.	Shri Anil Kumar, Vice-Chairman, Delhi Development Authority;	Member
4.	Shri Jagdish Sagar, Principal Secretary (UD), Govt. of NCT of Delhi;	Member
5.	Shri B.S.Minhas, Joint Secretary (UD), M/o Urban Affiars and Emp.;	Member
6.	Shri V.K.Duggal, Commissioner, MCD;	Member
7.	Shri I.A.Khan, Chairperson, NDMC;	Member
8.	Shri V.K.Duggal, General Manager, DESU;	Member
9.	Shri Rakesh Mohan, Addl. Commissioner (WS), MCD.	Member

After the Committee submitted its report in April 1997, the Court directed the Government to come out with its policy of regularization of various colonies and terms and conditions thereof. The Government of India worked out the terms and conditions and submitted an affidavit before the Court in

September 1998. The salient features of the proposed policy are as under:—

1. General Principles

1.1 Only those unauthorized colonies as were in existence on 31.3.1993, the extent depicted in the aerial photography, carried out at the instance of Government of NCT of Delhi, would be considered for regularization. However, the following types of colonies or parts thereof would not be considered for regularization :

(a) Colonies/parts of colonies falling in notified or reserved forest areas.
(b) Colonies/parts of colonies which pose hindrances in the provision of infrastructural facilities or fall in the area of alignment of existing/proposed railway lines, roads, water supply and sewerage lines and other utility works taken/required to be taken by any public authority.
(c) Colonies where more than 50 per cent plots are un-built on the date of aerial survey.
(d) No regularization will be done in respect of building being used for commercial purposes beyond ground floor and for purposes other than residential.

1.2 In all unauthorized colonies, whether on private or public land, regularization will be done subject to the preparation of proper layout and service plans in order to ensure that the minimum necessary feasible level of services and community facilities are provided.

1.3 No regularization would be done, whether on private or public land, if it violates the provisions of Ancient Monuments and Archeological Sites and Remains Act, 1958.

1.4 There would be no obligation on the part of the

Government, DDA/ the local body to allot alternate sites or flats to residents who are displaced on account of the provision of land for roads, civic amenities and community facilities.

1.5 In each colony it will be necessary to establish a Registered Residents Cooperative Society (henceforth called Resident Society) for coordination, preparation of layout and service plans, execution of developmental work and for liaison with the concerned local body/ DDA in respect of various issues pertaining to the regularization process.

1.6 The Resident Society of the unauthorized colony could take up works for provision of the infrastructural services and also make available the land for essential infrastructure and community facilities like roads, parks etc. The Resident Society of the unauthorized colony would take up works for providing civic services and also make available vacant land to the extent of 15 per cent of the area of the colony for providing community facilities. This land would be transferred in the name of local body/DDA. In colonies where such vacant land is not available cost of such land at L&DO rates would be deposited by Registered Society to the local body/DDA for provision of such services in an area nearest to the colony. The development of infrastructure/community facilities is essential for regularization of the colony.

1.7 The ownership of common facilities will vest with the concerned local body/DDA, as the case may be.

1.8 Every building in the unauthorized colony would be required to have building plan duly approved or regularized by the concerned local authority in accordance with the development control norms decided for such colonies.

1.9 In the case of unauthorized colonies on public lands occupied by non-affluent sections, the cost of land as per rate notified by LandDO at the time of regularization and if LandDO rates do not exist in the area, then the rates notified by DDA at the time of regularization together with a penalty of 10 per cent of the total land cost, would be recovered. In cases where the unauthorized colonies on public land are inhabited by affluent sections, the cost of land at the current market value on the basis of market rates prevailing in similar affluent but authorized colonies in the neighbourhood plus a penalty of 50 per cent on the same will be recovered. The affluent/non-affluent colonies have been categorized on the basis of following parameters: (a) location of the colony; (b) average plot size; (c) quality of construction, and (d) standard of living of the average inhabitant of the colony based on indicators such as use of air-conditioners cars etc. As per the aforesaid criteria, Anant Ram Dairy Colony and Mahendru Enclave fall under this category.

2. Procedure

2.1 Layout plans, land cost, penalty:

(a) The base map of the unauthorized colony will be provided by the local body/DDA to the Resident Society who will fix up the boundary on the plan and also get prepared the layout plan of the colony from a registered town planner. This layout plan would clearly show plot sizes built-up/vacant portions and provisions required for infrastructural, services/community facilities. The requirement of infrastructural, services/community facility will be assessed in consultation with local body/DDA. The Resident Society would then undertake developmental works of services as per the approved service plan of the colony and on completion of same would apply for regularization to the concerned local body/DDA.

(b) Alongwith the layout plan, co-operative society is required to submit the following:

(i) Complete list of members with plot Nos. in the resident society.

(ii) Bond indemnifying the local body/DDA in respect of all necessary measures for retrofitting against the seismic requirement and for structure stability of the building etc.

2.2 Since the development work is to be carried out by the societies themselves, therefore, no development charges will be deposited to the concerned local body. However, the processing fees for regularization of the layout plan will be charged as decided by the concerned local body/ DDA.

2.3 The construction on each individual plot is to be brought within the prescribed developmental control norms by the individual owner/Resident Society. However, it will not be a pre-condition to regularization of colony.

2.4 Recovery of land value and penalty for encroachment, unauthorized construction without approval of plan and building norms will be made by concerned local body/ DDA under whose jurisdiction the unauthorized colony to be regularized falls.

2.5 The land value will be collected by the concerned local body/DDA on behalf of land owning department/ agency. The amount so recovered will be credited to the account of respective land owning department/agency.

2.6 The penalties for encroachment on public land and unauthorized construction without approval of plan and building norms will be collected by the concerned local body/DDA and credited into a separate fund. From this fund and its own resources, DDA will under the guidance with directions of the Ministry of Urban Development and Poverty Alleviation, construct houses for economically weaker sections or carry out any other developmental work for public good such as development of park etc.

3. Other Provisions

3.1 Execution of developmental works will commence only after the approval of service plans by the concerned agency and submission of the layout plans alongwith the processing fees etc. to the concerned local body/ DDA.

3.2 The colony will be declared as regularized only after the execution of the infrastructure works as per approved services plan by the society.

3.3 In respect of unauthorized colonies to be regularized outside the urbanisable limits, suitable modifications to the Master Plan will be made, as may be necessary.

3.4 Action against unauthorized constructions which do not fulfil the conditions for regularization will be taken in a time bound manner by the concerned local body/DDA.

4. Registration of Residents' Co-operative Society

4.1 The formation of Resident Co-operative Society in each unauthorized colony to liaison with the concerned local body/DDA in various matters would be a precondition for considering the case for regularization.

4.2 The Resident Co-operative Society will prepare the layout/services plan in consultation with the concerned departments on the base provided by the concerned local body/DDA.

4.3 The Resident Co-operative Society will be required to furnish the following at the time of the submission of the layout plans :

(i) That, they will abide by the layout plans to be approved/regularized by the concerned local body as per development control norms, decided for the purpose.

(ii) The processing fees and other related charges are to be paid by the Society to the concerned local body/ DDA.

(iii) The Resident Co-operative Society of the unauthorized colonies would ensure that the provision of the services and land for essential infrastructure and community facilities like roads, parks etc. are available. In colonies where such land is not available, cost of 15 per cent of land at LandDO rates are deposited with local body/DDA for providing these services nearest to the colony. Also the development of the infrastructure is to be ensured before the regularization of the colony.

(iv) The list of the owners/occupants.

(v) Indemnity Bond.

5. Implementing Agencies

5.1 A separate cell will be created in the planning division of local bodies/DDA to carry out the work relating to regularization of unauthorized colonies.

5.2 Since the work related to regularization would involve preparation and implementation of development and service plans involving diverse agencies, each local authority will constitute an Inter-agency Coordination Committee under the chairmanship of Chairperson NDMC/Commissioner MCD/VC DDA and comprising of senior representative of DJB, DVB, TCPO, Divisional Commissioner, GNCTD etc. to guide, review and monitor the work pertaining to regularization and related matters.

6. Miscellaneous

6.1 Within the overall framework of these guidelines, if any clarification is required or if any doubt has got to be removed, instructions/advice of the Ministry of Urban Development and Poverty Alleviation, Government of India would be obtained.

6.2 While approving building plans or issuing occupation/completion certificates, separate indemnity bond indemnifying the local body/DDA is to be filed by the owner(s).

6.3 Unauthorized construction of any nature, not covered by these guidelines or within the provisions of Development Control Norms to be decided, would be strictly dealt with and demolished as per instructions issued earlier from time-to-time.

7. Development Control Norms

7.1 Since the prevailing bye-laws and norms cannot be employed in view of the deviations from prevailing norms, the following Development controls be made applicable:

(i) For plots facing road width less than 9.0 m./30ft., Ground coverage upto 100 per cent maximum, subject to the maximum, permissible FAR as per MPD/BBL and upto a maximum height of 8.0 m.

(ii) On the plots facing 9.0 ml./30ft. and above roads, the construction can go upto 12.0 m. Height. subject to maximum permissible FAR as per MPD/BBL.

(iii) No projection outside plot line, except sunshade of 0.60 m. on openings will be permissible.

(iv) For provision of service connections to each and every plot, minimum road width required should be 4.5 m. whenever the road width is less than 4.5 m., no individual service connection be provided. However, community service provision will be made and the land is to be provided by the society for the same.

(v) From fire safety point of view the length of the street/connecting road be limited to 100 m., maximum when approach road is less than 9 mts.

7.2 As far as the educational facilities are concerned, the minimum standards stipulated by the Director of Education, GNCTD would be considered adequate. Looking into the availability of the land, we may group together the facilities *e.g.* community hall, dispensary etc. However, all the land required for facilities and utilities will have to be provided by the Society of the concerned unauthorized colony.

7.3 For improvement of physical and social infrastructure, unauthorized colonies should get the modern services and amenities and should also be catered for their traditional cultural styles. Keeping in view the community facilities, the minimum standards are modified as follows :

Suggested Size for Facilities :

Sl. No.	*Items*	*Norms(Min.)*
1.	Primary School and Sr. Sec. School	As per the norms of Director of Education for recognition of such schools. Land component to be worked out accordingly.
2.	Community Bldg./Hall	200 m^2.
3.	Dispensary	200 m^2.
4.	ESS (Electric Sub-station)	As per DVB's requirement and site availability, DVB to also explore the pole mounted ESS in the eventuality of non-availability of land.

After guidelines were framed and filed in the Court by the Government, the Honourable High Court dismissed the Writ Petition on 27th February 2001 filed by Common Cause Society with the following directions :

(i) It would be appropriate if the Union of India, Ministry of Urban Affairs and Employment, Department of Urban Development, notifies colonies, which according to it are to be regularized and which cannot be regularized, in terms of General Principles, more particularly, paragraph (1.1) of the guidelines.

(ii) Till the modalities in terms of the guidelines are worked out, interim orders passed in CWP No. 4771/93 and connected petitions shall be operative.

(iii) By giving the directions-making observations, it shall not be construed as if we have expressed any opinion about the legality or otherwise of the guidelines in question.

Unauthorized construction is a regular feature in Delhi's landscape. Inspite of administrative instructions issued from time-to-time even at the highest level, unauthorized construction continues unabated all over Delhi. Field functionaries, Revenue Officials, and police are all responsible for the failure to check this phenomenon and encroachment on Government land. This has also led to the emergence of slums in the form of *jhuggi-jhompri* clusters. Various committees and commissions were set up from time-to-time to identify ways to battle this menace. In the recent past five such committees/commissions were set-up:

1. Justice Nanavati Commsiion.
2. Tejender Khanna Committee.
3. Mathur Committee.
4. Shrivastav Committee.
5. Dogra Committee.

Irrespective of the number of committees that may be formed, the reality is that it is not possible to carry out large-scale demolitions once we allow a certain number of *jhuggi-jhompri* clusters and unauthorized colonies to come up. Social, economic and political considerations are cited to suggest that demolition of such large-scale structures is not possible. Besides, the law and order problem in carrying out demolitions of such large scale settlements a plea is also made that such demolitions lead to national wastage when we are already short of housing stock. A somewhat similar view (given below) was expressed in the Justice Nanavati Commission Report (Page 103-104) in favour of regularization of unauthorized colonies:

> "If all these dwelling units are demolished then all the persons residing in these houses will become homeless. There is already a shortage of housing accommodation in Delhi and if these colonies/houses are demolished then the shortage of housing accommodation in Delhi will become worse. Thousands of houses will have to be demolished resulting in huge financial loss. The only positive benefit of such an action would be that it will act as a deterrent in future. Question again arises whether this would be worthwhile considering the huge economic loss and great amount of hardship and misery that the people residing in such unauthorized colonies/constructions will have to suffer. It would be almost criminal to demolish so many houses and make lakhs of persons homeless when there is already a shortage of housing accommodation. It would be unwise and unfair to adopt such a course. Wisdom would require a more intelligent and a better solution. Unauthorized colonies have been existing since years and the persons who were responsible for their coming up may not now be concerned with them any more. The occupants of such houses might have changed and persons residing therein now may not have flouted any of the developmental rules or the building regulations. To punish them by demolishing their dwelling units would be unfair and inequitable particularly when those dwelling units have been allowed to exist for so many years. It would be almost impossible for the Government to take such a drastic action in view of the social, economic and political consequences that would follow."

Unauthorized colonies normally come up on Government Land, Gaon Sabha Land, land notified for acquisition and private land. Some colonies come up partly on private land and partly on Gaon Sabha Land. In the past, there was widespread confusion among the public about title of these lands. People had made heavy investments of their hard earned money in good faith, believing the colonizers, but nevertheless were sometimes afraid about the land title. For removing doubts about the title of land on which these unauthorized colonies had come up the Lt. Governor of Delhi issued an order on 12th December 2007, clearly defining private land and Gaon Sabha Land.

I. *Government Land*: Land which has been awarded under the Land Acquisition Act, 1894 and its compensation has been taken by the ex-land owners, will be treated as Government Land, irrespective of the fact whether its possession has been taken over or not.

II. *Private Land:* Land for which award has been made under the Land Acquisition Act, 1894 but the land owner has not taken the compensation and possession of the land is still with the land owner, will be treated as private land.

III. *Gaon Sabha Land:* On coming into force The Land Reforms Act, 1954, all lands which vested in the Gaon Sabha, whether its possession was taken-over by the Government or not, will be treated as Government land. After enforcement of this Act, land vested with the Gaon Sabha under section 81 of the Act, will also be treated as Government Land.

After this notification of the Lt. Governor there was very clear identification of Government land and private land. Hence, there should be no confusion anymore regarding this issue. No interpretations are required because order of the Lt. Governor is very clear.

In October 2004, the Government invited applications for the regularization of unauthorized colonies that had come up in existence upto March 2002. 1432 applications were received.

In June 2006, by a public notice, applications were invited from those colonies which were in existence upto March 2002, and which also figured in the original list of 1071 colonies but could not apply for regularization against the earlier notice inviting applications. This time, an additional 107 applications were received. Thus, in all 1539 applications were received for the regularization of unauthorized colonies. Giving priority to this initiative the Government setup a Board on 20th June 2007, which was headed by the Chief Minister of Delhi, for the development of these colonies.

The Government of NCTD in its advertisements released in newspapers for the distribution of provisional certificates of regularization has expressed the belief that 50,00,000 people will benefit through the regularization of these colonies. The distribution of certificates was a major event for the Government and that's why these provisional certificates were issued in a function by Mrs. Sonia Gandhi, Chairperson of the Congress Party.

Regularization of unauthorized colonies has different connotations for different persons and groups. For the political parties it is an action which will determine the voting pattern, for colonisers what matters is only a notification or a certification of regularization. For the inhabitants the regularization means security and no threat of demolition, while for a property dealer it is a price rise in the property and for the common man it is simply an assurance. The issue first came up in 1983. It again came up at the Government level in 1993 when a list of such colonies was prepared. The process of regularization with assurances is still going on. NGOs also play an important part for or against and matter. The Courts, besides analysing the legality, also have to look into the whole issue in terms of social implications. During this course of time various committees are constituted for an assessment as well as to facilitate the decision.

Another point that bears consideration is that site conditions in these colonies are generally different from what is brought out on record. In most of the colonies a large number of plots are purchased not by the needy but on speculative considerations. A quick tour around these colonies will show a large number of vacant plots, plots with plinth construction, plots with *Kaccha* or *Pucca* boundary wall and plots with a boundary wall and small *Kaccha* room built inside to show occupancy.

Even the pricing of plots in these areas is determined by various factors. If the Government announces the provision of electricity, the rates will be increased by the colonizers from Rs. 500 to Rs. 1000 per sq. yd. Similarly, if there is an announcement about the construction of a road connecting the colony, the rates will go up by a certain amount. Again, rates will go up when there is construction of one road in the colony or construction of a drain in some part of the colony. The rates also went up by Rs. 500 to Rs. 1000 on the day when some of these colonies got connected with Metro Stations through the Metro Feeder Service. Thus, one can see that through this development process the rate goes up by announcement, introduction or execution of each developmental activity. The beneficiary is the colonizer and the broker. The actual user is always in the background. There are some unauthorized colonies in south Delhi where the rate has gone upto Rs. 40,000 to Rs. 60,000 per sq. yd. depending upon the location, connectivity and internal road plan.

Even after plans are submitted by the colonizers with the Government for regularization the colonies keep on expanding as the adjoining agricultural field is added in the purview by making another row of plots either in the same block or by calling it another next block. The innocent purchaser of these plots is generally not aware of this. These extensions thus again become unauthorized colonies for future regularization. The poor purchaser does not know that he might have to wait for regularization for as long as 15 to 20 years. Thus, the vicious cycle of these creation and subsequent regularization of unauthorized colonies goes on. If a survey is conducted of these colonies in terms of actual users the number of beneficiaries through regularization of unauthorized colonies will be much less than what the Government has come with. The Government also in its part cannot do repeated surveys because the situation keeps changing everyday. Surveys which were done in 1999-2000 have no relevance today either in terms of area of the colony, land title, ownership or occupancy pattern. If the Government is not able to provide housing at affordable price, it is impossible to check the growth of unauthorized colonies. For example, if DDA sells its residential land at the rate of Rs. 1,00,000 per sq. meter an average person would prefer to go to an unauthorized colony and buy a piece of land at the rate of Rs. 8000 to 10,000, even in much lesser developed areas where few urban facilities are available. He knows that the Government will provide the necessary infrastructure gradually. As the population of the city grows so will the growth pattern of these unauthorized colonies. The two parallel development models will continue; one for the "better" areas for those who can afford and the other for the "less desirable" areas who cannot afford. This is a historic fact and we have to accept it. Since an increase in population and the limited growth in new affordable housing is difficult to control, new unauthorized colonies will continue to emerge and the best course of action would be to regulate the developments by issuing licenses to the colonizers and determining land rates for the residential plots. The Government will have to intervene in the colonization process and pricing of land to look out for the interests of the actual needy people.

6 RE-SETTLEMENT OF SQUATTERS

The problem of squatters is common in all Indian cities. However, it is more prevalent in metropolitan cities due to the migration of people from rural areas of less developed states to those cities. The problem of encroachment on public land starts from day one when landless labourers from other states move to the city in search of employment. Generally the squatters are not choosy about the land they choose to squat on, though they would preferably like to be close to their native fellow men and workplace. From time to time the Government has drawn schemes for the re-location of squatters. The first such re-location programme started in 60's on the basis of a survey conducted by the Bharat Sevak Samaj to identify the squatters to find out the extent of the problem. Emergence of Jhuggy-Clusters, their formation, Clearance and Resettlement of Sqautters have been brought out in this chapter.

Delhi, which was a small city with a population of only 4.1 lakhs in 1911, grew to have population of 9.2 lakhs by 1941. However, with the Partition of the country and influx of the refugees from the West Pakistan in 1947 the population of Delhi increased to 17.4 lakhs by 1951. By 2001 city population went upto 143.7 lakhs and projected population of Delhi by 2021 is 230 lakhs. The increase in population over the years is given in Table 6-1.

When lakhs of refugees came to Delhi from West Pakistan after the Partition they squatted anywhere and everywhere. Even a place like Purana Qilla became a large refugee camp. Similarly, the area adjacent to Delhi University known as Kingsway Camp became home to a large number of refugees squatted. So was the case in areas like Karol Bagh and Jhandewalan. That was

Table 6.1 : Population Trend from 1911 to 2021 (Haven't we given this table already in an earlier chapter?)

Year	*Population (In Lakhs)*
1911	4.1
1921	4.9
1931	6.4
1941	9.2
1951	17.4
1961	26.6
1971	40.7
1981	62.2
1991	94.2
2001	143.7
2011	195.1 (Projected)
2021	220-230 (Projected)

the time when every one could see the plight of refugees. In a real sense we can't call them encroachers because they were pushed out by the circumstances created in West Pakistan. They included rich middle class people who had everything in life but had to leave behind their all assets and properties including their near and dear ones and come empty handed to the newly formed nation of India. Thus, they deserved sympathy and rehabilitation packages.

On the initiative of Pandit Jawahar Lal Nehru, the then Prime Minister of India, a survey was conducted of squatters in Delhi by the Bharat Sewak Samaj. The idea was to understand the extent of the problem in terms of the number of squatters on public land and draw a scheme for their rehabilitation. The detailed survey conducted by the Bharat Sewak Samaj revealed the extent of the squatting population and the land encroached upon. The problem was at a stage where it needed immediate solution. It was, therefore, decided to draw a plan for rehabilitation of squatters. Since availability of land was not a problem at the time the size of the plot to be allotted to each squatter was determined to be of 80 sq. yds. Under this scheme plots of this size were allotted in areas like Moti Bagh at Ring Road.

Thereafter, the allotment of 80 sq. yds was not found feasible because of the sheer number of squatters and it was therefore decided to construct tenements for *jhuggi-jhompri* dwellers. Under the scheme 384 tenements were constructed at Garhi Jharia Maria near East of Kailash. Besides these an additional 1408 tenements were constructed at Kalkaji and Ranjit Nagar (Khanpur) and 992 at Seelampur.

Subsequently, the construction of tenements for squatters was discontinued and it was decided to allot them only plots of 25 sq. yds. A comprehensive scheme known as *jhuggi-jhompri removal scheme* was undertaken in which besides the allotment of a plot of 25 sq. yds. norms were also laid down for the construction of toilet blocks, bathrooms, hand-pumps and other infrastructural facilities. After the scheme was drawn up, colonies like Madangir in South Delhi, Seelampur in East Delhi, Madipur in West Delhi were developed. Families were shifted to those locations from the city areas. Those who were shifted from Rahgarh Pura in Karol Bagh were re-settled in Madipur in 1968-69. Similarly those who were shifted from Bela Road Area were re-settled in Seelampur and those who were shifted from various parts in South Delhi were re-settled in Madangir.

Even after all these measures the problem of squatters and encroachment on Government land was assuming unmanageable proportions and hence it was decided to divide the squatters in two categories *i.e.* eligible squatters and ineligible squatters. The categorization of eligible and ineligible squatters was done on the basis of a cut-off date. To discourage the ineligible squatters they were shifted to far-flung areas of the city *i.e.* at the periphery of the city. It was also decided that norms of providing physical infrastructure like toilet blocks, bathrooms and hand-pump etc. would be at a lower scale for ineligible squatters. This was intended as a means to provide fewer facilities to ineligible squatters as compared to eligible squatters and also to shift them to the periphery of the city. These ineligible squatters were thus shifted to Seema Puri and New Seema Puri in East Delhi, Nangloi and Hastsal in West Delhi, and Khanpur and Tigri in South Delhi.

From mid-1975 to early 1977 a massive slum re-location programme was carried out in Delhi. The basic purpose of the programme was to clear the city of slums. The plan was to remove all *jhuggi-jhompri* from the city and rehabilitate all the squatters in various Re-settlement Colonies. Re-settlement Colonies were planned in all the four directions of the city. The plans of the colonies provided wide roads, lanes, parks, streetlights, drinking water, dispensaries, community centers and libraries. This physical and social infrastructure also existed in colonies, which had already come up in areas like Madipur, Nangloi, Seema Puri, Hastsal and Madangir.

The programme was attempted at such a massive scale that officers of all the departments were associated in the re-settlement programme. It was monitored by the then Vice–Chairman of Delhi Development Authority, Sh. Jagmohan. Daily reports were sought and work was evaluated regularly. During the period of 18 months 2,40,000 squatters were shifted from various parts of the city to 44 re-settlements colonies developed all-over Delhi. A few of the major Re-settlement Colonies to be named were Mangolpuri in West Delhi, Trilokpuri, Himmatpuri, Nandnagri and Gokulpuri in East Delhi, besides New Seema Puri at Shahdara Border and Khan Pur, and Tigri and Dakshin Puri / Dakshin Puri Extn. in South Delhi. An idea of the sheer scale of the programme can be drawn from the fact that the length of roads constructed in these Re-settlement Colonies was equal to the length of road from Delhi to Agra. Besides the 2,40,000 residential plots a large number of Commercial/Shop plots were also allotted. As an incentive to plan for a small family those who opted to go for sterilization were allotted a plot of 25 sq. yds. This incentive motivated a large number of people. Plots were also allotted for religious institutions. The details of residential plots in re-settlement colonies allotted up till February 1977 are given in Table 6.2.

Life in the Resettlement Colonies has completely changed the fate of its residents. There was a feeling that squatters were generally illiterate, poor and unhygienic group of people. This

Table 6.2 : Plots Allotted in the Re-settlement Colonies upto 1977

Sl. No.	*Name of Colony*	*Area in Acres*	*No. of Plots (25 sq. yds.)*
1.	Sunlight Colony	48.05	1675
2.	Sriniwas Puri	15.04	Tenements were constructed
3.	Garhi Village	7.68	Tenements were constructed
4.	Kalkaji	58.60	Tenements were constructed
5.	Madangir	139.20	6864
6.	Dakshin Puri Colony	77.90	6847
7.	Dakshin Puri Extn.	47.07	5634
8.	Tigri	38.08	2135
9.	Moti Bagh Ring Road	14.50	Tenements were constructed
10.	Pandav Nagar	45.47	1174 + 35
11.	Ranjit Nagar (Khan Pur)	6.00	Tenements were constructed
12.	Naraina (Inder Puri)	65.00	3943
13.	N.G. Road (A,D,E & C,F & G)	213.53	5716
14.	Addl Plots (N.G.Road) RandE Block etc.		2714
15.	Hastsal	40.95	3460+(60 Adll.Plots)
16.	Madipur	55.70	4612
17.	Nangloi Ph – I	30.23	1618
18.	Nangloi Ph – II	52.30	4361
19.	Nangloi Ph – III	11.00	752
20.	Nangloi Ph – IV (Jawala Puri)	53.81	3172
21.	Wazir Pur	30.70	4002
22.	Seelam Pur Ph.I and II		500
23.	Seelam Pur Ph.III and IV		4811
24.	Seelam Pur (Addl. Plots)		500
25.	Seema Puri Old	44.00	3626
26.	Seema Puri New (Ph.I,II & III)	17.74	3280
27.	West Khan Pur	7.15	1225
28.	Chowkhandi	8.55	1554
29.	Khayala Ph.I,II & III	20.0	3338
30.	Gokal Puri	14.86	2402
31.	Shakur Pur Ph. I & II	37.04	
32.	Shakur Pur Ph.III	7.91	7965
33.	Shakur Pur Ph. IV	6.27	
34.	Nand Nagri Ph. I	98.88	9960
35.	Nand Nagri Ph. II	31.13	
36.	Nand Nagri Block PandG Extn, EWS Qrts. (Weaver Colony)	5.02	1530
37.	Nand Nagri Extn.	12.35	2942
38.	Patpar Ganj Complex (Trilok Puri, Kalyan Puri, Khichri Pur)	815	25048
39.	Mangol Puri Ph. I	19.32	26884
40.	Mangol Puri Ph. II	23.67	
41.	Mangol Puri Ph. III	134.73	

(Contd...)

Table 6.2 : Plots Allotted in the Re-settlement Colonies upto 1977

42.	Sultan Puri	252.76	19693
43.	Sultan Puri (Addl. Plots)	89.41	153
44.	Mangla Puri	3.81	672 (Ph.II) 544 (Ph.I)
45.	Jhangir Puri	429.47	19216
46.	Kondli	15.55	1920
47.	Nehru Vihar		1992

contention was controverted by the numerous successes of people from these Re-settlement Colonies. When a study was conducted of Madipur area in 1974, after 67 years of their rehabilitation, it was found that the educational level was increasing. The number of school drop-outs had decreased and Madipur had produced its first graduate. Shri Sajjan Kumar, Member Parliament, who worked in this area during early 70's to help families that were trying to settle down in Madipur under a new environment and different lifestyle, represents the large outer Delhi Parliamentary Constituency today. Today, Madipur can be proud to have produced not only men in service and business-class but has also a dedicated parliamentarian, as one among them. This has been a real transformation and has given a new hope for the resettled refugee families. The Delhi Development Authority had set-up a community center in these colonies, which had a dispensary with a doctor and supporting staff, a TV Center for entertainment, a library for school children and a reading room for people of all age groups. This was a common platform replacing the traditional village Panchayat. The Community Center functioned all through seven days of the week so that facility was constantly available to the residents. The theme, mission and basic objective of the community centers was intended to provide all social assistance in terms of education and health needs.

When from 1975-77 2,40,000 families were shifted from slum conditions to these Re-settlement Colonies between 1975-77 few expected the colonies to develop so fast. The spirit of re-settlement was also a mission. The author himself is a witness to the conditions under which the re-settlement programme was carried out. He ensured that the families that were shifted to Re-settlement Colonies were actually given title papers of their plots and handed over physical possession of the plot on the same day to make the family realize their dream of owning property in Delhi. When families moved from the squatting areas to their new plots after sundown they were allotted the plots in the light of offical jeeps since there was no electricity in some of the areas while the development was going on. It was a very satisfying movement both for the author and for the families re-settled.

The sensitivity of this process could be felt even at the highest level. It was during a night in December 1976 that the then Vice-Chairman of the DDA, Sh. Jagmohan, rang upto find out the well-being of some families that had been shifted to Madangir on that day. It was 9.00 p.m. on that chilly night when the author went to the site to check up on the families. The 15-20 families had actually been shifted to Dakshin Puri. They were persuaded to move to a nearby Community Center building under construction. Since their belongings were lying in their new plots, they wanted to spend the night in the plots themselves. Upon the author's persuasion the women and children moved to the Community Center building under construction. The author got a lot of firewood from the nearby "Tall" (Coal and Wood Shop) so that the menfolk could light a bonfire to keep them warm during the night. These were brave people refugees who had lived through a partitition and spending a chilly night near a bonfire was a small issue compared to what they had been through earlier. When the author returned home from the site and rang up Shri Jagmohan at 1.00 a.m., he was eagerly awaiting the author's call to hear about the condition of those families (there were no mobile phones at that time). This shows the sincerity and sensitivity of the officers even at the top level in handling the re-settlement programmes. The author, therefore, repeatedly called the entire process a "re-location" and not a "dislocation" as was alleged by some people at the time.

The officers working on the re-settlement projects were also motivated because even the Vice–Chairman of the DDA would visit these colonies regularly. Trilokpuri Colony, a very large Re-settlement Colony in East Delhi, was named after one Senior Engineer Shri Trilok Singh. This example alone should be enough to exhibit the amount of motivation and strength the engineer and his team would have obtained in order to work for 12-14 hours a day.

The slum population in the *jhuggi-jhompri* clusters kept on increasing even while there was check on emergence of new *jhuggi-jhompri* clusters. Existing *jhuggi-jhompri* clusters were getting densified. Migrants coming to the city for the first time, pushed by the conditions of poverty and unemployment, get support from the relatives and members of the native hinterland. The presence of a relative or a friend or a community person from the same village is a great source of help for the new migrant in an unknown city.

The population growth in Delhi is on account of both migration and natural growth. Most of the squatters in *jhuggi-jhompri* clusters come to Delhi in search of employment from the neighbouring States of UP, Haryana and Rajasthan. In the 90's it was noticed that an increasingly large number of migrants to the city came from Bihar. Broadly the state-wise migration of squatters in Delhi is reflected in Table 6-3.

Table 6.3 : State-wise Migration: 1981-91

States	*Percentage of Migrants from 1981-91*
Uttar Pradesh	49.91 per cent
Haryana	11.82 per cent
Bihar	10.99 per cent
Rajasthan	6.11 per cent
Punjab	5.43 per cent
Others	15.68 per cent

(*Source :* Census of India 1991).

Growth of *jhuggies* has been noted as a regular feature in Delhi's landscape. A survey conducted in 1951 showed that there were 12,749 *jhuggies* at the time in Delhi. The number kept on increasing inspite of remedial action by the Government to provide alternative accommodation in the form of plots in various re-settlement colonies and preventive measures to check the emergence of new *jhuggi-jhompri* clusters. No amount of surveillance by the land owning agencies and the police has been able to curb the tendency of encroachment on Government land by *jhuggi* dwellers. Anyone who has come to the city in search of employment from any part of the country (more so from UP and Bihar) will squat somewhere or the other, mostly on some site not developed by the Government. The growth of *jhuggies*, which was at its highest during 1991 and 1994, is reflected in Table 6.4.

Table 6.4 : Growth of *Jhuggies* in Delhi

Year	*Number of Jhuggies*
1951	12759
1961	42815
1971	62594
1981	98709
1991	259344
1994	480929

(*Source*: M.N. Buch Committee Report).

A large-scale re-settlement programme to re-settle the squatters from Bela Road Area started in 1968-69. At that point of time squatters were also removed from Rahgarhpura and adjoining areas. The area around Nigam Bodh Ghat upto Old Railway Bridge was also cleared during 1968-69. Again during the Emergency period, *i.e.* from June 1975- early 1977, 2,40,000 *jhuggies* were removed and re-settled in 44 Re-settlement Colonies in areas like Madipur, Nangloi, Jawalapuri, Mangolpuri, Trilokpuri, Seemapuri, Tigri, Khanpur and Hastsal etc. Inspite of all these efforts 98,709 new *jhuggies* came up in the meanwhile. In 1990 when the Janta Government took over the then Prime Minister Shri V.P. Singh visited Bhoomiheen Camp (*jhuggi-jhompri* cluster) at Govind Puri and made an announcement that no *jhuggi* will be removed in Delhi without providing alternative accommodation. This very sentence of Shri V.P. Singh encouraged the encroachers and within four years about 2,21,585 more *jhuggies* came up raising the total number of *jhuggies* in Delhi to 4,80,000. It was a very difficult task for any Government agency to remove such a large number of *jhuggies* in the absence of alternative rehabilitation sites. In the 10 years between 1981-90 1,60,635 *jhuggies* came up on public land and after the announcement of Shri V.P. Singh another 2,21,585 *jhuggies* came up in just another four years. Thus, on an average 151 *jhuggies* came up daily on Government land.

Alongwith the growth in *jhuggies* the slum population in Delhi has also grown at a rapid speed. In 1981, about 15 lakhs people were living in slum conditions but by 1997 the number went upto 26.6 lakhs. It was projected that by 2011, 45 lakhs people will be living in slum areas. The growth trend of slum population is reflected in Table 6.5.

Table 6.5 : Growth of Slum Population

Year	*Population in Lakhs*
1981	15
1991	18
1994	24
1997	26.6
2001	32
2011	45

Source: Census of India 1981 and 1991, Society for Development Studies and High Level Committee on Unauthorized Colonies, Ministry of Urban Development.

The Slums and *Jhuggi-Jhompri* Department (commonly known as the Slum and JJ Department) was shuttled 2-3 times between the Municipal Corporation of Delhi and the Delhi Development Authority. From 1990 onwards, when the scheme of slum and *jhuggi-jhompri* removal was transferred from the Delhi Development Authority to the Municipal Corporation of Delhi, the work of clearance of encroached sites and the relocation of squatters came under the jurisdiction of the

Municipal Corporation of Delhi. From 1990 onwards the Slum Department allotted 39,634 plots of 18 sq. meter and 34,209 plots of 12.5 sq. meter. In all 73,843 plots have been allotted under the Resettlement Scheme to the squatters in various parts of the city who were shifted from encroached sites. In his process 221 sites encroached by the *jhuggi-Jhompri* clusters in various parts of the Delhi were removed and sites were cleared. Details of reclaimed sites are given in *(Annexure – 6/1)*. Thus, valuable Government land has been cleared for the projects for which it was earmarked. The colony wise details of plots allotted are given in Table 6.6.

Table 6.6 : Plots allotted under Resettlement Scheme after 1990

Sl. No.	*Re-settlement Colony/Site*	*Area in Acres*	*Plots Allotted*		*Total*
			18 sq.m.	*12.5 sq.m.*	
1.	Madan Pur Khadar	23.76	1290	1063	2353
2.	Tikri Khurd, Narela Site – II	5.50	497	—	497
3.	Tikri Khurd, Narela Site – I	25.00	1993 (-68)	214	2139
4.	Holumbi Kalan, Ph – II	70.00	3341	3897	7238
5.	Molar Band, Ph – I	27.40	2070	266	2336
6.	Molar Band, Ph – II	23.60	928	1534	2462
7.	Narela, Sub City	62.86	3474	3352	6826
8.	Holumbi Khurd	7.67	—	906	906
9.	Holumbi Khurd, Ph–I	30.00	1782	1040	2822
10.	Sector – 23, Rohini	2.23	—	236	236
11.	Sector – 24, Rohini	18.50	1472	—	1472
12.	Sector – 25, Rohini	14.82	1176	—	1176
13.	Sector – 26, Rohini Ph–IV	4.00	—	496	496
14.	Sector–26, Rohini	7.24	—	846	846
15.	Sector–3, Dwarka Ph–I	11.387	979	—	979
16.	Sector-3, Dwarka Ph–II	6.735	552	—	552
17.	Sahyoyg Vihar	14.114	1072 (+66)	—	1138
18.	Sector–I Dwarka	12.35	1029	—	1029
19.	Sector–VII, Dwarka	12.08	1043	—	1043
20.	Sector–III, Dwarka Ph-III	12.35	1001	—	1001

Sl. No.	*Re-settlement Colony/Site*	*Area in Acres*	*Plots Allotted*		*Total*
			18 sq.m.	*12.5 sq.m.*	
21.	Bakkarwal	49.36	2520	1532	4052
22.	Himmat Puri, Block–31	2.00	—	258	258
23.	Himmat Puri,	1.00	—	195	195
24.	Samaipur Badli	4.00	324	—	324
25.	Bhalswa Jahangir-puri, Ph–I	87.00	1965	1772	3737
26.	Binda Pur, Pocket–IV	13.56	1163	—	1163
27.	Bawana	87.00	3710	5552	9262
28.	Sector-16B, Dwarka Ph–II, Site-I	6.04	516	—	516
29.	Pocket-J, Sector-16 Rohini	11.6	303	—	303
30.	Sawda Ghewra, Ph–I	84.62	2930	4248	7178
31.	Sawda Ghewra, Ph–II	102.35	936 1570	1470 5332	2406 6902
	Total	840.519	39634	34209	73843

As the scheme for the re-settlement of squatters was the responsibility of the Slum and JJ Department of the Delhi Development Authority allotted land for squatters' of Re-settlement Colonies on rates fixed by the Government. It was more or less equal to the land acquisition rates. DDA was not satisfied with these rates because subsequent litigation by the land-owners for enhanced compensation of land went on in the Courts for years together. Appeals to the High Court could drag it further still. By the time DDA was liable to pay the enhanced compensation to Slum Department would not be a party to this additional financial liability. Therefore these days the Slum Department is acquiring the land directly through the Land Acquisition Collector/Land and Building Department of Government of NCTD after getting planning clearance from the Delhi Development Authority. This helps the Slum Department to acquire the land fast.

As a matter of procedure, the land owning agencies identify their land that is to be cleared of squatters. Then priorities are fixed for clearing the project sites where some hospitals, police stations or communication center is to come up. This is necessary because priority areas cannot wait to be cleared. A Joint Survey is conducted by the land owning department and the Slum Department, because the land owning agency/department has to pay the shifting charges at the rate of Rs. 29,000/- per family. The beneficiary has to pay only Rs.7,000 as his/her contribution. The rest of the amount comes from the Government grant. There are large areas where Joint Survey by the land owning agency and the Slum Department has been conducted and the land owning agency has also paid the shifting charges while the actual shifting of squatters by the Slum Department is yet to be conducted. The details of such land are given in Table 6.7.

Table 6.7 : *Jhuggi-Jhompri* clusters Surveyed for Relocation from1993-94 to 2006-07

Sl. No.	*Name of the JJ Clusters*	*Land Owning Agency*	*Amount Received (In Rs.)*	*No. of Jhuggies to be Relocated*
1.	Swami Daya Nand, Shahadara	MCD	25,20,000/-	128
2.	Wazir Pur	MCD	3,46,000/-	14
3.	Lucknow Road, Timar Pur	Police Deptt.	17,59,000/-	74
4.	G.T. Road, Burari	MCD	7,83,000/-	37
5.	A.E.O. from Plot No. 17, Rouse Avenue Area	CBSE	3,48,000/-	12
6.	Behind Meridein Hotel	NDMC	11,02,000/-	38
7.	Institutional Area, Lodhi Road	DDA	2,08,670/-	34
8.	Nizamuddin	DDA	48,42,000/-	200
9.	Aram Bagh	RML Hospital	13,29,000/-	58
10.	Kali Bari Marg, Sector-II, DIZ Area	CPWD	21,45,000/-	88
11.	Govt. Colony, Netaji Nagar	CPWD	3,80,000/-	17
12.	JJ Cluster behind Indian Express Building	CPWD	53,00,000/-	325
13.	J.P. Memorial Park Ferozeshah Kotla	Ministry of Culture	49,00,000/-	300
14.	Sanjay Camp Railway Line, Chanakya Puri	Railway	2,16,46,000/-	955

Sl. No.	*Name of the JJ Clusters*	*Land Owning Agency*	*Amount Received (In Rs.)*	*No. of Jhuggies to be Relocated*
15.	Arjun Das Camp, Bangali Camp, back of House No. 2, Tuglaq Road and 21 A, Aurangjeb Road	NDMC	1,08,69,000/-	579
16.	Asaf Ali Road Plo. No. 1122/23	MCD	36,21,000/-	63
17.	B-122 and147, Okhla Indl. Area	DDA	36,21,000/-	150
18.	Telecommunication JJ Cluster	Telecom munication Dept.	1,42,50,000/-	700
19.	Plot No. 25 Loha Mandi, Naraina	DDA	15,37,000/-	102
20.	S. Educational Society	DDA	17,60,000/-	75
21.	Guru Ravidass Camp	MCD	2,85,000/-	16
22.	Bengali Camp Okhla Ph-I	DDA	12,78,000/-	51
23.	G.T.Karnal Road, Ashok Vihar	DDA	2,93,68,000/-	1146
24.	Hari Nagar	CPWD	7,80,000/-	30
25.	Kanak Durga Camp Sector-12, R.K.Puram	LandDO	74,64,000/- 1,59,69,000/-	940
26.	Shanker Camp Sector-13, R.K.Puram	CPWD	18,99,000/-	80
27.	New Sanjay Camp Okhla	DDA	9,86,000/-	34
28.	South Campus Dhaula Kuan	Delhi University	34,60,000/-	344
29.	Southern Ridge (Bhatti Mines)	Forest Deptt.	10,70,97,000/-	3500
30.	Lado Sarai	DDA	4,06,000/-	100
31.	Jaipur Golden, Rohini	DDA	1,80,53,000/-	800
32.	CEWS, Kalyan Bhavan, Vasant Kunj	Social Welfare Board	46,60,000/-	235
33.	Pragati Fly Over	DTTDC	31,80,000/-	156
34.	Railway Safety Zones	Railway	9,09,41,000/-	3200
35.	Bilas Pur Camp, Molad Bandh	NTPC	4,00,37,000/-	1726
	Total			**16307**

Prior to the present scheme of squatter relocation, the squatters were required to pay only the license fee of Rs. 7/- and Re.1/- towards scavenging charges per month. No lump sum amount was charged from the beneficiary. The scheme was fully funded by Government. As per estimate, in the 44 Resettlement Colonies developed upto 1977 about Rs. 80 lakhs per year are recovered as licence fee. From time-to-time the Government has announced plans to grant leasehold rights to such allottees.

Recently the Delhi Government has taken a decision to provide squatter's families with built up flats instead of plots. These flats will be provided on a leasehold basis. The Delhi Development Authority has also decided to undertake in-situ development. It has identified some *jhuggi-Jhompri* clusters for that purpose. The area will be developed by private builders who will be allowed additional FAR and also commercial space to be disposed of by them. They will construct tenements for all the squatters in the cluster. It is yet to be seen how the programme takes off because a similar programme in Katputtli Colony near Shadi Pur Depot was going on for the last 7-8 years but did not work. An open approach is required on the part of the planners and bureaucrats. If the Government cannot solve the problem of squatters because of the funds involved, there is no harm in entering into private partnerships. This is important since city development has to be experimental to work-out new rehabilitation models.

From April 1990 to March 2008, 221 *jhuggi-jhompri* clusters have been removed from various parts of the city by the Slum Department of the Municipal Corporation of Delhi. The affected families have been relocated in different developed colonies. (Details are given in ***Annexure- 6***)

The resettlement scheme has undergone various changes from time to time based on the new policy evolved after Shri V.P. Singh, the then Prime Minister, announced in January 1990 while visiting Bhoomiheen Camp at Govindpuri that Ration Cards will be issued to all the *Jhuggi* dwellers and no squatter will be removed without providing alternative allotment. A subsequent survey was conducted by the Food and Civil Supply Department of the Delhi Government. In the first phase 2.60 lakhs families were identified in 929 *jhuggi-Jhompri* clusters as on January 31, 1990. However the Slum and JJ Department prepared a list of 1080 *jhuggi-jhompri* clusters as on 31st March 1994 where there were 4,80,929 families.

Now since *jhuggies* could only be shifted upon provision of alternative allotment, the clusters that were proposed to be removed were the ones where the land owning agency contributes shifting charges. In other cases where *jhuggies* were removed immediately, *in-situ* an upgradation programme was to be carried out. This was to provide basic facility and improve the environment. The minimum basic facilities included construction of pay and use Jan Suvidha Complexes containing toilets and baths and also providing mobile toilet vans in the *jhuggi-jhompri* clusters irrespective of the land title.

Under the programme of re-location where the land owning agency contributes Rs. 29,000 per plot besides share of the beneficiary, it was planned for the development of sites and services with plots of 18 sq. meters each with a 7 sq. meters undivided share in open courtyard as per the cluster Court planning concept. The total area allocated for each squatter family for re-settlement was 25 sq. meters in aggregate. The re-settlement complexes are an integral part of the new Residential Scheme of the DDA. Under this scheme a site measuring about 5 hectare was to be utilized for providing plots and achieving a density of 200 units per hectare. There is also provision for community facilities like Primary School, Shishu Vikas Kendra, Basti Vikas Kendra, Open Space, Community Utilities like Dhalau etc. Full coverage of 18 sq. meters is permitted to the beneficiary family on the ground-floor and subsequently when resources permit and depending upon the affordability of the beneficiary they can construct further on the ground-floor. Independent WC seat and bathroom on the upper floor with cooking shelf are an integral part of the dwelling unit that serve to make the unit a self content residential unit.

Since most of the land allotted to the Slum Department for re-settlement of squatters is part of the layout plans of the DDA, the Slum Department is responsible for the provision of infrastructural facilities within the layout of the re-settlement complex. The peripheral services are to be taken care of by the Delhi Development Authority as part of its integrated development. This arrangement was with reference to managing the re-settlement project within the budgetary limit.

Before removing a *jhuggi-jhompri* cluster the number of eligible squatters is determined by the Joint Survey conducted by the officials of the Slum Department and the Land Owning Agency. This is essential to ascertain because the Land Owning Agency has to pay the shifting charges. Ineligible squatters are removed by the Land Owning Agency to get possession of the whole site. The salient features of the New Resettlement Scheme that came into force in 1990-91 include: —

(a) Re-location of squatters situated on project sites required by the Land Owning Agencies.
(b) Only those squatter families will be eligible for alternative plot that are Indian Nationals and are living in the *jhuggi-jhompri* cluster as on 31.01.1990 and hold a valid Ration Card. The eligible families to be allotted plot of 18 sq. meters with 7 sq. meters undivided share in open courtyard as per the Cluster-Court-Town-House Planning concept.
(c) DDA to provide 20 per cent of re-sidential land @ Rs. 825/- per sq. metres of the net plotted area.
(d) To meet the re-location cost and re-settlement under the scheme, Slum Department to be provided with a sum of Rs. 23,000/- per family, *viz.* Rs. 10,000/- out of the plan funds per squatter family to be resettled along with Rs. 10,000/- to be paid in advance by the land owning agency and Rs. 10000/- by the respective beneficiary.
(e) Slum and JJ Department will construct on a plot of 18 sq. metres upto plinth level alongwith WC seat. This will be out of house building loan of Rs. 15,000/- to be sanctioned to each family by DCHFS/HUDCO.
(f) Resettlement is to be done by setting up multi-purpose cooperative societies covering about 200 families in each society. Allotment of sites and service plots to be made on leasehold basis through cooperative societies.

The above casting formula was later further revised raising the cost to Rs. 4,400/- per plot in view of the higher cost of land acquisition. The funding formula was also revised. Now the land owning agency had to contribute Rs. 29,000/- per family. Rs. 5,000/- was to be paid by the beneficiary family and Rs. 10000/- was to come from plan support.

The scheme has been under implementation since 1990-91. The Delhi Government had been providing plan support as envisaged in the scheme. Till March 2002 39,731 families were shifted from various *jhuggi-jhompri* cluster and re-settled in Dwarka, Rohini, Narela, Molad Bandh, Holumbi Kalan, Holumbi Khurd, Bhalswa and Bakarwala.

The relocation scheme has undergone further changes. The Slum Department had been providing WC with the plinth level plot on the assumption that shelter loan will simultaneously become available from DCHFS/HUDCO. In view of the decision of the High Court of Delhi to allot plots to squatters on the license fee only the provision of plinth and WC has been dispensed within the Future Development Scheme. Additionally, in order to provide toilet facilities the Slum Department is now providing community toilet and bath complexes in the re-located sites till the beneficiaries make their own arrangements of WC on the allotted plot. The provision of loan through HUDCO was ensured by Sh. Jagmohan, the then Minister of Urban Development, when a large number of families were shifted to Narela. He wanted them to be given financial support so that they would be able to construct their houses by purchasing building material and pooling their family labour. By arranging loan support most of the squatter families could construct their houses within a reasonable time and this gave them a new hope and sense of owning a house in Delhi.

When the cost of plots was raised from Rs. 23,000 to Rs. 44,000, besides the increase in the land acquisition rate, it was also noted that the expenditure on services had also gone up. This was additional expenditure on land and provision of facilities. The cost of development of each plot then worked out to Rs. 70,000/-. As a result of this the whole funding pattern required revision. Besides the eligibility criteria remaining the same (*i.e.* the beneficiary should be citizen of India, beneficiary and his dependent should not own residential plot in Delhi) it was also made clear that transfer of possession would amount to automatic termination of the license without notice and would result in cancellation and re-entry on the plot by the Slum and JJ Department. Under the new scheme the license may be granted by charging interest free cash security of Rs. 5,000/- from the licensee, with a license fee of Rs. 200/- per year, which is to be charged for ten years at the first instance. To recognize the right of women it was also decided that license will be given in the joint name of wife and husband, the first name being that of the wife. The licensee will be issued an identity card of the license including names of the family members with photos of the licensee and family members.

Under the latest policy those who are squatting on public land on 31.12.1998 but after 31.01.1990 will also be allotted a plot of 12 sq. meters. They are treated as post 90 eligible squatters. The cut-off date, determined to be 31.12.1998, was approved and conveyed by the Government of India, Ministry of Urban Development and Poverty Eleviation *vide* its communication number K-19014/4196-TD-II-B/VOL-III dated 13.10.2000. The Ministry had conveyed that it has been decided that the cut off date for eligible beneficiaries is extended from 31.01.1990 to 31.12.1998. It also approved allotments of 18 sq. meter plots to-pre-1990 squatters and 12 sq. meters to post-1990 squatters.

The Slum and JJ Department of the Municipal Corporation of Delhi provides basic facilities in the resettlement areas while the provision of peripheral and trunk services are to be taken care of by the concerned agency like Delhi Jal Board and Electricity Agencies. In addition, social infrastructure in the form of transport, education, health care and fair price shops etc. are to be provided by the Government of NCTD.

Under the present Re settlement Scheme plots of sizes of 18 sq. meters and 12.5 sq. meters are allotted. Again this categorization is for eligible and ineligible squatters. Those who were squatting on public land before 31st January 1990 are treated as eligible squatters and are entitled to an alternative plot of 18 sq. meters. Those squatters who possess a Ration

Card of post -1990 and upto December 1998 are entitled to a plot of 12.5 sq. meter. The Slum Department resorts to *in-situ* development where land owning agency does not need the land in near future and gives a no-objection certificate to the effect that the cluster may be upgraded. Since the implementation of the scheme from 1990-91 demonstrative projects of *in-situ* up-gradation were implemented at Pryog Vihar in West Delhi and at Ekta Vihar, R.K. Puram, South Delhi. One such project is also undertaken at Shanti Vihar. At Shahbad Daulatpur also 4,600 families have been covered under the scheme. Even where no *in-situ* development is done, civic amenities like water supply, streetlight, roads and storm water drains etc. are provided in the *jhuggi-jhompri* clusters.

For improving the environment in the *jhuggi-jhompri* clusters, various environmental improvement and social schemes, such as the construction of pay and use Jan Suvidha Complexes to curb the habit of open defecation, and Basti Vikas Kendras and Shishu Vikas Kendra to meet the social and health need of the children, have been set-up in slum clusters. The Slum Department has so far shifted about 60,000 families from 1990 onwards to well developed Re-settlement Colonies like Molar Band, Madan Pur Khadar, Dwarka, Rohini, Bakarwala, Bawana, Narela, Holumbi Kalan and Bhalswa. A number of requests are also pending with the Slum Department from the land owning agencies where more shifting is required. About 40 such clusters where there are about 15,000 families have been identified need re-location and the land owning agencies have already paid the shifting charges.

Also, under a new policy to construct EWS flats the Slum Department is planning to construct 6,896 flats at Dwarka, Rohini and Sawda Ghewra Ph–III. In addition the Slum Department also proposes to construct 400 flats at Dev Nagar for affected families in the Walled City. It also proposes to construct 15,000 flats at Bhalswa. The Slum Department is also planning to get additional 250 acres of land for its Re-settlement Scheme.

Slum clusters in various parts of the city and their subsequent re-location have deep social and economic implications. Clusters also have political support — that is why the slum population is termed as a "vote bank".

Wherever there are slums close to residential areas the property value of the neighbourhood area, especially the portion in front of the slum settlement, gets affected. In Allakhnanda the existence of a slum cluster proved a nuisance to the allottees of self-financing flats. The slum dwellers used to come to the DDA flat site for defecation early in the morning. Besides being a health hazard this activity also created a very filthy and unhygienic condition in the area. There was a case where because of these conditions an allottee of the flat was so desperate that she wanted to sell the flat and move away. It was difficult for her to find a buyer and get a reasonable price of the flat. She was also scared of lodging a complaint against the slum dwellers due to fear of retribution.

Similarly, in Ashok Vihar there are beautiful MIG Flats on one side of the railway track while a large *jhuggi-jhompri* clusters had come up on the other side of it. These squatters also use the space between the DDA flats and the railway track for defecation. The problem was so acute that it created social tension in the area. When the Government finally decided to remove the *jhuggi-jhompri* clusters the squatters resorted to violence and police had to resort to firing. Further problems arose when the authorities decided that in order to ensure that the squatters do not use the space between DDA flats and Railway Track for defecation proper latrine blocks should be constructed for them. When land for the latrine block was identified on the other side of the *jhuggi-jhompri* clusters there was protest from the Factory Owners Association of Ashok Vihar.

These are a few instances to demonstrate how the existence of slums adjacent to planned areas of the middle class society leads to social tension and violence. The law-abiding citizens, who have paid for a good living environment, have to suffer. Problems like these cannot be solved easily. They are part of the reality of urban life, where rich and poor have to co-exist either in tension or in peace.

Similarly there are problems involved in the re-location of squatters at the new sites. If you shift them close to a fully developed colony or close to village *abadi* there is resistance. In one case when families were to be shifted on Government Land (Gaon Sabha Land) under the re-settlement programme there was heavy resistance from the villagers. The villagers didn't allow the squatters to be their neighbours because of differing socio-economic strata, backgrounds and ways of living. It was extremely difficult for the authorities to go ahead in re-settling the slum dwellers.

Because of illiteracy, unemployment and unhygienic living conditions crime rate is high in slum areas but it is also observed that given an opportunity these people have potential to upgrade their lives and contribute to society. In areas like Madipur, Raghubir Nagar and Madangir, squatter families have not only constructed beautiful two-three storey houses but have also improved their living condition through economic development. Family income has increased. Children have acquired education and have entered even the professional fields. Today one can see the growth of a car-owning population in the Resettlement Colonies, which were developed over a period of time by the DDA.

The policy of the Government that no *jhuggi* will be removed without providing alternative accommodation has also caused inconvenience and economic loss to the land-owners. If the alternative plots for settlement are not available with the Slum Department, residential or commercial plots even of small size cannot be vacated. In one such case a plot of Punjab and Sindh Bank in Paschim Vihar could not be built because there were about half a dozen *jhuggies*. Though the Bank was willing to pay the shifting charges no alternative plots for the squatters were available with the Department. Thus, the Bank plot remained encroached and unutilized. There was a similar case of institutional use in the Qutub Institutional Area but the authorities finally resolved it.

As it is the responsibility of the individual land owning agency to shift the *jhuggies* from its land some agencies do not agree to contribute their share of re-location charges requires under the Relocation Scheme. When Platform Number 12 at the New Delhi Railway Station towards Ajmeri Gate side was to be laid the Railway Authorities did not agree to pay the shifting charges and forcefully removed the squatters to clear the railway line area. Their plea was that once they pay for squatters shifting from their land, they won't be able to clear their Railway Land in other parts of the country, which was a valid reason. However subsequently the Railway Authorities also realized that if they want to clear their valuable land in areas like Chanakya Puri and other safety zone areas they would have to work within the framework of the relocation policy. Therefore thereafter for removal of *jhuggies* from other areas they paid the shifting charges to the Slum Department, similar to what is being done by other land-owning agencies. For shifting 955 *jhuggies* from Chanakya Puri, the railway has paid Rs. 2,16,46,000 and for shifting 3200 *jhuggies* from other safety zone areas in Delhi, it has paid Rs. 9,09,41,000 to the Slum Department.

As on date there are about 850 *jhuggi-jhompri* clusters that contain approximately 5 lakh *jhuggies*. In other words about 25 lakhs people are living in these clusters. The problem is not so simple because of the amount of land required and the finances needed for physical and social infrastructure. After a thoughtful consideration a serious view should be taken on this problem. The solution cannot be implemented on a year-to-year basis. It has to be a long-term scheme as part of comprehensive plan. Even if we make efforts to ensure that no new *jhuggi* comes up in Delhi reality suggests otherwise. Unemployment and depressed economic conditions in some parts of the country push people to the city. Whether city is receptive or not is their concern. Even if they are unwanted entrants in the city they have no option. It is their basic democratuce right to exist, which the planners must appreciate.

7 LAND AS A RESOURCE

Non-utilization of Land

Protection of land in Delhi has always been a serious problem. There is a general tendency in the public to show disrespect to the law. Wherever there is vacant/unutilized land, it becomes a temptation to the land grabbers, *jhuggi* dwellers and builders. Vast areas of land are found unutilized in various parts of the city. Land owning agencies do not have proper records or a Plan for its utilization. There is no 'Action Plan' with the departments for utilization of such lands. Even when Courts desire to have such information, facts are worked out in such a way that no land is shown as vacant, but rather, quite unrealistically, all the land is shown as planned for development. Acquisition of Land, its Protection and Stock taking etc. have been analyzed in detail in this chapter.

One can understand that the development of city and sub-city takes 15-20 years but, at the same time, there should be some system by which all land, which is acquired and forms part of a layout plan is properly accounted for and utilized. However, this is not being done. In east Delhi and south Delhi areas, where acquisition started as early as in 1959, 1961 and 1965, still vast land pockets are vacant and are available for development. Rohini, where land acquisition was started in 1980-81 reflects the same condition. Large areas of land remain unutilized even in fully developed colonies. Nobody accepts the responsibility as a Project Manager. Once the land is acquired, it is the Project Manager who should take charge of the land and ensure its protection, planning and development as well as its disposal. However, this is not in fact being carried out in reality.

Engineers are not willing to take charge of the land unless a Lay-out Plan has been prepared. They do not feel concerned and are not serious about the non-utilization of these land sites. Site Engineers as Manager of the Project are perhaps more afraid of the land getting encroached rather than ensuring its utilization in time. They feel that their job is to take a clean slate and then begin their plans. But as Project Managers, they should be taking charge of the land as it is. Often, while the process of acquisition of land is accompanied by Court cases and some land generally gets involved in litigation processes. It is not always necessary that whole chunk of acquired land will be handed over by the Land Acquisition Collector after acquisition in one go. During the process of acquisition, some land gets built up unauthorizedly. The Land Acquisition Collector is supposed to remove those unauthorized structures and hand-over vacant possession of the land. The Land Acquisition Collector perhaps has no interest in the projects of Delhi Development Authority. He, therefore, tries to hand-over vacant land. On the other hand, Engineers do not accept even that land where there are few simple boundary walls, even though, this kind of land can clearly be termed as vacant land and Engineers can start development over there. Engineers would like demolition to be carried out even on such land where there might be a well located, because they feel that wells too are structures and therefore, they refuse to consider the land as vacant. They do not feel that this can be utilized by them as a source of water for the project. Even Planners do not keep note of these advantages while drawing the Lay-out Plan. In places where there are trees, they can be and should be incorporated in the Lay-out Plan, as a green area or a park. Planners and Engineers should know that wells and trees, if any, on the acquired land are DDA's property as the land acquisition collector pays the compensation to the land owner for these properties/facilities. Thus we can, and advisably must use existent natural and human-made structures as sources for development, rather than as hindrances in planning.

Cases have come to notice where boundary walls constructed towards the roadside are treated by the engineers as built up area and not vacant area. And only on this plea, they have refused to take-over the possession of the land without realizing that boundary wall on the road-side will help to save the land from encroachment. As soon as the boundary wall is removed, encroachers on the road-side will start encroaching the land. Moreover, this is not the end of the game. Even after demolition of such structures, there is reluctance on the part of the engineers and horticulturists to take-over possession of the land. They want the *malba* or the debris of the demolition also to be removed. These are only excuses, which show lack of interest towards common goal, lack of interest towards a laid down objective and lack of interest towards the visionary target.

It is noticed at several places that even when some demolitions are carried out to remove the encroachments, lands are not taken-over by the Executing Departments on the plea that whole land has not become available. Similarly, Architects will not draw the Plan till the whole land area is available. Getting the entire land by making free from Court cases and removing structures is a difficult job and cannot be done always in one move. Architects and Planners should work in such a way that whatever land becomes available should be utilized as soon as it is available and as and when additional land becomes available by removing encroachments or by getting Court orders in favour of the Government, it should be incorporated into the design and planning at various stages of availability.

About 80-90 Engineering Offices spread all-over Delhi, have a large force of Junior Engineers. Each Junior Engineer can identify the vacant land, utilized land, partly utilized land, land being misused and land getting encroached. The concerned Executive Engineer should then at his personal level draw an action plan. Architects should draw simple plans and start utilizing this land. An exercise to identify all vacant land must be done and all lands should be utilized in two years.

All the District Centres provided in the Master Plan have not been constructed. Land for several District Centres, which have not been planned, was acquired long back. Each District Centre is constructed on a piece of land measuring 40 to 80 acres. Protection of such large pieces of land for 15-20 years is not possible. As a result of this, valuable commercial land in areas like Dilshad Garden and Shastri Park etc. has been lost to encroachers. Delay in developing this land also encourages misuse of residential premises for commercial purpose. It is significant to note that if the Delhi Development Authority is not able to provide commercial space required, shops are likely to come up in the houses. Such illegal development, on the one hand, affects the revenue of Delhi Development Authority and, on the other hand, creates traffic problems for the areas where residential premises are converted to commercial use causing inconvenience to the law abiding neighbours.

Government Departments lack of zeal and spirit, which can take one to the top. No one wants to take responsibility or show responsiveness. They are all part of a system. But any system functions effectively only when responsibility is accepted and one owns the project in a sincere manner.

Encroachment Removal

Land which gets encroached upon is held by the people with vested interests. Vested interest can be of commercial or political nature. Retrieving these encroached lands is not a simple exercise. Massive demolition programmes have to be organized for the removal of such encroachments. The intensity of pressures and problems varies from area to area. If there are commercial encroachments, resistance in the form of public pressure from the local residents is less as compared to the residential encroachments, especially in the *jhuggi jhompri* clusters and unauthorized colonies. Encroachments of a commercial nature are generally in the shape of *pucca* shops and markets. Sometimes there are massive commercial structures, which cannot be demolished in a day or two. After demolition, removal of *malba* is another problem. Generally police assistance is available on the day of the demolition of the unauthorized structures on Government land. Thereafter, however, when engineers have to clear the debris and remove the demolished structure, no police assistance is provided to them. Working at the demolition site without police assistance at this stage is difficult. The affected shop owners or builders try to stall the development action with the help of the local political leaders.

When one such massive demolition was carried out on G.T. Karnal Road in North Delhi in 1993, the structure was constructed on an area of about 5000 sq.yards. It was a massive double storey structure made of cement and concrete. It was part of the G.T.Karnal Road Industrial Area. When the landowners lost the Court case, DDA took immediate action to demolish the structure. This structure was unauthorized however, the shops were purchased by large business houses and other traders. Even removal of business stocks from these shops was a massive job. The presence of a large police force and bulldozers created some impact, and raised fear and concern among the shopkeepers who started removing their goods on their own. DDA gave them sufficient time to do so and the demolition operation was started after the goods had been removed by the shopkeepers. It was a difficult task to demolish the concrete pillars with the bulldozers to bring down the structure. At about 4-4.30 p.m. a person came with a stay order reported to have been issued by a Court in the Tis Hazari. On carefully checking the paper, it was found that it was a forged paper, which was produced at the site to stop the demolition. There was no stamp of the Court on the paper. This is just one of the examples of the kinds of tactics that are employed by the affected persons to stop the demolition. Their whole emphasis is generally on getting the demolition stopped either through political pressure or by approaching the Courts.

Incomplete information is provided to the Courts in order to secure stay orders. In the mentioned case since senior officers were present at the time of demolition, they could see that the order produced was not genuine. Had only junior functionaries been present, demolition would have been stopped as soon as this false paper was produced. By doing so the land encroachers would have succeeded in their motives.

Retrieval of land is very difficult and so is its disposal. The above mentioned structure was so massive that the removal of debris would have taken months. As the Engineering Department takes over possession of vacant land only, they did not take-over possession of this land. Consequently the land remained unattended for nearly 8-9 years. The Land Disposal Department comes into action only when a layout plan of the site is prepared and details of plots to be auctioned are made available to them. Thus even though the Land Management Department acted swiftly in public interest and took over possession of the acquired land as soon as the matter was decided by the Court, the Development and Disposal Department failed to act in the same spirit. As a result an extremely valuable plot of land remained undeveloped and unutilized for years together. The best course would have been to auction the 5000 sq. yards of plot as a single plot on as is where is basis. The *malba* would have been removed by the auction purchaser. This is one such example to show how difficult it is to remove encroachments, reclaim Government land and ensure its timely disposal and utilization.

There are many other such cases, which prove how difficult it is to manage valuable urban land. Had this land been in the possession of a private person, he would have made crores of rupees out of it. Government agencies move at their own speed, look for procedures, go by certain systems without looking forward to the main objective as there is no specified accountability.

Stock-Taking of Project Land

Problems of urban land which have not been included in the lay-out plans are very complicated and peculiar. All the acquired land of a particular revenue estate is not included in the lay-out plan. Some uneven corners remain left out. These are very valuable pieces of land in terms of their market value. At the same time after the project is completed, nobody is aware of its utilization.

Similarly, planning process gets delayed in the proposals where the whole land required for the project is not made available to the Planning or Engineering Department. There are instances where the entire land could not be made available in one got because some land got involved in litigation and in some cases possession of land was not handed over by the concerned Land Acquisition Collector on account of its built up nature.

Again there are cases where land is acquired but its possession is not handed over for years together by the Land Acquisition Collector as the ex-land owner move various Courts. In these cases, the concerned Land Acquisition Collector and Land and Building Department are the main respondents. Delhi Development Authority is not the main party though it is the main affected party. Compensation is paid by the Delhi Development Authority and moreover, such delays result in halting the various development projects of DDA. The other two Departments do not have the same stake and interest as the Delhi Development Authority has. Revenue records and the Land Acquisition Record, which are generally summoned by the Courts in such cases lie with the Land Acquisition Collectors and Land and Building Department, Government of the NCTD. The Delhi Development Authority does not have possession of these records and therefore, has to request the Land Acquisition Collector and Land and Building Department to produce such record in the Courts whenever summoned.

There are a number of cases where land which is not handed over by the Land Acquisition Collector to the Delhi Development Authority even after acquisition because of litigation. Land is misused and construction is carried out unauthorizedly By, the time, the litigation is over and the matter is decided in favour of the Government, no more vacant land is available at the site. It gets built up and sometimes even transferred from one hand to another.

Another noticeable tendency of ex-land owners is to address applications to various quarters like the Lt. Governor, Delhi, Chief Minister and other such officers, with requests for de-notification of their acquired land. In some cases, the Delhi Development Authority writes to the Land and Building Department, Government of NCTD, to request the concerned Land Acquisition Collector to hand-over the possession of the acquired land, a plea is taken that the matter is before the Court. In many cases, Courts also give directions that the matter may be considered by the De-notification Committee. There are a number of cases referred to the De-notification Committee, which otherwise the Courts would not have referred to this Committee, had the possession of these lands been transferred to the Delhi Development Authority in time. On the one hand, the Delhi Development Authority is not able to execute its projects as a whole piece of acquired land is not handed over, while on the other hand, the very sanctity of the project gets disturbed and sometimes even the whole road alignment and provision of services is affected by delayed transfer to and delayed acceptance of land possession by the concerned DDA Departments.

Cases are also noticed at times where huge structures are raised unauthorizedly and Land Acquisition Collector is not able to hand-over vacant possession of these lands even after acquisition. Such structures are used for various purposes including education, and even health care. School buildings or hospitals have been constructed unauthorizedly against their land-use and building bye-laws. There are unauthorizedly built structures where hospitals and dispensaries are functioning and the Land Acquisition Collector is not able to hand-over possession. Additionally, there are many religious structures which have been constructed unauthorizedly. Some religious structures which affect even major road alignments move applications that alignments of the road should be changed so that those plots of land are not taken over by the Land Acquisition Collector. Although it is also a fact that such structures are built on their own land and not on Government land, however, these have been constructed without following the building bye-laws and without the getting sanctions for their Building Plan. All this affects the overall city planning and project at the micro-level.

Similarly, unauthorized construction in the form of colonization by the vested interests near village *abadi* as well as on the lands, which are notified for acquisition, is being carried out day in and day out. It is not the common person but rather the colonizer who is to blame. Large areas of land are being covered by this kind of colonization. The number of structures is very small but these are constructed in a scattered manner so that no large piece of vacant land is left to be taken-over by the land acquiring authorities. Most of the single room structures are constructed with a view to show the built-up status of the area. In many cases, there is no occupancy. In other cases, there are only *chowkidar* (watchman) huts and boundary walls. All this is an attempt to stall the land acquisition process and hamper the planned development of the city. Authorities have to be strict to ensure regularization of such colonies. There is one such colony in Rohini, North Delhi called Prahalad Vihar where request was to de-notify about 113 acres land when in reality, only about 5 to 6 acres of that plot of land was actually covered with constructed structures. The colonizer even ensured to arrange a visit of the Union Minister of Urban Development to impress upon the residents and the staff of the Delhi Development Authority that he is resourceful and can manage the release of land from acquisition. In such cases if land is released it is not the common man but the colonizer who benefits whose land stock value increases many times enriching him over night. The idea behind this move was to get the land de-notified so that it could be sold at high urban prices. This private agency had not yet succeeded administratively and therefore, has gone to Court. Had this land become available to the Delhi

Development Authority, it would have constructed more than 6000 flats for its waiting registrants. Not only do the registrants have to wait, in addition, they will have to pay new cost for flats which increases day by day. Because of colonizers and stay orders, it is the poor common man who suffers.

In South Delhi, there are large beautiful green areas developed by the Delhi Development Authority. These are very pleasant to the eyes and give a sense of aesthetic landscaping. Areas around Mehrauli, Ladha Sarai and Lado Sarai present green features. Unfortunately, in between these large green areas, there are small patches of land, which have not been handed over to the Delhi Development Authority by the Land Acquisition Collector because the land owners try to slow down the land acquisition process by initiating Court cases. They make all sorts of misuses of the land in violations of the building bye-laws as well as violating the Court orders. In 1996, the Hon'ble Supreme Court of India had ordered that all misuses in the form of building material from the land adjacent to this road going from Mehrauli to Andheria Mor should be removed. All these misuses were removed. Land was fenced and the Ridge Management Board had to ensure that it is not misused. Misuse was removed even from the unacquired lands because the use of the area as per the Master Plan is green and no commercial activity of selling building materials is permitted. After 6-7 years of the original demolition and acquisition, some unscrupulous building material sellers again started misusing the land in violation of the orders of the Supreme Court of India.

In many areas, a project land cannot be utilized as in between there are small structures or pieces of land where stay orders have been granted by the Courts. These small structures are generally reported to be part of some Unauthorized Colonies which are expecting regularization by the Government.

A few small structures affect the execution of a City's important project on 1500-acre land. Whenever effort is made to remove some structures, the politicians right upto the Minister level would jump into it and stall the action of Delhi

Development Authority. Politicians are always keen to side with the voters rather than care for planned city development. Perhaps they lack that vision to see the city of the future, the vision to see the city of hope, they have no vision to see a city, which will provide glory and prosperity. If some officers in the administration do try to take action, they have to face the consequences. Strange are the ways in this country that one who wants to do something for the city, one who wants to do something for society, one who wants to implement the laws is made to suffer beyond redemption. This happens at all levels, shifting of Shri Jagmohan, Minister from Urban Development is an example of this kind.

A slow planning process is also responsible for an overall delay in planning, implementation and execution of Government lands. This further adds to the project cost. The burden ultimately falls on the common people. Large areas of land earmarked for District Centres and Community Centres in Mayur Vihar, Dilshad Garden, Shastri Park, Paschim Puri, Rohtak Road, Rohini and other parts of the city are lying unutilized years after their acquisition. Vacant lands cannot be protected for 15-20 years, these should be utilized within a maximum of 5-6 years. In Dilshad Garden, almost half of the land earmarked for the District Centre has been encroached. Similarly, in the Shastri Park District Centre, East Delhi near the Interstate Bus Terminal, quite a large piece of land has been encroached upon by the construction of a *Masjid* (mosque) and *Kabristan* (graveyard). The department should spend so much time, money, effort and energy to acquire land only if it has a sincere intention to protect it from encroachment and develop it to the betterment of the city. Currently, land is acquired only because the Delhi Development Authority has to meet the city's requirement. About 1500 acres land which was acquired in Rohini and physical possession handed over by the Land Acquisition Collector in May 2000 was finally taken over by the Engineering Department for starting development activities after nearly 20 months. Engineers were reluctant to take-over the land unless the complete lay-out was made available to them.

Nobody wants to own the project of a particular plot of land because there is no project manager. The ideal situation, like in the case of private builder's company, would have been that as soon as the land is acquired and handed over to the Delhi Development Authority by the Land Acquisition Collector, it should be taken-over by the Engineering Department on the same day and the concerned engineer should assume the role of Project Manager. From day one, this Project Manager should take care of land problems, legal matters, encroachment crisis and coordinate with facilitators like planners and architects. He or she should also coordinate with other agencies like the Delhi Jal Board and the Electricity Department. Vacant land which was to be developed for infrastructural facilities is still lying unutilized. There are attempts and complaints of land being encroached upon and unauthorized activity continues. Unless land is taken-over by the Project Manager, its proper and timely utilization cannot be ensured. In such situation, there should be a single officer who is competent and responsible enough to take decisions concerning that particular piece of land. If there is no Project Manager then no individual officer feels professionally committed to the end target. If there is any encroachment, he writes to the Land Protection Department, which will then work in conjunction with the Police Department. Sometimes the police is available and at other times it is unavailable. If police force is not available at a certain date set for demolition by DDA, then once again a fresh demolition programme is fixed which might take months and during this intervening period, more unauthorized construction and encroachment takes place. Even when the police is available, it is not necessary that all the encroachments and unauthorized structures are removed on the same day itself. The encroachment removal machinery is slow and insufficient to handle the sprawling unauthorized construction while on the other hand the pace of encroachment which we notice all-over the city is too fast and unless the process to halt encroachment is not stepped up, we will lose the remaining beauty and breathing space of our capital city to such unplanned construction.

8 LAND PROTECTION

Protection of land in city like Delhi is similar to fighting a battle. On the one hand, various Government agencies issue statements that Government land should be protected and on the other whenever operations to remove the encroachments from Government land are planned, there is hindrance from political parties and their workers, at times even at the level of Ministers, Cabinet Ministers and Chief Ministers. Therefore, it is needless to say that removal of *jhuggies* and other encroachments is not as simple as it appears to be. During an on-going Parliament Session, generally, such removal operations get slowed down to avoid unnecessary criticism of the ruling party in the Parliament. Again, before Assembly Elections or National Elections, removal of *jhuggies* slows down because of political considerations. The process of removal of encroachments from Government land once again gets retarded during the annual examinations because plea is taken that dis-location of populace, including students and their families should not be carried out at this stage. Again during the months of May and June using the pretext of extreme heat, political parties come to the rescue of encroachers. So is the case during the rainy season. Political workers and parties have all sympathy for the land encroachers and rather than helping a local body such as DDA to protect its land and assist in its land reinforcing process, they find ways to stall the sincere efforts of the land owning agencies like DDA to remove encroachments from its land. This chapter deals with Protection of Land and specific case studies about Encroachment Removal besides the Types of Land and reasons for Unauthorized Construction and misuse of land.

Jhuggi dwellers are being acknowledged as being a very

strong group even at the local level. Even when a survey is carried out to identify the eligible and non-eligible squatters, squatters create problems and offer resistance. Even for shifting a small cluster of *jhuggies* to clear its land, DDA has to face resistance not only from local political workers but from State level leaders as well. They all talk about fixing responsibility for land encroachment however, they themselves shelter and provide protection to the land encroachers and land grabbers. It is really very unfortunate but true.

Jhuggi dwellers who squat on the public land get sympathy from political parties. Orders are passed that no *jhuggi* will be removed without providing alternative allotment. A residential plot of 18 sq. metres is allotted to a *jhuggi* dweller where his contribution is as small as Rs.7,000/-. The value of an 18 sq.m. plot in Delhi is between Rupees 1 to 1.5 lakh. On the other hand, a law-abiding citizen, who got registered with Delhi Development Authority in 1981 for an allotment of a plot of 26 sq. meters, is still waiting in queue. This is agonizing for the honest tax-paying citizens. No political party will suggest that land encroachers *i.e. jhuggi* dwellers should not be given alternative allotment. They are land encroachers and still they have all advantages because of their voting right.

During 1975 to early 1977, about 2.4 lakh *jhuggies* were removed by Delhi Development Authority from its land as well as from land owned by various other land owning agencies. These *jhuggi* dwellers were re-settled in various Re-settlement Colonies developed all-over Delhi. They were supposed to pay a nominal license fee of Rs.7/- per month. However, despite being an affordable amount, even this was not paid. This was a massive re-location programme unparalleled in human history. Nowhere in any other city in the world, a relocation programme on this massive scale had been planned and carried out. All the Government land was made free of encroachments. Land was utilized for various projects. Vast areas of land in Hauz Khas, Kalkaji, Mahrauli and Yamuna river front were developed as green. This was a laudable job done at that time. However, in

January, 1990, when Shri V. P. Singh, after taking over as Prime Minister of the Nation, visited *Bhumiheen* (landless) Camp in Kalkaji, Govindpuri area, announced that no *jhuggi* will be removed without providing alternative allotment. As per survey carried out at that time there were 2.6 lakh *jhuggies* in Delhi, which reflected that on an average 20,000 *jhuggies* came up every year from 1977-1990. After the announcement of the Prime Minister, there was a sudden increase in *jhuggi* clusters as well as a growth of new *jhuggies* was witnessed in the existing *jhuggi-jhompri* clusters. By 1998, the number of *jhuggies* in Delhi had gone upto about 4,80,000. This reflected a trend of about 30,000 *jhuggies* every year from 1990-1998 as against 20,000 *jhuggies* every year prior to the announcement made by the Prime Minister that no *jhuggi* will be removed without providing alternative allotment. It worked as an incentive for *jhuggi* dwellers, as they could now get plots of land legally in exchange for their illegally constructed *jhuggies*.

In Khazuri Khas, a trans-Yamuna area, during the occurrence of a flood, *jhuggi* dwellers vacated the land, came on the roadside. When water receded, not only they re-squatted on the Government land but in turn started constructing *pucca* and semi-*pucca* houses instead of-*jhuggies*. It was learnt that some agency had given an assistance of Rs.5,000/- to each *jhuggi* dweller. Inspite of the best efforts of the Delhi Development Authority and even after installing a barrier and not allowing building material, construction activity continued. Truckloads of bricks were off loaded at the Wazirabad Road and then carried to the individual plot sites. The Delhi Development Authority had been seeking police help to ensure that the entry of building material should not be allowed. However, inspite of its efforts, unauthorized activities continued. When an attempt was made to remove the encroachments, the police had to resort to strict measures in order to control the violent encroachers. Thus, this problem is not limited to encroachment of land but extends itself to become a law and order issue. All political parties and political workers sympathize with *jhuggi* dwellers. They unjustifiably blame the enforcement agencies and land owning agencies which want to enforce the rule of law and protect the Government land.

A similar situation was also noticed in the Chilla Dallupura area where a road was to be widened to give proper connectivity for smooth flowing traffic. Not only did the encroachers resist this but they even approached Parliamentary Committees and other Government machinery to stall the action of the Delhi Development Authority to remove the encroachments and construct the road.

By clearing some land adjacent to the East-End Apartments in east Delhi, the Delhi Development Authority had to reclaim Government land which was needed for providing the required social and physical infrastructure to the residents. However, the land encroachers had gauged up. They were being supported by the local political workers and parties, so even though they had no legal right on the land and they were squatting on it openly and freely. When the clearance operation was planned, local residents with the help of political workers created a law and order problem. To control the mob, the police had to resort to strict action and in the process one person died. Once again, the matter was simply one of land encroachment but had rather escalated into that of law and order disruption.

It is unfortunate that everywhere the Government agencies try to protect their land, this kind of violent mob creates a law and order problem and manages to generate political sympathy. It is a very unhealthy trend. By sympathizing and supporting the land encroachers and law breakers, what kind of society we are going to create, only the future can tell.

Similarly, in Batla House near Okhla in 1991-92, unauthorized construction activity was expanding towards the Yamuna river-side. As it is a totally Muslim inhabited area, the local field staff was afraid of the minority community, and the junior level field functionaries were feeling helpless. They could hardly do anything except reporting the matter to the department regarding unauthorized construction. The department on the other hand, discussed the matter at various levels but found it difficult to demolish the structures. Day in and day out, unauthorized construction was being carried out. Government land was being encroached upon and the river-bed land was being filled by mud and *malba* and houses were being constructed day and night without caring for the strength of their foundation. The department planned a demolition and a massive police force was organized to this effect. There was only one entry point to enter this area. On the one side, there was whole settlement coming up Unauthorizedly and flowing on the other side was the river Yamuna. On the third side, there was again a settlement — the Oklha village and it was only on the fourth side that there was a small road passing through the Jamia Millia Islamia University leading to this site. The law-breakers were not afraid of anybody, they were fearlessly encroaching Government land and constructing unsafe structures. Many of these constructions were 3 to 4 storeys high. There were small lanes, which would have made it impossible for the fire-tenders to reach in times of a mishap. These were some of the situations, which the local staff had to deal with under tension and terror. The demolition operation to remove encroachment had hardly begun with the police with the SHOs of 3-4 Police Stations, when the residents started throwing stones at the demolition workers and the police. They had already collected the stones in advance on their roof-tops. They were strongly resisting the removal of encroachments. The situation grew very serious as the police had to resort to the use of tear gas shells. As there was only one entry point for the colony, if that was blocked, the Delhi Development Authority staff was trapped. However, thanks to the police who acted with courage under their senior officers, the safety of the Delhi Development Authority staff was ensured. This could be made possible only after taking into custody some miscreants. However, despite such efforts, unfortunately, the Delhi Development Authority could not remove the encroachments and very little of the total encroached area could be reclaimed.

Batla House is located in Okhla. This unauthorized colony is located between Jamia Millia Islamia Higher Secondary School and the river Yamuna going towards the Okhla Barrage. During the early 90's there were attempts to encroach upon this Government land and build unauthorizedly on the land under acquisition. This area, which was totally a Muslim concentrated region was demarcated as a Development Area of Delhi Development Authority notified under the Delhi Development Act. This Act implies that no building activity can be carried out there without proper sanction of a building plan. However, inspite of this Act, unauthorized construction was going on day in and day out. Junior Engineers and other field functionaries of the Delhi Development Authority were scared to intervene. Land in the river-bed was being filled with *malba*. Construction of houses over such filled land is not safe but over the years three to four storeyed houses came up. Various attempts of the Delhi Development Authority to demolish these unauthorized structures were unsuccessful.

Similarly, a lot of land falling between the Agra Canal and the Yamuna River near Kalindi Kunj was also colonized unauthorizedly. A large structure with a boundary wall covering a lot of land was constructed by the Jamiat Ul Hind. When an effort was made to check this unauthorized activity, once again with a totally Muslim concentration, a prominent local leader of Muslim community reached the site and did not allow the demolition of the unauthorized structures to be carried out. This colony is known as Abul Fazal Enclave. As on date, almost the entire area right upto Road No. 13 going from Sarita Vihar to Noida near Kalindi Kunj is built up. This unauthorized colonilization exists without any infrastructure. The Government will be expected to regularize such areas in due course of time and provide infrastructure for which these private builders would have left no land. How can one expect to develop schools, hospitals, dispensaries, police stations and milk booths etc when no land for such facilities is left by the colonizers who want to sell every inch of their land. In case of fire there will be no escape for the residents of Batla House and Abul Fazal Enclave because the required infrastructure is not available. The builders and encroachers are all interested only in promoting their own interests. Even land from which National Highway No. 2 is to pass has been built unauthorizedly by raising unauthorized structures including the so-called school. Nobody thinks of the city, the facilities, the roads, which give connectivity and all essential lifelines of any community, and city.

Encroachments in this area continued, construction of unauthorized and unsafe houses still continued. Today the entire area is built-up. It is difficult for the local staff to dare and plan a demolition action. When it was found that the demolition of unauthorized structures is not possible, the DDA decided to construct a boundary so that the encroachments do not expand any further towards the river. This might be a form of damage control, but this is not the solution. The perfect solution in a democratic set-up is that citizens must respect the law. But in a situation like the one in Delhi, law breakers, land encroachers and land grabbers get political patronage and protection.

Unauthorized Construction

Demolition

Demolition of unauthorized construction either on Government land or in the development area is difficult, on account of two reasons: — 1. Identification of land, and 2. Nature of unauthorized construction. There are various types of lands which are under the charge, management and care of the DDA. These are:

(i) Nazul Land
(ii) DDA's Acquired Land
(iii) Ministry of Rehabilitation Land (called MOR land)
(iv) Land and Development Office Land (called L and DO land)
(v) Development Area (this land is declared as Development area and is not necessarily acquired).

For the purpose of protection and care of land there is specific

Department in Delhi Development Authority, which is called Land Management Department. Its two sub-Departments are:

(i) Land Acquisition and Land Records.
(ii) Land Protection

Land of various categories as mentioned above is managed by separate units under the charge of respective Joint Directors/ Deputy Directors. When unauthorized construction or encroachment is to be removed from any land, the matter is referred to the concern Joint Director/Deputy Director of the land protection branch. There are zonal offices of the land protection department in the following areas:

(i) North Zone (all the areas of North Delhi in North of Rohtak Road upto Majnu Ka Tilla except Rohini scheme area).
(ii) East Zone (all land in East Delhi on the eastern side of the river upto UP Border).
(iii) South-East Zone (all land from the West of Yamuna River upto Aurobindo Marg. and upto Haryana Border on the southern side).
(iv) South-West Zone (all land from West of Aurobindo Marg to Dhaula Kuan and upto Haryana Border on the southern side).
(v) West Zone (all land in the West Delhi right from Dhaula Kuan, Janak Puri and upto Rohtak Road except Dwarka Project area).
(vi) Rohini Zone (all the area of Rohini Project).
(vii) Dwarka Zone (all the area of Dwarka Project).
(viii) Central Zone (all areas in the Central Delhi like Kashmiri Gate, Daryaganj, Karol Bagh and Sadar Bazar etc.).
(ix) Coordination. This branch is for coordination of the activities of various Branches in the Land Management Department including Land Protection Zonal Offices. This branch is also headed by a Joint Director/Deputy Director.

Now the number of land protection zones for field

operations has been reduced to 6 zones by merging the Central Zone and Dwarka Zone with South-east and South-west Zones, and of course the coordination branch for over-all control is in addition to the field zone.

During 2006-07 DDA could carry out only 402 demolition operations and removed 4388 *Kacha*, *Pucca* and semi-*Pucca* structures. The number of structures, which come up during the period vastly exceed the number of structures, removed during any given year. This results from a continuous process of adding more unauthorized structures and encroachments resulting in unauthorized colonization and emergence of *jhuggi-jhompri* clusters.

Weekly demolition programmes are drawn by the zonal offices of Land Protection Department. While making programmes, the Zonal Officers are expected to lay down the priorities in view of the fact that at some locations encroachments are to be removed immediately. For instance, in certain cases the land is to be cleared of the encroachment immediately on vacation of stay order from a Court. This is done on urgent priority basis so that the encroacher does not get time and opportunity to obtain another stay order. This is for important project areas where construction of road and sewer line etc. is held up. In some cases priority has to be laid on the ground that clearance operation for the site was fixed on several occasions earlier also but because of non-availability of police force it could not be carried out. There are many other reasons, which call for priority fixing of the demolition-clearance programme.

The concerned Branch Officers managing various types of land like Nazul Land, DDA's acquired land, land and development office, MOR, and development area have to keep regular record of the total land under their charge in terms of land encroached, land under litigation and land which is prone to encroachment. There are areas, which are built up, but very small vacant land pieces are available. Protection and utilization of these areas is difficult because of no connectivity being available. There are serious attempts by land encroachers to encroach such lands which are then followed up by a move to get stay orders from the Courts against demolition.

Similarly there are areas, which are called Development Areas. Before land is notified for acquisition under section 4 of the land acquisition act, the whole area is declared and notified as Development Area. The purpose of declaring the area as Development Area is that no building activity of any sort can come up without obtaining the approval of the competent authority. Though this land is still private land and is only notified for acquisition however it has to be protected for the project. If some structures come up after the area having been declared as a designated Development Area then the concerned branch immediately takes action to issue notice and then the competent officers pass the demolition order after holding a hearing. After the demolition orders are passed by the competent officer these are sent to the Zonal Joint Director/Deputy Director of the area. It is seen that the unauthorized construction in the designated Development Area is much more then the cases booked and demolition orders passed. One major reason for slow demolition process is that one Junior Engineer has to look after a large chunk of land. In addition the identification of the unauthorized structure with reference to identification of land is generally difficult because the Jr. Engineer is not the Revenue Official. He is therefore not able to identify the unauthorized structure with reference to Revenue Khasra number of the village land. As a result of which the number of cases where demolition is to be done in the development areas pile up every day resulting in the emergence and development of unauthorized colonies all over Delhi in the Development Area.

However, responsibility of the land protection in terms of misuse and unauthorized colonilization for the area, which is not declared as development area lies with the Municipal Corporation of Delhi. Even the Revenue Department of the as of Delhi can take action where agricultural land is misused for non-agricultural purposes. Generally no action is taken by them. If action taken it is not sufficient because of the extent of the problem and lack of will. This also leads to unauthorized colonilization. Even the Archeology Department is supposed to take action for unauthorized activity on the land falling within certain limits of historical monuments but they have also totally failed. Development of Christian Colony near Qutub Minar is one such example where a colony has come up near Qutub Minar within the restricted area but the Archeological Department did not do anything. If this could happen with a national monument of the stature of the Qutub Minar which is visited by thousands of Indian and Foreign tourist's daily we can understand the plight of other monuments of various historical periods which are surrounded by unauthorized residential and commercial settlements.

After getting intimation from the concerned land owning branch, the demolition programme is fixed by the concerned Zonal Deputy Director of the area. There is no secrecy to these programmes because intimation is sent to the police, concerned land owning agency, the contractor who has to arrange bulldozer, transport including extra labour if required and the Revenue Officials of Delhi Government if possession of land after its acquisition is to be taken after removing the encroachments. Though it is the responsibility of the Land Acquisition Collector to hand over vacant possession of acquired land to the DDA, but in practice since the Land Acquisition Collector is not equipped in terms of infrastructure, such encroachment removal action is undertaken by the DDA on behalf of the Land Acquisition Collector. Proposals for removal of encroachment and demolition also comes from the Site Engineers and Horticulture Department for removal of encroachment from the project site as well as from the areas to be developed as green for parks.

When demolition is attempted the concerned field functionaries of the Land Use Department are also expected to be present at site and assist in identifying and declaring the encroached land as encroached. This seems to be idealistic situation but in reality the site conditions are different as well as difficult. Proper demarcation of the site under dispute is most important and essential part of the whole process but this can also pose as a severe drawback at times if field functionaries are not conversant with the land status. The Deputy Director concerned must visit the site before fixing a demolition programme. However they leave this job to the lowest Field Functionaries like Patwaris and Field Investigators. Non-identification of site at times raises dispute and either the demolition is postponed, or it is half done. This leads to wastage of efforts and loss of money spent in arranging labour force, machinery, staff and valuable time of police force. In such cases accountability always needs to be fixed because by all means, the department must protect its land.

Not even half of demolition programmes fixed for the week are carried out. This applies to all areas in the city. In many cases the demolition programme is postpone on the plea that the required police force is not available. In other cases due to non-availability of outer force. In major demolition operations or sensitive areas inhabited by particular community or areas in the proximity of Village *Abadi*, local police is assisted by the outer police force *i.e.* Central Reserve Police Force. At one point of time Delhi Development Authority had its own demolition squad but it could only assist the local police because the mobile demolition squad of the DDA under the Deputy Superintendent of Police did not have the powers of the police station. The mobile demolition squad of the DDA therefore could not work independently of the local police. This mobile demolition squad was on DDA's payroll. The practice of keeping mobile demolition squad was discontinued. When again after a few years it was felt that DDA would be able to carry out atleast small demolition programmes if it had some police force at its disposal, again a proposal to have independent mobile police squad for DDA could not materialize because the Delhi Police besides other conditions wanted Staff Quarters for the squad members. DDA could not agree to this condition because its own staff had not been provided staff quarters to a very satisfactory level. Moreover law and order is mainly the responsibility of the police and therefore it seemed inappropriate and preposterous that DDA pay their salary bills.

Police has its own law and order priority. At times it is busy in the festival season like Dussehra, Diwali, Durga Pooja and Id etc. At other times it is busy on the VIP routes when foreign dignitaries visit the country. It is also busy for a number of days before Independence Day and Republic Day. During such periods assistance to the DDA for a demolition operation is not a priority subject. Therefore demolition programmes are not fixed on these occasions. Similarly during three Parliament Sessions *i.e.* Budget Session, Monsoon Session and Winter Session demolition work gets slowed down. Again prior to the national and assembly elections, demolitions are not planned and done. The reason is obvious. The general plea or excuse is taken that staff will update its land record during this period. Whatever be the reason, what ends up happening is that demolitions are not carried consistently throughout the year. It is these occasions when demolition process is slowed down or demolitions are not done that unauthorized construction and encroachment gains immense pace. Records show that most of the cases regarding unauthorized construction in the flats and unauthorized colonilization is carried out during this period.

Unscrupulous persons have various means of carrying out unauthorized construction. One such method is using the plea that the old structure which is weak is being rebuilt. In areas like Paharganj close to New Delhi Railway Station such unauthorized construction takes place. The area on the one side of the road towards Sadar Bazaar is a Development Area of DDA whereas the other side of the area towards New Delhi Railway Station is marked outside the Development Area of the DDA and is under the jurisdiction of the Municipal Corporation of Delhi. Too much mixing of the land creates confusion with regard to the working jurisdiction of the local bodies. A number of hotels have come up in this area unauthorizedly. The lanes are so narrow that demolition with bulldozer is not possible. Whereas using the manual process of demolition to demolish a three-four story building is difficult and time consuming. In such cases then the demolition squad is only able to damage the unauthorized construction and not demolish. Similarly all areas around Jama Masjid, Darya Ganj, Chawri Bazar and Sadar Bazar have similar character. These are the factors, which cause jurisdiction confusion leading to unauthorized construction and giving an opportunity to the field staff for their corrupt practices.

Reasons for Unauthorized Construction and Misuse

Our planning norms in terms of provision of commercial space were not realistic. Over the years with increase in individual and family income purchasing power has increased. As a result, more consumer retail outlets and luxury goods disposal centers were needed. This was not kept in mind by the planners, in areas like Lajpat Nagar, Kalkaji, Malviya Nagar and many more such areas.

9 MANAGEMENT OF URBAN LAND

Land is a very valuable resource and urban land especially is a significant asset. Therefore, it needs to be managed properly. This involves a twofold exercise – maintaining proper urban land records and managing urban land efficiently. Unlike agricultural land, the status of urban land keeps changing very fast in terms of its ownership, its size, its use and its value etc. Therefore maintaining urban land records becomes even more essential. They need to be updated every now and then; however, it is difficult to prescribe a fixed time period for such an update. Similarly, managing land at various sites is a Herculean task because of its value added status. In urban areas, there are attempts to encroach upon the land, to involve Government departments in litigation, to create third party interests and last but not the least, to change the whole character of land by overnight construction and changing its use. These are the conditions that cause real and complex problems for Urban Planners and Urban Land Managers. An attempt has been made in this chapter to elaborate upon and dwell in detail on the various issues involved in maintaining urban land records and managing urban land. The discussion of these issues has further been related to critical field situations in order to make it more practical and engaging.

The trend of rapid urban growth is noticed in all the major metropolises in the country. Delhi, which had a population of only 4 lakhs in 1901, has also grown to a large metropolis. Between 1901 and 1947 the city followed a gradual pattern of increase. It was only in 1947 when a large influx of refugees came into Delhi that it registered a sudden increase in its urban population. By the end of the century, the population of Delhi has risen to one crore thirty-five lakhs. In fact, there are few cities in the world that parallel such sustained trends of population growth. There is a tremendous pressure on the city's land on account of this tremendous increase in population. Housing activities and other networks of institutional services and infrastructure have not been able to keep pace with the burgeoning population. In general, if urban infrastructure and facilities do not keep pace with the growing population of a city, it leads to the emergence of slums and the generation of social tension, both of which have been noticed in Delhi.

The Delhi Development Authority has been managing large areas of various categories of lands in the city. It also ensures the planned development of the city by acquiring land and disposing of it by allotment and auction. Similarly, DDA also facilitates commercial development by the allotment and auction of commercial plots. It has also allotted plots under Rohini Residential Scheme and constructed more than 3,00,000 flats of various categories like: Janta, Low Income Group, Middle Income Group, Self Financing Category – 2 and Self-Financing Category – 3. There is no doubt that the Authority has allotted residences at affordable prices but at the same time its slow process of land development, disposal and construction of flats has created conditions non-congenial for planned development, which have resulted in unauthorized development, encroachment of public land and unplanned growth of the city.

The various kinds of lands that are managed by the Delhi Development Authority, include :

1. Nazul Land (Nazul I)
2. Ministry of Rehabilitation Land
3. Land and Development Office Land
4. Acquired Land
5. Gaon Sabha Land

Nazul Lands are those lands, which came under the Delhi Improvement Trust as part of an agreement between the

Secretary of State for India in Council and the Delhi Improvement Trust. This agreement was executed on 31st March 1937. Properties of the Government in the following 23 Nazul Revenue Estates were placed at the disposal of the Delhi Improvement Trust under section 54A of the United Provinces Town Improvement Act, 1919, as extended to the province of Delhi. A copy of the Nazul agreement of 31st March 1937 transferring these Nazul Revenue Estates and other properties is given below :

List of 23 Nazul I Revenue Estates

1. Naiwala
2. Basti Rehgar
3. Karol Bagh
4. Bagh Raoji
5. Shidipura
6. Jhandewala
7. Qadam Sharif
8. Paharganj
9. Burn Bastion Road
10. Garstin Bastion Road
11. Daryaganj South
12. Chiragh North
13. Chiragh South
14. Jhilmila Tahirpur
15. Inderpat
16. Arakpur Bagh Mochi
17. Aliganj
18. Southern Ridge
19. Sadar Bazar North
20. Sadar Bazar South
21. Inside City Walls
22. Daryaganj North.......
23. The Bela Road

Excludes those portions of these estates which fall within the limits of the Fort Notified Area Committee.

When the Delhi Development Authority came into being, it inherited all the properties of the erstwhile Delhi Improvement Trust including the 23 Nazul Revenue Estates listed above.

These lands are managed as per provisions of the Nazul Agreement in 1937. The DDA has a separate branch that deals with all these lands and properties.

Besides these lands, the Delhi Development Authority also deals with land which is referred to as MOR Land (Ministry of Rehabilitation Land). The Rehabilitation Department in the Ministry, which was part of Ministry of Supply and Rehabilitation, has been closed. Since there was no machinery within the Government to deal with these lands it was, therefore, decided by the Government of India's Ministry of Supply and Rehabilitation in September 1982 to transfer unutilized lands within the urban/urbanisable limits of Delhi/New Delhi under the charge of the erstwhile Department of Rehabilitation to the Delhi Development Authority. The Department of Rehabilitation, Ministry of Supply and Rehabilitation, Government of India, therefore, *vide* its letter dated 2nd September 1982 wrote to the Delhi Development Authority transferring all the unutilized lands within the urban/urbanisable limits of Delhi/New Delhi under the charge of the Department to the DDA and the DDA on its part agreed to take-over those lands on an as is where is basis upon payment of Rs. 30 Crore. (**Annexure 9/2**)

The transferred lands measured approximately 1020 acres in size. Broad details of surveyed and un-surveyed lands were also provided alongwith the list of such lands. The lands were scattered all-over Delhi, mainly in the rehabilitation colonies although some valuable plots were present in areas like Defence Colonies and Nizamuddin. By disposing off the plots through auction DDA not only earned a lot of money, much more than the package price, but also imbalanced the land pricing structure. Thus, it can be said that the DDA has swayed from its social objective with regards to the MOR Lands.

Another category of land that DDA has been managing is called Land and Development Office. These lands belong to the Land and Development Office, Ministry of Urban Development but were transferred to the Delhi Development Authority by a Notification No. S.O.1810 issued on 20.7.1974 and Notification No. S.O.4719 21.8.1975 for care and maintenance and to be kept as "green" lands. (**Annexure 9/3 and 9/4**).

The lands were transferred to the DDA for management under section 22 (1) of the Delhi Development Act, subject to the conditions that DDA shall not make or cause or permit to be made any construction on these lands and shall, when required by the Government, replace the land or any portion thereof as may be required by the Government. In all there are 121 sites of various sizes ranging from 2 acres to about 20 acres. Most of these sites are present in R.K. Puram, Nizamuddin, Diplomatic Enclave and Sarojini Nagar etc. Though DDA protects the land no watch and ward charges are paid by the Land and Development Office. It is difficult to protect the land given Delhi's ground realities and at times some of the land does get encroached upon. DDA is handling this job as part of its land management exercise.

The most important type of land that the Delhi Development Authority is dealing with is the land acquired by the DDA itself (Nazul II Land). DDA regularly acquires land for the planned development of the city. The Land Acquisition Act empowers the Government to acquire land for any public purpose. The purpose of planned development, for which land is acquired by the Delhi Development Authority, is to promote quality of life by securing appropriate use of land in accordance with development policies. Land acquisition, its development and disposal is performed under the policy of large scale acquisition, development and disposal of land communicated by the Government to the then Chief Commissioner of Delhi *vide* letter dated 2.5.1961. It suggested that about 8000 acre of land should be acquired, in the first instance, under the provision of the Land Acquisition Act, 1894. DDA has been acquiring, developing, utilizing and disposing of land since then. So far 75,435.71 acre of land has been acquired and placed at the disposal of the Delhi Development Authority under section 22(1) of DDA Act, 1957 from April 1961 to March 2008. (See **Annexure 9/5**).

Upon the acquisition of village land the villages are declared as urban villages. The Gaon Sabha lands of such villages are placed at the disposal of the DDA. These lands are transferred by the Government to the DDA under section 22 (1) of the Delhi Development Act 1957 for the purpose of development and maintenance as "green" lands. Such lands are transferred to the DDA from time-to-time. Out of 362 villages in Delhi, 135 villages have been declared as urbanized villages. The transfer of Gaon Sabha land is generally done in groups. One notification which was issued on 24.8.1974 transferred Gaon Sabha Land of 48 villages to the DDA **(Annexure 9/6)**. Thereafter Gaon Sabha Land of more villages was transferred by subsequent notifications.

When transfer is made to the DDA by notification, though on paper the whole Gaon Sabha Land stands transferred but in reality only clear vacant land comes to the DDA. It is upto the SDM of the area to transfer the remaining land after removing any encroachments on them. Since this process is not followed in many areas the land remains encroached even at the transfer stage.

Thus, all these lands have to be managed by DDA in terms of protection, planning, utilization and disposal by various means. It has to develop the appropriate mechanisms in such a way that the whole concept of land as a resource remains valid and available for the proper planning and development of the city. In view of the fact that there is a tendency on the part of the public to keep an eye on vacant land and encroach upon it, it is necessary on the part of the DDA to guard against these ill-intended plans of land encroachers and protect its valuable land.

Delhi is already short of housing stock. While framing the Second Master Plan for Delhi, it was assessed that from 1981 to 1991 the city required a little over seven lakh houses, whereas the requirement for the following decade *i.e.* 1991 to 2001 was over nine lakh houses.

Since the city's civic administration has not been geared up and equipped enough to keep pace with the growing population a number of squatters' settlements and unauthorized colonies have formed all-over Delhi during the last 45-50 years. A survey conducted by the Civil Supplies Department of the National Capital Territory of Delhi in January, 1990 revealed that there were 2,60,000 *jhuggies* (shanties) in 929 *jhuggi-jhompri* clusters spread all-over Delhi. On an average, about one lakh squatters come to Delhi every year. Besides these squatters, there are also others who are slightly better off and thus can afford to move to unauthorized colonies.

Squatting or encroachment of land has different meanings for different categories of people. While some would sympathize with *jhuggi*-dwellers, others will refer to the general tendency on the part of squatters in terms such as "encroachment of public land". Some sections of the society have strong views about the squatters' community and believe that squatters encroach public land only to get alternative sites, which they then generally sell and subsequently re-squat on public land. Still others, with a bureaucratic approach, look at the problem from a different angle and suggest harsh measures to remove the squatters' settlements. The political strata react to the issue from a completely different perspective and advocate for the re-settlement of squatters and payment of compensation for dislocation.

There are some areas that are more prone to encroachment because of relavitely advantaged locations. Such areas are generally located at the fringes of urban villages. Normally land around urban villages stands transferred to the Development Agency either through acquisition or transfer of Gaon Sabha Land. However, but not only is such Government land encroached upon but in the majority of the cases it is exploited for commercial and industrial use against the prescribed land-use pattern. Professional land grabbers raise large commercial complexes upon green areas provided around urban villages. Unless land around urban villages is utilized immediately after acquisition the threat of encroachment and unauthorized construction will persist and affect the orderly development of the area.

While keeping in view the value of urban land there should

be flexibility in the land-use pattern. Areas that are prone to encroachment and are of vital commercial value should not be left undeveloped since pressing urban forces would go by the felt-needs and not the real needs of the neighbouring community. If the felt-need of the area is to develop a particular piece of land for commercial, household or industrial use, the philosophy of idealistic urban planning of keeping the piece of land as green will not be sustainable. Sooner or later forceful attempts will be made to exploit the land for the felt-need of the neighbourhood. Thus, the planning process must keep pace with changing urban needs.

Because of the scarcity of land in urban areas and the increasing land values on account of its use for residential, commercial, industrial and institutional purposes, the pressure on land is mounting up and resulting in encroachment and unauthorized construction. Even the nature and type of encroachment depends on the prescribed land-use and its location. Urban land, which has tremendous commercial potential, is more prone to encroachment. Although land grabbers are generally aware of the risk involved in such activities they frequently drag the matter to the Court, due to the land's tremendous value, thus taking benefit of slackness on the part of the administrative machinery. The land grabbers take calculated risks and come up with heavy investments. Non-maintenance of proper records of urban land, multiplicity of authorities, lack of coordination between various departments and the lack of an urge at various levels in the administrative setup to fight against the land mafia are some of the major factors resulting in land encroachment.

There is no well-set and established system for maintaining urban land records, like revenue records in villages. Unless large municipal corporations and development authorities evolve some set of norms and design formats to achieve uniformity in maintaining urban land records this problem is going to persist and it will adversely affect the progressive functioning of developmental agencies.

Non-maintenance of the inventory of land is another weak point in urban organizations' system of working. Municipal authorities keep records of the properties only from the point of view of house-tax collection. Industrial corporations maintain details of industrial units and are not concerned with any vacant undeveloped land within or around these industrial units. While large authorities like the Delhi Development Authority keep records of their acquired land small pockets of land belonging to other organizations like the Land and Development Office, Ministry of Rehabilitation, Railways, Municipal Corporation of Delhi and New Delhi Municipal Council do not figure in their inventory. Without a complete inventory of all urban land no organization can know the ownership of those small undeveloped pieces of land that belong to other agencies. Furthermore, there is a non-superimposition of development plans on the *Shajra* [Shajra is a revenue map that gives details of land of each Khasra (plot)]. Plans are also susceptible to misclassification and misuse by land racketeers. Land-owning agencies do not seem to be appreciative of the significance of maintaining land inventory, either in terms of its present value or its future resource potential, even though this process is essential for them.

The emergence of *jhuggi-jhompri* clusters and development of unauthorized colonies has led to tremendous pressure on urban lands in Delhi. Although the concerned agencies keep on trying to ensure protection of their land urban forces are much stronger than them. Economic and political factors also play a significant role in the formation of slum clusters and development of unauthorized colonies. Delays in land acquisition, ill-fought Court cases, lack of coordination between various developmental organizations and working priorities of various agencies are some of the major reasons for land encroachment and the emergence of unauthorized colonies. Some of the major land owning agencies in Delhi, which include the Delhi Development Authority, Land and Development Office, Rehabilitation Department, Municipal Corporation of Delhi, Delhi Administration, Cantonment Board and the

Railways, do not have regular working machinery for the management of land.

The management of land is considered to be an important component of urban planning and development. Unless land is properly accounted for, acquired when required, planned and developed speedily, a lot of urban land is likely to be lost. Land encroachments and unauthorized constructions not only take away valuable urban land but also affect the execution of major public utility projects such as the construction of roads, electric sub-stations, parks and facility centers etc. Land Management thus needs to be assigned considerable importance in the overall urban scenario. It should be reoriented to keep pace with the urban growth and ground realities influenced by economic forces and political considerations. Political parties and politically-supported local groups and organizations generally stand in the way of demolition of unauthorized construction and removal of encroachments on public land for political considerations. This phenomenon is observed even more freqeuently close to Assembly or national elections.

As mentioned above, developmental agencies and other major land-owning organizations such as the Railways, Aviation Department and Cantonment Board need special land management machinery. Their staff needs to be professionally trained. Rules and laws need to be created and amended when required to assist the land managers and conditions need to be created to discourage the tendency of encroachment on public land. Public awareness against land encroachment and unauthorized construction should be created through the media. The press should help in restoring respect for the law and should deplore the act of encroachment of public land required for urban infrastructure and neighbourhood facilities.

If land management is not considered as an important and basic area of urban development then shortage of urban land as a potential resource is likely to severely affect the overall planning and development of large urban centers.

There should be no rigidity about land-use plans with respect to immediate utilization of small land pockets. This should help to provide for more institutional services. The task of the land manager is not only to provide land to the planners and engineers but also to ensure its proper and expeditious utilization.

Generally, land management implies taking care of acquired land, developed or undeveloped. The role of the urban land manager starts much earlier. He should get involved in the process of urban development right at the initial stage, when a plan is conceived. He has to be a front line professional functionary and tie up with other departments and organizations.

Another major area where the land manager has to concentrate actively is to ensure that the unacquired small pockets of land in large schemes are acquired as early as possible. Although, it is difficult for the land manager to singularly go ahead because of vested interests and lack of the required urge at various inter-organizational levels forming part of a private and public working system, he must, however, make concerted efforts by tying up at appropriate levels to ensure timely acquisition of such small unacquired pieces of land. If these small land pieces are not acquired in time, unscrupulous elements involved in land deals will damage the character of the whole urban project by carrying out unauthorized building activities in these pockets. Thus, the urban land manager needs support not only from the revenue and management experts but also from top executives in the urban administrative framework.

Most of the land in urban areas generally gets squatted upon because of negligence on the part of the land-owning agencies. As utilization of land involves its stock taking, preparation of plans, execution of projects, disposal of properties and overall coordination between various departments, it is essential that there should be a proper project team to monitor these activities and the land manager can be an important functionary of such a team. The planning, execution and land disposal process should be dynamic to keep pace with increasing demand. Unless the pace of development is accelerated, unauthorized construction and encroachment on public land will continue as a parallel urban activity.

Even the pattern of crime in urban areas is shifting towards offences connected with land. "Land Mafia" is a common terminology being used in large urban centers to refer to the various unscrupulous individuals and groups who encroach upon public land.

The problem of urban land management will, thus, have to be looked at from a broad perspective in order to take into account the overall scenario of the Ideal Planning concept and contend with the powerful and uncontrolled urban forces. An un-contended situation is going to create disharmony and disorder in the urban social fabric; crime rate will go up, families will break apart, children and aged people will live in a state of uncertainty, discontentment will demonstrate its degenerating effect and will result in an overall decline in urban social life.

Land Acquisition Problems

Large areas of land are notified as development areas, before notification of land under section 4 of Land Acquisition Act, 1894. During the process land acquisition, which takes about 3 years attempts, are made for unauthorized colonilization. When actually land is acquired then there are patches of land, which are built up, and some portions of land are under stay. As a result of this the project for which land is acquired cannot take off in time. Roads are held up, sewer lines cannot be laid. It all leads to increase the development cost and the poor allottee has to suffer.

As a result of encroachment on Government Land, unauthorized construction in the development areas and unauthorized construction on the DDA land, the number of cases which need demolition pile up every month. This is the state when inspite of having drawn Master Plan and the Area Plans the city has grown in an unauthorized manner i.e. why we call Unauthorized Development of a planned city.

Removal of encroachment from Government land and taking over possession of the acquired land is not only a problem of land but it is a law and order problem. What we saw in Greater

Noida and Singur recently where land was acquired, is a situation in most of the areas. It is not only compensation for acquisition of land rather it is an issue of rehabilitation of the families, it is an issue of employment, it is an issue of livelihood for those who become landless. The issue has to be handled in a different way. A simple legal approach will not work when the prices of land all-around metropolitan cities and small towns are going up the compensation for acquisition of land has to be liberal with some rehabilitation package.

Shortage of Urban Land

Over the years the population of Delhi has increased manifold. On an average about 50 per cent decadal increase in population was noticed in Delhi from 1961 onwards. Population pressure leads to urban land shortage. New townships cannot be planned on conventional planning norms, which provide for a large circulation space and green areas. Similarly, institutional requirement also needs to be re-determined in view of increasing pressure on urban lands.

In early 1950's large areas were earmarked for schools and local municipal hospitals in the Rehabilitation Colonies. Similarly large sites were earmarked for the Delhi Water Supply and Sewerage Disposal Department, the Electricity Department and the Delhi Transport Corporation. There was no scarcity of urban land in those days.

When the first notification for acquisition of 34,000 acre of land was issued in 1959, the land acquisition rate was very low. Over the years there was gradual increase in this land acquisition rate. In 1990 land acquisition rate was fixed as under:

1.	Agricultural Land	Rs. 4.65 per acre
2.	Land in River-bed.	Rs. 1.25 per acre

The next notification fixing the rate for acquisition of land was issued in 1998 and again in 2001. The rate fixed through these two notifications was :

	Rate Fixed in 1998	*Rate Fixed in 2001*
1.	Rs. 11.20 lakhs per acre for all agricultural land (excluding) lands situated in river-bed between the forward bunds.	Rs.15,70,000/- per acre for all agricultural land (excluding lands situated in river-bed between the forward bunds).
1.	Rs. 3.60 lakhs per acre for the land situated in the river-bed between the forward bunds.	Rs. 5,05,000/- per acre for the land situated in the river-bed between the forward bunds.

Thereafter the rates of agricultural land were notified in 2005 as under:

Rs. 17,58,400 per acre for all agricultural land (excluding) lands situated in river bed between the forward bunds.

2. Rs. 5,70,000 per acre for the the land situated in the river-bed between the forward bunds.

In addition the land-owners also get solatium @ 30 per cent of the acquisition rate.

In between, when the rate was not notified, Land Acquisition Collectors were awarding the rate as notified in the last order, however, the Court of the Additional District Judge, where applications were filed by the ex-land owners, were giving an annual increase of 12 per cent per annum. Thus even when the land acquisition rate was not notified, the Courts had been allowing a 12 per cent increase. This increase was also upheld by the High Court and accepted by the Land Requisition Department. Additionally, it is to be noted that the notification for fixing the land rate also provides for a 10 per cent increase every year.

The major problem in land acquisition was low rate or non-revision of acquisition rate from year to year. When rates for every thing were going up and even for Government control commodities were increasing how can we expect the agricultural land-owners to transfer their land with no increase. If cost of construction is going up, cost of building material is going up, cost of labour is going up, how can we say that the cost of land has not gone up. In all fairness agricultural land-owners must be suitably compensated for their land. Moreover payment of compensation is not made in time. These were very agitating factors for the land-owners. Sh. Vijay Kapoor, the then Lt. Governor of Delhi strongly believed in un-conventional Land Acquisition process in view of the fast changing economic conditions and urban land value. He was a strong believer that the land-owner should be made as a partner in the Development Process so that he transfers his land willingly for the urban development. He had suggested that planners should workout the system whereby certain amount of developed land will go back to the land-owner and in this process he becomes partner of land quisition and development exercise. This he felt would smoothen the Land Acquisition Process, avoid litigation and help in fast urban development. He had very progressive and practical views on land aqusition and urban land-use pattern. As the land-owners do not get adequate and timely compensation for their agricultural land they always prefer to sell the land to the Private Builder rather than to be acquired by the Government especially after change in the land policy for allotment of alternative residential plots. Now upto certain size no alternative residential plot is allotted to the ex-land owner and after a certain size the area of the alternative residential plot is considerably reduced. This was done to discourage those who used to buy small plots with the intention to get alternative residential plot following acquisition of their land. This alternative allotment was in addition to the land compensation. The intention was to give allotment of alternative residential plots to the local land owners whose land was acquired. But over the years speculative vested interest had jumped into take undue benefit of the scheme.

Planning requirements have to be regulated keeping in view the ground realities. While preparing the First and Second Master Plan for Delhi, nobody had visualized the actual requirement for parking space. Car owning capacity of Delhiites has increased manifold with improvement in economic status. Now instead of parks, residents look for parking space. In many areas the Local Residents' Welfare Associations with the help of Municipal Authorities have reduced the park area in front of their houses to create more parking space. In early 60's very few families owned private cars. Today there are a large number of families, which own more than one car. It is no more a mere status symbol. middle Class and low-income group people can afford to own private vehicles. As on date there are about 56 lakhs vehicles in Delhi. All this requires lot of parking space.

In the flats constructed by the Delhi Development Authority car garages were provided only for category three flats of self-financing scheme. Scooter garages were provided for two bedroom self-financing/middle income group flats. No parking provision was made for the low-income and Janta Category flats. Today what to talk of middle income-group flat owners, car owning population is mounting up in lower income-group and Janta Category flats. In areas like Madan Gir in South Delhi one can see that the allotees have constructed three-four storeys flats with dozens of cars parked in the lanes and road sides.

With the increase of population density in the older colonies, as against one family there are 3-4 families in one plot and everyone owns a car. Places like Kailash Colony and Greater Kailash are jam-packed in the evening and there is hardly any space for vehicles to roll through roads, which are even otherwise quite narrow. In this scenario, one has to thank the automobile companies that instead of producing big cars like the Ambassador have come in the market with small cars covering less road and parking space. This suggests that the planning process should take into account the economic standard and potential economic growth. So is the case with commercial space where the requirement has shot up drastically due to more purchasing power.

In the Re-settlement Colonies, where plots of 25 sq.yards were allotted in early 60's and mid-70's we find houses with basements and 4 floors upward. On the one hand it shows prosperity and improvement in the economic standard and on the other hand it calls for the planners to give new dimensions to future planning.

In some schools, which were constructed in the 1950's, part of the play-ground land has been utilized for establishing local

Government Offices. This is a good decision on the part of civic bodies and local administration to utilize the excess land of schools for creating institutional infrastructure. Some such properly utilized areas are noticeable in Lajpat Nagar, South Delhi, wherein the school play-field an office of the Municipal Corporation of Delhi (Central Zone) has been built. A similar approach for optimum utilization of urban land to create more institutional space needs to be adopted in other parts of the city as well.

Delhi Development Authority has decided to allot plot of 2 acres instead of 4 acres for Senior. Secondary Schools. This is the right decision considering the need of the time. This economizing in the use of land represents the general trend of planning in the city, especially in view of new innovations and technological developments, which help in earmarking less space for electric sub-stations and sewerage disposal plants. Back in the 1950s and 60s, it was hard to imagine that the land allotted to the Delhi Transport Corporation will prove to be a luxury in 1990's and early 21st century. This is indeed the time to give serious thought to optimum utilization of these valuable urban lands and rethink its usage patterns.

If commercial activities on the road-sides are regulated properly, then the land earmarked for roads right away can be reduced. As matters stand today, half of the road is generally either encroached or is held up because of Unauthorized Parking. Most of the roads are encroached either by the *Rehriwalas* reducing the actual drive way or by unauthorizely parked vehicles. Congestion at Yusuf Sarai Market reflects this situation where inspite of three lanes road width on either side of the road hardly two lanes on each side are available. Remaining road portion is occupied by the parked vehicles. So is the case in areas like Rajouri Garden and Fateh Nagar in West Delhi.

Traffic management is another important aspect of urban planning. Traffic managers should come out with new traffic management options to regulate traffic and ensure that the right of way remains available for a smooth flow of traffic. This will help avoid accidents, ensure speedy movement of vehicles, thereby saving time and fuel consumption.

This is the time when we have to think about these small issues which although may not appear very important to everyone, are in fact significant and therefore, cannot be ignored. Citizens should be prepared to pay for better urban services. If a hawker has to pay for temporarily occupying the space and a car-owner has to pay parking charges for parking the car in a parking lot during the day time, why should he not pay while he parks his car during night along the road-side. Everyone has to contribute for civic services. It pinches only when one group of people pay for the other in the name of subsidy to disadvantageous group. Similarly, house-tax payment needs to be streamlined. As on date only about 8 lakhs properties are taxed as against nearly 38 lakhs properties. If people can spend lakhs of rupees on constructing houses and furnishing them with best available materials, then why should they not pay to the Civic Bodies? Civil administration must plan to take all properties into their tax net. It will certainly help to generate more funds for better parks, educational and health facilities and an improved environment.

Urban land must be managed in a very professional manner. It has to be combination of old Revenue Records as well as new updation. Each piece of land if not yet utilized on account of encroachment, litigation or any other reason must be identified in the property registers for future disposal. The cost of protecting vacant land is much more specially when such lands are lost by encroachment. Since there is already shortage of urban land all unutilized lands planned or unplanned, developed or undeveloped must be stock listed for future disposal. There should be a target fixed for disposal of such lands. The Delhi Development Authority should also prepare an inventory of such lands with notional price, so that at the end of the year the value of such properties must be reflected in the balance sheet. This is not being done as on date, as a result of which the DDA is not aware of its total assets. A simple land-costing exercise is, therefore, is very essential to make the land-owning agencies aware of their financial potential and financial assets in terms of undeveloped, unutilized, unsold properties.

1. Encroached Structures Removed

2. Park Developed at the Reclaimed Site.

3. Park Developed After Removing the Encroachment.

4. Jhuggi-Cluster at Nehru Place.

5. Unauthorized Settlement near Lotus Temple.

6. Unauthorized Structures Removed—near Mool Chand Flyover.

7. Green Development after Encroachment Removal–Mool Chand Flyover.

8. Encroachment near Qutub Minar.

9. Green Land Encroached.

10. Commercial use of Green Land.

11. Religious misuse of Green Land.

12. Violation of Land use.

13. Green Site Developed—Ladha Sarai.

14. Unauthorized settlement near historic Qutub Minar

15. Jhuggies in River Bed Area.

16. Jhuggies in Yamuna River.

17. Early Stage of Settlement in a Resettlement Colony.

18. Self help Housing in Resettlement Colony.

19. Life Starts in Resettlement Colony.

20. Life in full swing in Resettlement Colony.

21. Resettlement Colony comes up fully.

22. Life is properly Planned—Resettlement Colony.

23. Massive Housing Development and road network in Dwarka.

24. Veer Awas in Dwarka.

25. Cooperative Group Housing Society flats in Dwarka.

26. LIG Flats in Rohini.

27. New Architectural Designs in Rohini-LIG, MIG Flats.

28. Massive Flats Construction in Rohini.

29. Road Network in Rohini Residential Estate.

30. Residential Area in Vasant Kunj.

31. DDA Flats in Vasant Kunj calm atmosphere.

32. Land Encroached in Vasant Kunj Road side area.

10 CRITICAL LAND ISSUES

Land is very valuable asset in urban settings. Its value is not determined just by its size but also by its location and use. Similarly, its status is also an important determinant of its value. A plot of land close to a major road would be priced much higher than a plot situated in a small narrow lane. Similarly, land adjacent to a posh locality will be much more valuable than a piece of land adjacent to a village or a *jhuggi-jhompri* cluster or an unauthorized colony. Similarly, if the land-use as commercial its value will be much more than the residential, institutional or industrial use. If land is free from acquisition it has a different value, than the land which is under notification of acquisition. Land involved in litigation will not fetch an amount equal to the land which is free from litigation and has a clear title. These are some very critical land issues which determine the value and use of land. This chapter discusses issues such as urban land record, land problems and land litigation.

Urban Land Record

A record of land in the rural set-up has a long history. The revenue records maintained in India since long cover each piece of land irrespective of whether it is village *Abadi, Gaon Sabha* land or private agricultural land. The name of the land-owner for each *Khasra* number is reflected in the *Khasra Girdavari* and these records are updated periodically. Similarly record of urban land is maintained in terms of plot number existing in a particular colony or locality. However updating of property-owner record is also done when required. The actual problem of land record comes in urban areas when after acquisition of land, it looses its rural identification reflected in the revenue record of the village, then it is no more known by a particular *Khasra* number. It becomes part of a lay-out plan. Some part of the *Khasra* number area becomes part of road portion, some residential plot or some institutional area. The problem of identification of land at times becomes subject of Court matter. It is therefore very essential that the layout plans should be super-imposed on the *Khasra* maps and proper ownership record of *Khasra* number as well as property number in terms of super imposition of the layout plan on the *Shajra* map should be part of regular land record.

Record of rural agricultural land is maintained through a proper, well-defined system developed through years of experience by the revenue officials. This system tries to ensure that there is uniformity in the format used for maintaining records of agricultural land thus facilitating a smooth functioning and enabling the system to stand the test of time. However, on the other hand, there is no proper system for keeping record of urban lands. More so, when the land is at the transitional stage, *i.e.*, its status is being changed from that of rural to urban in character and usage. A basic problem in making urban land records is that the layout plans are not superimposed on the *Shajra* maps.

During the 1950's, massive land acquisition was planned and about 34,000 acres of agricultural land was notified for acquisition under the Land Acquisition Act. This land was notified by the revenue boundaries without reference to *Khasra* number and specific area in each *Khasra*. If, by mistake, some land was left out, when the notification under Section-6 of the Land Acquisition Act was issued, and this invariably created problems. Disputes are being raised even after 40 years of the initial notification. For example, there have been many cases where one fine morning a person comes to the concerned official and reports that his unacquired land falls within the green district near Nehru Place. He produces some papers to show ownership of the land. It is likely that his land might have been utilised in the construction of some road. Such manipulative individuals know how to manage the Revenue officials to show that unacquired land falls in the developed District Green Area. In such a case, the individual's next step normally is to write to the authorities for possession of land. Delhi Development Authority, on its part, examines the site position of the land claimed by the petitioner. Generally, such land forms part of development projects and stands utilized either in a park, or road alignment or in some other utility area. In case it is found that land is unacquired and has been utilized in the project/scheme, Delhi Development Authority takes up the case for its acquisition with the Land Acquisition Collector through the Land and Building Department.

There are instances where sometimes people were able to prove through the revenue records that their small piece of land remains unacquired and they submitted the Building Plan for sanction. If this plan is not sanctioned, they move an application in the Court and get orders in their favour that the Building Plan may be sanctioned by the Delhi Development Authority or the Municipal Corporation of Delhi as the case may be depending upon the area jurisdiction. At times, Courts pass orders saying that either the land be acquired within a specified time (usually it is 4 to 6 months) or else the building plan of the petitioner may be sanctioned. In such cases, although Delhi Development Authority immediately takes up the case with the Land Acquisition Collector through the Land and Building Department, Government of National Capital Territory of Delhi to acquire that particular piece of land however, since it is to be acquired by the Land Acquisition Collector who does not work under Delhi Development Authority, his working priorities differ and he works in a way that is detrimental to the interest of Delhi Development Authority or any other relevant Government agency. Thus consequently, in many cases, land is not acquired within the time permitted by the Court. Delhi Development Authority has to follow up vigorously with the Land Acquisition Collector through the Land and Building Department for its timely acquisition. At times very valuable urban land is involved in this kind of litigation. We have quite few such cases in areas like Hauz Khas and Nehru Place. Land being of commercial use as per plan, vested interests become more active to stall and delay the land acquisition process in the Land and Building Department as well as in the Office of the Land Acquisition Collector.

Such cases were also noticed in other parts of the city where small land pieces remained unacquired for one reason or another. At one site in Rohini even where the road had been constructed, a piece of land was found unacquired and the land-owner was in a position to create problems for the Government.

The question of how some land remains unacquired or how people come to know about their unacquired land after 20-30 years of the original acquisition process is complicated. Revenue officials dig out such cases by going through the land acquisition awards of the 1950s and 60s and records of land with *Khasra* numbers, which were not notified under Section-6 of the Land Acquisition Act or were not included in the Award by the Land Acquisition Collector. This is highly valuable information and is given to the land-owners, to lodge their claim before the department or to move the Court pleading that the land should be restored to them by the Delhi Development Authority.

It is noticed that in most of such cases, land is not acquired within the time granted by the Courts because in Delhi, the land development authority is not the land acquiring authority. It has to depend upon the Land Acquisition Collector who is part of the Government of National Capital Territory of Delhi. Revenue officials of the land acquisition office who are not on the roles of the Delhi Development Authority have no professional commitment with the DDA and thus can play to the advantage of the land-owners.

In areas where large human settlements have come up over the years demarcation of unacquired land and left-over small pieces of land is extremely difficult. Fixed demarcation points like wells etc., are not available. Planners should ensure that, if possible, fixed points should be preserved by incorporating in the green development. If there is a well, it should be part of the green development. The Department can get the advantage of a free tube-well, at the same time, it can serve as a fixed point for demarcation in case of any land dispute in the future.

The best course to avoid future urban land disputes is that all lay-out plans should be superimposed on the *Shajra* maps before these are approved. It should be made mandatory on the part of planning agencies to do so.

This system will also help to recover enhanced compensation from the actual beneficiaries. As on date since lay-out plans are not superimposed on the *Shajra* maps, enhanced compensation cannot be recovered from the individual land-owners. It will help to identify the beneficiary for recovery of enhanced compensation. At the same time to overcome this situation of recovery from individuals, the Delhi Development Authority provides for in-built mechanism in the costing formula by including at the initial stage some percentage of enhanced compensation of land in the costing details of the project.

Land compensation is enhanced by the Court in cases where petition is filed in the Courts. Sometimes it is enhanced after a gap of 10-15 years. It is enhanced at the level of Additional District Judge and High Court, and can also be enhanced by the Supreme Court. As a planning body, Delhi Development Authority does make provision in its costing formula to include certain portions of enhanced compensation. This is not actual but is based on the trend of enhanced compensation and past experience.

Disputes about land title continue even after land has been acquired and the project is through. There are numerous examples of such land disputes. Many a times, Revenue Officials do not agree to the same demarcation. Delhi Development Authority staff tries to prove that the land has been acquired and that it stands in its possession. Whereas a private party through the help of the Revenue Official of SDM's Office tries to prove that his unacquired land has been utilised by the Delhi Development Authority. He moves the Court for taking over possession of such land. In one such case, in Vasant Kunj when in the demarcation it was proved that the builder had constructed on the land already acquired by the Delhi Development Authority, a large scale demolition was carried out in 1992 and a huge commercial complex with more than 50 shops was demolished. It is a different issue that this land has not yet been utilised by the User Department. One recent case happened in East Delhi, where a petitioner moved an application that part of his un-acquired land has been allotted by the Delhi Development Authority to a Government Institution. Such issues create demarcation problems. Had the lay-out plan been superimposed on the *Shajra* map, all such problems could have been avoided. In that case, there was no need for any demarcation of such lands.

Though, Delhi Development Authority had broadly drawn its lay-out plan of Rohini and Dwarka on the *Shajra* maps, however, in South and East Delhi, where initial development started in the 1950s and 60s, no lay-out plan was superimposed on the *Shajra* maps, therefore such land disputes are more noticeable in South and East Delhi.

There are several land-owning agencies in Delhi. Similarly, there are various types of lands owned by different agencies. Large areas of land were acquired by the Government when the national capital was shifted from Calcutta to Delhi in 1911. Land, for this new capital, was acquired in 1908. Thereafter, land was also acquired by the Delhi Improvement Trust, Delhi Development Authority, when it came into existence, also started acquiring large areas of land. In addition, land is also owned by various other Government Departments such as the Irrigation and Flood Control Department of the Government of National Capital Territory of Delhi, Public Works Department of Govt. of NCTD, Central Public Works Department, Land and Development Office, Ministry of Rehabilitation, Custodian Land, Railway Land, New Delhi Municipal Committee and Cantonment Board land.

Sometimes it becomes difficult to identify the agency, which holds the ownership of a certain piece of land. In addition to all these categories, there is *Gram Sabha* land also. Besides *Gram Sabha* lands in villages the other major land-owning Departments are Land and Development Office and Delhi Development Authority. Some land is also managed by the Ridge Management Board, even in the River-bed on a stretch of land from Wazirabad in the North upto Okhla Barrage in South, land is owned by various Departments like Land and Development Office, Irrigation and Flood Control Department, Central Public Works Department, *Nazul*-I Land which came from Delhi Improvement Trust, Delhi Development Authority's acquired land, land owned by Metro, Delhi Noida Toll Bridge and U.P. Canal Department Land. Identification and demarcation of all these lands is not a simple issue.

Similarly, in many areas, it is difficult to identify whether a particular plot of land is Custodian Land, *Nazul*-I Land, Ministry of Rehabilitation Land, Land and Development Office Land, *Gram Sabha* Land or Development Authority's acquired land.

Urban land being of great value, such land disputes will certainly increase in the future. The best way to avoid these disputes is that *Shajra* maps should indicate the type of land it is and lay-out plans should be superimposed on these *Shajra* maps before these are finally approved.

So far 101074.32 acre land is managed by the Delhi Development Authority. Category-wise details are given below :

1.	Nazul-I land which came from the erstwhile Delhi Improvement Trust.	—	22383.12 Acre.
2.	Land acquired by the Delhi Development Authority.	—	75435.71 Acre
3.	Land taken from the Ministry of Rehabilitation in 1983 under a Package deal of Rs.30 crores.	—	1020 Acre.
4.	Land and Development Office. Land for care and maintenance since 1974 and 1975.	—	2564.627Acre.

Land Problems

Urban land, especially in a city like Delhi, is very valuable therefore, this land should be put to use within a specified workable time schedule. Planners should draw the working plans coinciding with the land acquisition process. It should be so synchronized that as soon as land is acquired, working drawings should be available to the site engineers to take up the work. Land should be simultaneously taken-over by the Project Engineers and developmental activities should start from day one. Currently, such working modules are present in cities like Bangalore. Such working modules require that a budgetary provision for developmental activities, deployment of security for protection of land, a small vigilant team of Officers to handle revenue and legal matters should start working together, simultaneously from day one.

It is a common working feature of Delhi Development Authority projects that inspite of the fact that the land is taken over by the Project Engineers, if in case, somebody just squats over the project land, claims its title or moves the Court, the Project Engineer, instead of acting as project chief and ensuring protection of land, starts making references to the Revenue Department or the Land Protection Department. The Project Engineer, as an officer in-charge at site, should not allow any person to interfere in the project and to stall the work by alleging ownership of the land. The Project Engineer should be well aware of the fact that after acquisition, the Land Acquisition Collector has transferred the land to him. Thus, it becomes Government land. Large areas of land, which remain unutilised for years together, attract land grabbers. On a visit to any part of the city in South, East, North or West Delhi, one can see large stretches of land lying vacant everywhere. The Government land-owning agency such as Delhi Development Authority should prepare the lay-out plan at the land acquisition stage itself. Delhi Development Authority's sign boards have been displayed at most of the vacant sites in the city but there is no presence of any site office for any local inquiries. No official or Government functionary is generally available at site. There is no activity reflecting any sign of development over these large tracts of land.

Land on the left side of the Ring Road near Nehru Vihar, on the other side of the Wazirabad Bridge, has been lying vacant and unutilized for years together. It is totally unprotected without any fencing or board of the land-owning department. Going up, further towards the North of this site, more undeveloped land of similar nature is available. Some of this land might belong to other departments like PWD or Flood etc. The very fact that this land remains unutilised, is an open invitation to the land encroachers. This land perhaps was not encroached fully because of its topography and its being a low lying area where water stagnates during most of the year.

A little further, to the North, the Dhirpur Project reflects the same story, where a network of roads was laid long back. There is still no other developmental activity except the construction of roads. Utilization of land includes disposal of land, construction of roads, provision of social infrastructure like hospitals, schools, police stations, fire services and milk-booths etc. This institutional framework is yet to come up. This is one of those projects which is monitored by the concerned Project Engineer. Still disposal and development of land has not been taken up. The working setup of the organization is compartmentalized where the Project Engineer does not feel concerned for the total development and utilization of the land. He thinks his job would be over by laying down the sewer and by constructing roads and fixing electric poles and carrying out other physical development at the site. As a Project Manager, someone has to be responsible from A to Z of the project, *i.e.*, from the initial development of land till its final disposal. Unless this concept is made part of professional ethics, we are not likely to achieve the desired results.

We have urban planners, architects, engineers and administrators but we do not have project managers who should account for all the development and disposal activities. Similarly, a large chunk of land is found undeveloped in the Jahangirpuri area. A stretch of land on the left side of the Outer Ring Road near Jahangirpuri can be seen while travelling on that road.

Non-utilization of land and the slow process of development

has caused tremendous loss in terms of its delay cost. Between the Dhirpur Nirankari Complex and Jahangirpuri, a large chunk of land, which is more than 300 acres and belongs to the Delhi Jal Board has been lying vacant for years together. Luckily, it did not get encroached, primarily, because it is away from the main city area. Secondly, there were no settlements around this area.

A large piece of land, which is reported to be for commercial use on the left side of the Outer Ring Road, as one crosses the G.T. Road, is lying in an unattended manner. There are attempts for its encroachment. Small shanty type unauthorized settlements and *jhuggi-jhompri* clusters have already intruded on the area. If this land is not utilized immediately, it is likely to be lost to squatters.

If there is not much scope for commercial development as commercial activities have come up in the residential areas themselves, then such large plots reserved for this purpose should be utilized for residential and institutional purposes. There is dire need to have more residential accommodation in the city. When it is found that people are not interested in going to far flung areas like Narela – 10-15 kilometers from this site, it seems logical that these lands be used for residential purposes.

Land is encroached not only by the squatters looking for a place to live, but encroachment by religious institutions is also quite common. In East Delhi, a large part of a park was lost as the neighbourhood Muslim population started using it as a burial ground or *Kabristan*. The local Horticulture Staff found itself helpless when they were told by the local residents that dead bodies of 2 or 3 children were buried at that site. Gradually a few more dead bodies were reported to have been buried in the park. Instead of burying these bodies in one corner, they were buried in a spread-out and scattered manner. In this process, about half an acre land was lost. If the burial ground was a community need, a reference by the local residents should have been made to the concerned department, which would have considered their requirement and made provision for the same in that area. It could not be ascertained whether the bodies were actually buried or whether false graves were created to give the impression of a graveyard by creating mounds of soil. Similar misuse of land and encroachment was noticed in Shastri Park in East Delhi where land was earmarked for the District Commercial Centre. It was very valuable commercial land but as it remained unutilised for years, land encroachers felt that they could have their own way on that land. Some land was encroached by constructing a *Masjid* (mosque) and some by the construction of temples.

Urban Land Management may not appear to be a very specialized subject but it is a very complicated area of management. It is not merely keeping a record of urban land as it goes much deeper and wider in scope than simple record-keeping. Details of land notified under Section 4 of the Land Acquisition Act by the Land Acquisition Collector, details of land notified under Section 6 of Land Acquisition Act and details of land actually acquired are the first stage of the inventory process. Even after acquisition, all the land is not transferred. Some land is involved in litigation, some land is held up because it is unauthorizedly built up and the Land Acquisition Collector has to organize a demolition programme with the help of the police. In other instances, where there are boundary walls and small, unoccupied rooms with a purpose to show habilitation, Delhi Development Authority's Revenue Officials would like the Land Acquisition Collector to hand-over possession of this land, but at the same time, another department dealing with protection of DDA land, tries to bring it on record that land under such structures is considered built-up. Sometimes this gives advantage to the landowners to move the Courts and obtain stay order. Thus evidently, lack of coordination between two departments causes delay in taking-over the final possession of the land.

There are instances when a particular piece of land is notified under Section 4 of Land Acquisition Act alongwith other large areas, but by mistake or by someone's manipulative actions it is left out of the notification under Section 6 of the Land Acquisition Act. The Land Acquisition Collector after having noticed the mistake includes this piece of land in the final award. Though the award is legally complete and the land is transferred by the Land Acquisition Collector to the Delhi Development Authority, the owner of the specific piece of land moves to the Court on the plea that since the land was not included under Section 6 of the Land Acquisition Act, it cannot form part of the award. Thus litigation starts and delays the execution of the project for which the land was originally acquired. These are some of the unforeseen problems in Urban Land Management.

There are a number of cases where initially land was notified under Section 4 of the Land Acquisition Act by a boundary identification instead of giving each and every *Khasra* number. This implies that all land falling within such boundary identification would be notified under Section 6 of the Land Acquisition Act and would be included in the award. But there are cases where the land is left out under the second and third stages of the land acquisition process. This could possibly be a genuine mistake or error on the part of the functionary, but such mistakes are fatal as they affect the execution of projects and also add to the litigation. As the value of urban land has gone up phenomenally, sometimes even builders get involved in these litigations. All this adds to the project cost as land is notified afresh. Since compensation for land is workable from the date of notification of land under Section 4 of the Land Acquisition Act, the ex-land owner gets more compensation than is his due.

As has been stressed elsewhere in this book, to avoid such problems of land status in the future, lay-out plans should be approved only when these are superimposed on the *Shajra* maps. Unless the lay-out plan is properly superimposed on these *Shajra* maps, it should not be approved.

With the fast pace of urban development and ever-expanding urban activities, fixed points which are required for demarcation of land by the revenue officials are missing. Old wells, cremation grounds as far as possible should be retained as fixed points. If this is not always possible, atleast lay-out plans should be properly superimposed on the *Shajra* maps so that if subsequently someone comes with a claim that a particular piece of land owned by him is not acquired by the Government, for that matter, the Government should be able to link it with its utilization plan and its utilization pattern. If it has been utilized in some other public utility area, the Government has a strong case to request the Court to allow its acquisition. If it forms part of some residential area, perhaps the ex-landowner would try to establish his claim before the Courts that he should be allowed to use the land for his residence. The Delhi Development Authority on its part tries to acquire this land to ensure its proper planning for general public and civic development.

Land Litigation

Court cases concerning land matters have tremendous financial implications. Urban land is highly valuable. By misusing the judicial process, attempts are made by the litigants to drag the litigation, thus delaying the matter till an opportune time, which suits them, arrives. Delhi Development Authority being a large body has various operational departments. Sometimes the litigants try to confuse the issues by involving various departments. Getting comments from Lands, Engineering, Planning and Horticulture Department etc. takes time. At the same time, in such a situation, it appears as if no department has ownership of the matter. The emphasis is lost. Even the Courts have noticed this kind of coordination problem and the resulting delay. When in one such case the reply was not filed in the Court in time because comments were expected from the Planning Department, the Court imposed a fine with the orders that this may be recovered from the Officers of the Planning and Land Department. The varied nature of cases makes the work jurisdiction unclear even to the Panel Lawyers. Even the Office of the Chief Legal Adviser does not have a clear picture as to which department owns a particular case. There is confusion between land acquisition and land protection and this results in a wrong marking of papers thereby delaying the entire case. For matters of record, every officer whether junior or senior tries to pass on the papers rather than resorting to informal discussion or telephonic talk which certainly helps to clarify the points and to expedite the matters. A wrong reference made to one officer from the Chief Legal Officer's Department, at times, delays the matter for one or two weeks. Even, the Law Officer, who handle the matters of land acquisition and land protection, at times do not draw the lines of identity between Court cases of two Departments.

The most common reason for delay in handling Court cases is in those matters where the petitioner makes reference about utilization of land either for green development or fencing by the Engineering Department or for developmental activities taken up by the Project Engineers. The other two departments, which are generally concerned with land matters are Planning and Architecture. In land acquisition matters, land-use, lay-out plan and panel development plan are important factors. When petition is referred to these departments one by one for providing information relating to their departments, the matter gets delayed. Generally, the first department to whom reference is made will see the next date of hearing and after constant follow up, they send the file back to the Law Officer or to the Lands Department or to the Zonal Lawyer, generally, a day before the date of hearing, without realizing that comments were required to be given immediately because there are other departments who are also required to contribute. A day before the date of hearing, the Panel Lawyer is not able to formulate the reply that too when comments on various points raised in the petition relating to Planning, Architecture and Engineering Department remain un-replied. A reference is again made to the other Departments for their comments. It is also observed that Court matters are not given required priority and comments are given by the lowest functionary in the department. Senior Officers through whom the file passes is just to obtain their signature without any material and valuable contribution. These sketchy comments are not enough for the Law Officer or the Panel Lawyer to help them in drafting the replies. All this gives advantage to the petitioner and disadvantage to the organization. It is only in very few cases, which are of vital importance and are handled at the level of the Head of the Department that a proper track is kept. The matter is followed up with the panel lawyers as senior advocates are engaged and are briefed. These cases are taken care of properly and generally decided in the organization's favour.

Another reason for a not proper follow-up of the cases is the large number of panel lawyers. If there are about half a dozen Panel Lawyers dealing with the cases of one department, it is easy for the Head of the Department and next in command to remain in touch with the panel lawyer directly or through the Law Officers. If the number, as is the case now, higher than this optimum then it is difficult to follow-up with the Panel Lawyers. Clubbing of cases also helps in follow-up. If cases of one nature or cases of one area are entrusted to one Panel Lawyer, it is easy for the department to follow up and contribute properly by holding regular conferences with the senior advocates. This practice is being followed in land acquisition matters and cases of similar nature in areas like River-bed and Rohini Project which have been clubbed and are being contested properly. This helps to save time of and also better involves the executing agencies like Engineering, Architectural and Planning.

Another reason which is somewhat related to Court cases and follow-up action is that once a matter is decided by the Court either by dismissing the request for de-notification or passing order for acquisition of land then, specific time period, various agencies and departments do not come together for giving finality to the orders. After the dismissal of the case of the petitioner, DDA has to take-over possession of the land. In normal course, it should be possible to take-over possession of land within a week. But unfortunately, as various departments and agencies like Land and Building Department, Government of NCTD, Land Acquisition Collector of the area, Police, Demolition Squad and Land Acquisition Branch are involved, it becomes difficult to bring all these agencies together assigning priority to the job. Many a times, when the date is fixed for taking-over possession, the Land Protection Branch, which has to tie-up is already committed to some other problem. Sometimes the police force is not available because they need more advance notice. Once the problem is postponed, it takes another 3-4 weeks that too only with proper follow-up to re-fix the programme for taking-over possession. All this delays the actual acquisition of land because acquisition is completed only when possession is handed-over to the Delhi Development Authority by the Land Acquisition Collector.

Another reason for this delay is the indifferent attitude of the lower functionaries. It is not possible to take-up each and every case at the highest level. The Deputy Directors or Tehsildars do not exhibit the sense of priority and commitment for achieving the objectives of the Authority and this, results in delay. In many cases, because of stay orders granted by the Courts, Projects are held up and delayed. If the Project Manager and Engineers take up the job of project handling independently, they can be more effective. However, in practice, it is not so. Instead of keeping liaison with the concerned advocates to know the day to day information of the cases, they prefer to have information about the Court cases through the indirect route *i.e.* after each hearing, they write to the Lands Department inquiring about the Court proceedings and asking what stage the Court case is at. The best course for them would be to get in touch with the Panel Lawyer, speak to him a day or two before the date of hearing and offer any assistance required. They should attend the Court with all relevant record, information and documents to show how the stay order is delaying the project and how the public exchequer will suffer by delaying the execution of the project. If all this is done, cases can be decided fast and judgments can be passed in favour of the Organization. But this initiative is lacking. However, wherever some Project Managers have shown concern and were associated with the Land Department and the advocates, DDA was successful in getting the stay orders vacated and matters were decided in its favour.

A small piece of land under stay at times holds up the entire Project. Such was the instance at Bhikajikama Place and the District Centre in Rohini where projects were held up because someone had gone to the Court and got the stay order. Even where matters are settled and acquisition is complete, once again greedy trouble mongers go to Court and get stay orders. This is extremely unfortunate to say the least. Individual interest cannot be more important than the national interest. There are cases where litigation has been going on for the last 15 years. It is all against public interest. Litigation should not be a source of legalizing the illegal work. Follow-up of Court cases in the District Courts belongs to the level of the Junior Law Officer. In most of the cases relating to land, factual position being in favour of the Organization, matters are decided for the DDA. But a little more care at the level of the Branch Officers can certainly help to see that proper item by item comments and other documentary evidence is made available to the Panel Lawyers and cases can be decided speedily.

In the Supreme Court, the number of cases being limited, these are generally handled properly at the level of the Head of the Department. Senior advocates are engaged and they are briefed properly. The issues of law are clear. It is only in the High Court where the Department has to involve the Project Managers to act as real Project Managers rather than Engineers, Architects and Planners, that they should feel concerned for the Court cases. They should be actively associated and brief the Panel Lawyers. They should provide them with all record and documents including Plans. The financial implication for delay should be properly spelt out. Inter-departmental coordination is very essential for speedy settlements of these matters. In land acquisition matters, basically, it is not DDA but the Land

Acquisition Collector who is to provide information. Land is acquired by the Land Acquisition Collector, Government of NCTD on behalf of the Delhi Development Authority. Although the Land Acquisition Collector and Land and Building Department, Government of NCTD notifying the acquisition of land, may not feel concerned to the extent DDA feels but they need to be involved and an understanding at the senior level should be built so that whatever information is asked for by the Court about notification of land and issuing the award is made available by the Land Acquisition Collector. The loser in any case is not the Land Acquisition Collector but the Delhi Development Authority and, therefore, it has to be more cautious and vigilant and an understanding and communication at a regular basis at the senior level between the officers of two departments is necessary to avoid unpleasant situation, defaults and delays.

Urban land is a highly priced commodity. Delhi has limited land. Its value is determined by its use. It should be the duty of each department like DDA, Public Works Department, SDMs of the Area, Municipal Corporation of Delhi and the police to ensure that no land in any form be allowed to fall to encroachment or misuse. Different departments and agencies should not pass the blame on each other. Each agency, rather each official in the agency should feel personally concerned in Land Protection. When the matters are before the Courts each department should assist the other to present the records before the Courts. Today management of land is a very specialized area of urban development. A special cadre of officers should be created and the developmental authorities and municipal bodies should have dedicated teams of such officers. The officers should be well equipped in areas like land records, revenue, infrastructure and urban finances. The growth of future urban centers will depend on our policies and programmes relating to urban development and urban management.

11 PRESERVING YAMUNA

Rivers have always played very important role in the socio-economic life of the cities. Besides source of trade and commerce, rivers with religious sanctity have contributed in the social and religious life of the people. A new role, which rivers can assume, is of sport and tourism. Even the establishment of early human settlements was near the rivers primarily because of water. Indraprastha was built on the riverbank. So was the case when Shahjahanabad was built. The Britishers also selected land for its new capital when they shifted the capital of India from Calcutta to New Delhi in 1911, close to Yamuna River what we call today the Burari Area. The coronation pillar in whatever form it is today is testimony of this effect. River is generally the lifeline of the city. It is source of water supply. It is also major lung space between urban masses on two sides. However indiscriminate urban growth of all sorts especially unauthorized industrial waste flowing through various industrial estates and dirty water flowing the Yamuna River has disrupted environmental balance. It is shame to admit that today river is virtually converted into a dirty drain. The Yamuna has high level of water pollution, which is mainly untreated sewage and waste flowing from industrial and residential settlements. This chapter deals with the problem of pollution in River Yamuna and efforts made to deal with the same.

Two significant geographical elements in the natural environment of the city are ridge and River Yamuna. From the legendary city of the Indraparastha to 21st Century Delhi we have seen changes less of developmental nature and more of decay. Shahjahanabad the classic old city was built during 17th

Century by the Mughal Emperor Shahjahan. It was located on the western bank of the river. The river played dominant and utilitarian role in Shahjahanabad's urban form. Water supply, transportation and water channels used to flow in the city through Chandni Chowk canals. River was flowing touching the Red Fort. That was the beauty of the monument and the river as well subsequently with the passage of time and development of the city road was built between the Red Fort and the river what we call today as the Ring Road. This Ring Road, which is parallel to the River Yamuna from South to North, acted as barrier between the settlements and the river.

Before reaching the Wazirabad Barrage, the River Yamuna flows with its pure water and sanctity. One can see clean and pure water near Burari and Wazirabad and one is able to enjoy the freshness of its waters and its vibrant waves near Burari. The river enters the city at Pallah to the North of Delhi Border. It covers a distance of about 45 kms. upto Okhla *via* Wazirabad.

The residents of Delhi know that the Yamuna seizes to be a river after crossing Burari and Wazirabad. The large stretch of land between the two *Bundhs* or small dams right from the Wazirabad Barrage upto Okhla is owned by various Government agencies. Some land in this area is still privately owned and has not come under the Government's possession. Various kinds of activities are noticed in the area between the two *Bundhs* which is commonly known as the river-bed area. The majority of the land from the Wazirabad Bridge upto Old Railway Bridge is owned by the Land and Development Office, Ministry of Urban Development and the Nazul-I land, belongs to the Delhi Development Authority and was handed down to it by the erstwhile Delhi Improvement Trust. Similarly, majority of the land from Old Railway Bridge upto the Nizamuddin Bridge is again Land and Development Office land and the Nazul-I Land.

There are many Government agencies which own the land in the river-bed area. These include the Land and Development Office, the Central Public Works Department, the Public Works Department, the Delhi Development Authority, Railways, the

Delhi Vidyut Board and the Metro Rail, besides privately owned land. A large stretch of land towards the eastern side of the Yamuna River but within the protected bunds, belongs to U.P. Canal Department.

Some land in the river-bed area has been allotted to a few religious institutions. A large piece of L&DO land near the Wazirabad Bridge is allotted to an institution known as Nanaksar. Similarly, a large piece of land to the North of the Nizamuddin Bridge is allotted to the Swami Narain Mandir where a large temple complex has come up. Now even the village complex for stay of athletes and sports persons who would come to participate in the Commonwealth Games in 2010 is also being built there. However there were objections and strong agitations from the environmentalists against construction of a village complex over there. A *Bundh* has been re-enforced for the safety of the village complex and also for Swami Narain Temple. Swami Narain Temple is a real feature and a landmark in the city.

A large number of Religious Institutions and *Dharamshalas* (charitable guest houses) are located between Ring Road and the river, towards the northern side of the Old Railway Bridge. Similarly, a number of *Samadhis* of political leaders have been laid out on the land between Old Railway Bridge upto the Raj Ghat Power Station.

To de-congest the Mathura Road from Ashram crossing to Faridabad, a new National Highway is proposed to be constructed linking Maharani Bagh Ring Road area to Faridabad alongwith the river and the Agra Canal. This project will be undertaken in two phases. Phase-I will cover a stretch from Maharani Bagh to Jasola. Major part of the land for this road stretch is already with the Public Works Department, GNCTD, which is to construct the roads. Land in this area, which was owned by the DDA and formed part of the road alignment has already been handed over to the Public Works Department, GNCTD.

East Delhi is connected with rest of the city by bridges over the River Yamuna. Besides the Wazirabad Bridge, three more bridges over the Yamuna River have been constructed near the Inter-State Bus Terminal (ISBT), ITO and Nizamuddin. The Nizamuddin and the ITO Bridges were recently widened by constructing additional bridges parallel to the existing to ease the flow of traffic from the trans-Yamuna areas. Recently another bridge from Gita Colony to the Samadhi Area at Raj Ghat has been constructed to give additional relief to the trans-Yamuna Area. Four Pontoon Bridges one near the Tibetan Colony, close to Wazirabad, one in the vicinity of Raj Ghat, one near Bhairon Road and another one close to Sarai Kale Khan connecting Mayur Vihar have also been constructed. Unauthorized commercial activities have come up on either side of these Pontoon Bridges. Recently, the New Delhi Noida Toll Bridge was also built connecting Maharani Bagh with New Okhla Industrial Development Authority.

It was during the 1950s, that Government land in the river-bed area was given to the Peasants Cooperative Societies under the "Grow more Food" programmes. It was an excellent idea at the time, but now agriculturists have further transferred the land to others. Some land was disposed off, where unauthorized activities in the form of *Jhuggi-Jumpri* clusters and semi-*Pucca* and *Pucca* structures had come up.

Land from the Nizamuddin Bridge to Okhla Barrage was private land. A large part of this land was acquired by the Delhi Development Authority during 1990-92, however, possession of all this acquired land has not come to the Delhi Development Authority because of litigation and stay orders granted by the Courts. In this process of land acquisition, a large number of unauthorized settlements towards the Okhla and Jogabai areas have come up. These unauthorized builders are not deterred by the threat of floods. Day in and day out they fill up the river-bed, create huge landfill areas and have raised unauthorized structures against all the land-governing laws and bye-laws. The area being very densely built-up and occupied by the Muslim community, no demolition could be organized successfully (as has also been demonstrated in the chapter on Land Protection).

The Authorities assessed the delicate law and order situation in that area and therefore, have not been able to check the ever-increasing unauthorized construction. What this situation required was a strong and sincere administrative will, which should have and could have nipped this problem in the bud itself, so that it didn't gain such a great momentum and become an indestructible and irreversible development later on.

Even on the northern side of the ITO Bridge, a large Unauthorized Colony known as Hathi Colony had come up. Almost all the structures were of *Pucca* and semi-*Pucca* nature including the religious structures which had come up. No such colony should have come up in the river-bed area. Even while the guidelines for regularization of unauthorized colonies were drawn it was decided that colonies in the river-bed area will not be regularized. Similarly a large number of *jhuggies* had come up in the river-bed area on the stretch of land between the Old Railway Bridge upto ITO. Some *jhuggies* near ITO were removed when the Secretariat Building of the Delhi Government was operationalised. Another *jhuggi-jumpri* cluster had come up near Bhairon Road between Ring Road and the Yamuna.

Besides land encroached by the *jhuggies* in the river-bed area there was always threat of encroachment by the religious institutions because once these come up subsequent demolition becomes difficult. This has been the case with religious structures all-over the city. A major religious structure was attempted on the North of ISBT Bridge which was immediately removed with the help of the Court and strict action by the authorities. The structure was known as Moni Baba Temple. The demolition was so difficult that large contingent of staff and police was required to remove the structure. Had timely action not been taken, temple would have come up and subsequent removal would have been difficult.

Land on the either side of Inter-state Bus Terminal Bridge is Government Land. In land records it is known as Nazul Land as it came to DDA alongwith all the land of the erstwhile Delhi Improvement Trust. Most of the land was with the agriculturist who was given this land in 60's under the Grow More Food Programme. On the northern side of the Inter-State Bus Terminal Flyover after crossing the river portion, someone known as Moni Baba started constructing a large temple. It was of a peculiar design and shape. It was a circular wall of 27 inch thickness and about 12 ft. high with covering an area of about 2000 sq. meters. It was quite close to the bridges. Even when construction was going on notice and warnings were issued but they kept on building the structure. One Union Minister was pattern of the institution involved in construction of the temple. Source of funding was not known. One Moni Baba (one who did not speak) was the person who had some followers and was instrumental in construction of the temple. Only the boundary wall had been constructed and idols had been brought which were to be installed. DDA moved an application before the High Court of Delhi and Court ordered to remove the upcoming structure. Copy of the order was served on the Union Minister who was pattern of the organization. It was necessary to remove the structure because once it comes up fully and a temple is set up, future widening of this important bridge would not be possible. Otherwise also it was Government Land and ex-farmers had no legal right to sell or give it to the Moni Baba for construction of temple.

This was a very difficult demolition because of the nature, use and design of the structure. This was one demolition where all the machinery of the Department and large number of police force was required. The demolition programme was fixed at the weekend. It was also fixed for night as a strategy. Demolition squad of all the zones alongwith all the officers assembled at Vikas Minar at 6.00 p.m. Though the operation was to start after 9.00 p.m. but once the staff goes home they might not return by 9.00 p.m. Some of them being residents of distant areas. Arrangement for their dinner was also done. This was one demolition where Chief Engineer Electrical was also involved directly as machinery and generators were to be used.

All precautions were taken to see that the demolition is done properly. Four bulldozers were requisitioned seeing the massiveness of the structure. Four large generators were arranged for lighting arrangement. Large ropes besides divers were also arranged because in the nearby pond some one might jumping. Staff has given special training for this demolition. Three-four persons were also trained who had to perform as *Pujaris* and remove the idols which had not been *'STHAPITID'* (installed). Demolition squad with all the officers started from Vikas Sadan under police protection at 10.00 p.m. Traffic on the ISBT Bridge was stopped. As a first step Moni Baba was taken into custody. Large Police Force was deployed at demolition site. On reaching the site, staff members who performed as *Pujaris* and other members of the demolition squad removed their shoes and respectfully removed those idols, which were planned to be installed in next two-three days. These were respectfully kept in a vehicle and taken to a temple near civil lines, under the police escort. A video film was made when the demolition squad performed prayer and removed the idols and placed in the vehicles alongwith the staff.

Thereafter the demolition started. Since it was a thick circular wall first dent from outside was difficult. Once one part of the wall was punctured actual demolition began. Staff and police were keeping vigilant eye that nothing untoward happens. Four large bulldozers worked from 9 to 10 hours throughout the night to demolish a big thick wall. The traffic on either side of the ISBT Bridge was not allowed till 9.00 to 9.30 a.m. next day. By that time the site had been cleared, unauthorized structure removed, DDA encroached land reclaimed and order of the High Court implemented.

This is an example to illustrate that how difficult at times it is to carry out demolition to save Government land. This demolition was possible only in a Curfew like condition by stopping complete traffic on the major road. Since religious structure was being attempted the demolition squad had to take care of religious sentiments also. Once the idols were installed demolition would have been difficult. Execution of this demolition programme was very difficult task. It could be made possible by proper planning, execution and assistance of all the concerned departments.

Large scale encroachments in the form of squatter settlements and semi-*Pucca* structures came up in the river-bed area. Reportedly, there were about 34,000 *jhuggies* in the river-bed, covering an area of more than 100 acres. These 34,000 *jhuggies* were in about thirteen clusters as per details given in Table 11.1

Table 11.1 : *Jhuggi* Clusters which Existed in Yamuna River-Bed (now removed)

Sl. No.	*Name of Estate*	*Name of Cluster*	*Area Appx.*	*Nos.of Jhuggies Appx.*
1.	Bela Estate	1. Sanjay Amar Colony 2. Indira Camp 3. Dholak Basti 4. Tejpal Bagichi 5. Kanchanpuri 6. Indira Colony 7. Mool Chand Basti	39 Acr.	18000 DDA Land- 7000 PWD Land- 7000 Railways Land- 1000 DVB Land- 3000
2.	Chiraga Janubi	1. Rajeev Camp Thokar No.21 2. J.J. Camp Thokar 16 3. J.J.Camp -do- 8 Laxmi Nagar. 4. Indira Camp Rain-well No.5 Vikas Marg	59 Acr.	12000 PWD Land- 8000 UP Canal Land-3700 Railway Land- 300
3.	Inderprastha	1. Nangla Machi JJ Cluster 2. Gautampuri	11.50 Acr.	3800 on DVB Land- 3000 LandDO Land- 800
			109.5 Acr.	33,800

Now all the *jhuggies* from the river-bed area have been removed and the site has been cleared of encroachments. Thanks to the intervention of the High Court of Delhi, which has played a social role in preserving the ecology of the city and ensuring to maintain the sanctity of the river.

The land-owning agencies not only could not protect their land because this was not a priority area for them, there being no residential or commercial projects, could not even remove the *jhuggies* inspite of the fact that the squatters were using it for all purposes. Even religious structure had come up within the slum settlements. The shifting process by the land-owning agencies was slow and without any specific target date to clear the whole river-bed area. The High Court of Delhi had issued orders in the case of Okhla Factory Owners Association *v.s.* GNCTD (Government of National Capital Territory of Delhi) in CWP No. 4441 of 1994 to clear the Yamuna River-bed area within two months. The High Court Order reads as :

"In CWP. 4441 of 1994 this Court passed a judgment dated 29.11.2002 and considering all the aspects and taking relevant material into consideration, it was observed that pursuant to the scheme which has been formulated by the respondents, that is, the Union of India as well as the Government of NCT of Delhi, and the yardsticks for allotment of land to the *Jhuggi* dwellers, the Government would require approximately 3,000 hectares of land, and land to that extent, is not available in Delhi. It was also observed that the tardy nature of progress for re-allocation would require almost 272 years to re-settle the slum dwellers taking into consideration the persons who are squatting upto 1998. What has happened from 1998 till date may make this figure of 272 years even more. The judgment has also taken into consideration that for requirement of 3,000 hectares of land, the Delhi Development Authority has acquired only 7,500 acres of land and whopping sum of acquisition cost of the said 7,500 acres of land is approximately Rs.1,72,500,00.00 and development cost for the said required land would be Rs.42 thousand crores.

We have been told that the Government of NCT of Delhi and the Union of India have filed an SLP against the said judgement. Therefore, we are not passing any order with that aspect of the matter.

What is required to be done in the present situation in this never ending drama of illegal encroachment in this capital city of our Republic-River Yamuna which is a major source of water has been polluted like never before. Yamuna-Bed and both the sides of the river have been encroached by unscrupulous persons with the connivance of the authorities. Yamuna-Bed as well as its embankment has to be cleared from such encroachments. Rivers are perennial source of life and throughout the civilized world, rivers, its water and its surroundings have not only been preserved, beautified but special efforts have been made to see that the river flow is free from pollution and environmental degradation. The Yamuna River has been polluted not only on account of dumping of waste, including industrial waste, medical waste as well as discharge of unhygienic material but the Yamuna Bed and its embankment have been unauthorizedly and illegally encroached by construction of *Pucca* houses, *Jhuggies* and places for religious worship, which cannot be permitted any more. As a matter of fact, under the garb of reallocation, encroachers are paid premium for further encroachment. Delhi with its present population of twenty million people can take no more. In view of the encroachment and construction of *Jhuggies/Pucca* structure in the Yamuna Bed and its embankment with no drainage facility, sewerage water and other filth is discharged in Yamuna water. The citizens of Delhi are silent spectators to this state of affairs. No efforts have been made by the authorities to remove such unauthorized habitation from Yamuna-Bed and its embankment.

We, therefore, direct all the authorities concerned, i.e., DDA, MCD, PWD, DJB as well as the Central Government to forthwith remove all the unauthorized structures, *Jhuggies,* places of worship and/or any other structure which are unauthorizedly put in Yamuna-Bed and its embankment, within two months from today."

All the acquired land could not be handed over to the DDA by the Land Acquition Collecter as there was stay order from the Court in some cases. There are cases where the Court has ordered to maintain *status-quo* even for the land which has been acquired and placed at the disposal of the DDA. Development of this land has not been done due to such litigation and Court orders.

As mentioned earlier in this chapter the river has been converted into a drain by flow of sewer and industrial waste. The Master Plan of Delhi has also listed the following 22 drains falling in River Yamuna :

1. Najafgarh Drain
2. Magazine Road Drain
3. Sweeper Colony Drain
4. Khyber Pass Drain
5. Metcalfe Drain
6. Kudsia Bagh Drain
7. Moat Drain
8. Trans-Yamuna MCD Drain
9. Mori Gate Drain
10. Civil Mill Drain
11. Power House Drain
12. Sen Nursing Home Drain
13. Drain No. 14
14. Barapullah Drain
15. Maharani Bagh Drain
16. Kalkaji Drain
17. Okhla Drain
18. Tughlakabad Drain
19. Shahdara Drain
20. Sarita Vihar Drain
21. LPG Bottling Plant Drain
22. Tehkhand Drain

From Wazirabad Bairaz to Badarpur Border on 48 km. long Yamuna stretch there are 17 Nallahas, which flow in the river. 70 per cent of the Yamuna pollution is from Najafgarh Drain. About 42 small or big Nallahas carrying all sorts of wastes enter the Najafgarh Drain at several points. It is said that Najafgarh Drain, which is most polluted drain today, was at one point of time a clean stream of River. This is reflected in the document of the Central Pollution Control Board on "Our Rivers". Sahibi

River originating from Alwar area was an attractive lake of 10 km. at Dhassa village. This lake was connected to Yamuna in 1965.

Najafgarh drain is catchment area for 38 small and big drains. whereas 72 drains flow in the Shahdara Drain. There are about 1500 unauthorized colonies and 1200 *Jhuggi-Jhompari* clusters in Delhi. There is no provision of sewer in these settlements. As a result of which waste from these settlements reaches the Yamuna to pollut it further.

In the name of clean Yamuna, plans have been drawn. Some were implemented half heartedly with no result. Departments express helplessness on their part. There is no combined effort to clean the river. So for Rs. 902 crore have been spent by the Delhi Jal Board, Yamuna Vikas Board, Industry Department of Government of National Capital Territory of Delhi, Municipal Corporation of Delhi and other Government Departments/ Agencies. Major amount is spent in laying down the sewer lines, treatment plants, increasing their capacity, connecting drain with treatment plants and in carrying out development related schemes in Yamuna and setting up treatments plants in industrial area.

A scheme was also prepared to carry the water of various drains in a large drain parallel to the Yamuna River so that the waste and drain water does not mix up with the River Water. This was not accepted. For changing the trunk sewer lines, Government of India will provide Rs. 387.17 crore in the second phase of Yamuna Action Plan.

The Yamuna Vikas Board expects that pollution from the river would be removed within three-four years. As per this scheme on both sides parallel to Najafgarh and Shahdara Drains, 115 km. long sewer pipeline will be laid down. These parallel lines will be connected to nearby sewage treatment plant. By this process residential and industrial waste instead of going straight in the Yamuna will go in the treatment plants through sewer lines and only clean water will flow in the river. Supplementary drains will be connected to sewage system of Bela Road and Ring Road. Under this scheme 22 km. area of Yamuna from Wazirabad Bairaz to Okhla Bairaz will be covered.

Though there was flood this year in the river, but generally it is after a gap of about 10-15 years. The adjoining areas have been properly protected by 10 embankments (*Bandh*). These embankments are at the level of 207 –216 meter height. Besides this there are three barrages (Wazirabad Barrage, ITO Barrage, and Okhla Barrage) on 23rd September 2008 when the level of the Yamuna River went upto 206 meters, it could not cross the embankment because of their height. The Nallahs flowing in the Yamuna were also blocked so that by back flow water should not enter the city. The length and height of 10 embankments protecting the city from floods are given in Table 11.2.

Table 11.2 : The Length and Height of Embankment (*Bandh*) Protecting the city from Floods

Sl. No.	*Embankment (Bandh)*	*Length in km*	*Height in Meter*	*Area Protected*
1.	Pallah to Wazirabad	18.36	2016.20	Wazirabad
2.	Left Forward	5.750	211.80	Sonia Vihar
3.	S.M. *Bandh*	11.9	209	Shahdara
4.	Jagatpur *Bandh*	4.388	211	Jagatpur
5.	Yamuna Bazar *Bandh*	600	209.10	Nigambodh Ghat
6.	Yamuna Bazar Marginal	1.1	207.98	Yamuna Bazar
7.	Mughal *Bandh*	2.7	208.45	ISBT
8.	Power House *Bandh*	2.3	207.14	Rajghat, Daryaganj
9.	Left Marginal *Bandh*	6.7	207.42	Khajuri Khas
10.	Madan Pur Khadar *Bandh*	3.5	201.42	Yamuna Down Stream

When river front is contained within the *Bandhs*, land outside the *Bandh* can be utilized and should be utilized for green, recreation and community activities.

The Government must work out a time frame in consultation with all concerned agencies for the development and utilization of land within the two *Bandhs* for the stretch from the Wazirabad bridge to Okhla Barrage as it forms a vast land resource and can prove invaluable in the city's development. Urban land could not be left unutilised or under-utilized. Additional *Bandhs* can be constructed to ensure that more land becomes available for various uses. Keeping in view the flood studies of past 50 years, the Government must work out a plan to utilize the vast urban lands in the river-bed area atleast for 6-8 months in a year when the land is usable. This is in the center of the city where land values are very high. The land is approachable from various directions. East Delhi, which is on the eastern side of the Yamuna River, will also get a fillip by the development of commercial, institutional and recreational activities in this area. Various architectural and environmental features, which are of educational interest, can be created in this area.

We should not allow the river-bed land to be encroached upon. The Courts are already for the protection of Government land so the concerned land-owning authorities must take advantage of the atmosphere around. Interests such as appeasement of voters should not detract us. We must see through the next 500 years and not just 5 electoral years.

A large tract of land in the river-bed area is also under cultivation. It is only during the monsoon *i.e.* about 2-3 months of the year that one can actually see the river flowing. For almost 9 months in a year, it is only a dry patch where dirty water flows from major city drains. In a stretch of about 22 kilometers from Wazirabad to Okhla which is about 2-3 kilometers wide, a beautiful Green Development Area with recreational and other use could have been conceived and planned. Failure to do so had led to unauthorized cultivation, development of unauthorized colonies and emergence of *jhuggi* clusters.

The Government must act firmly to protect the sanctity of this river, which has been covered in our religious scriptures. Serious concern must be shown to check new *jhuggies* to come up in its bed and on its banks.

Every one expresses concern for Yamuna getting polluted. Even Supreme Court of India has shown its concern. The situation has not improved. It is very unfortunate that in a city like Delhi, which is Cosmopolitan in character and national capital, we could not ensure Yamuna's flow with clean water. People have religious sentiments attached to the Yamuna like Ganga River but still nothing is done at public level to pool efforts to clean the river. Administration only refers to proposals, programmes, funds and at the end of the day comes out with statistics, which have no meaning.

For ensuring that River Yamuna is kept clean even the Supreme Court expressed its concern from time-to-time. Bhure Lal Committee, which monitors progress of cleanliness of Yamuna, has reflected on the Government by placing facts through its reports before the Supreme Court but there is no change in the situation.

The Yamuna has vast areas. 9700-hectare land is in the river-bed. Beautiful green areas can be developed on either side of the river on the *Bandh*. This should be creative and aesthetic development with various themes depicting our history and culture right from the era of Pandwas. Our great history of tolerance and secular character of the nation should be reflected through development of soft and pleasing nature. Playgrounds for various play activities and sports can be created which can be used from 8 to 10 months of the year because whole area between the two Bundhs of the river is flooded only during Monsoon, when there is excessive flood which is generally once in two decades. This area should not be left unutilized. Beautiful picnic spots should be developed with floral creations. Let us do so to make the Yamuna a living feature as part of our life

We all want Yamuna should be clean. Like ridge. river is also a godly feature of the city. We have not been able to incorporate the Yamuna River in our life, in our urban culture, in our thought, in our aesthetic sense and in our fabric of ethnicity. As we care for our homes, we should care for Yamuna. Let it be part of our thought. Its purity should be restored. Its dignity should be respected and its use as sports and religious feature should be restored. We should resolve to do so. All right minded people should unite as Government and its machinery has failed to do so. Let our children and youth take the lead to give lost dignity and honour to the Yamuna.

12 TRAFFIC MANAGEMENT

Roads are the lifeline of a city. The smooth flow of traffic is essential for travelling from one place to another. Travelling should not only be safe and involve minimal time but it should also be relaxing and tension-free. Unfortunately, in Delhi there is no concept of lane driving, no respect for traffic rules and no sense of road discipline. The Supreme Court, on its part, has played a vital social role by ensuring the introduction of CNG within a time-frame whereby the city's air pollution has been brought under control. The Supreme Court has also helped in regulating the traffic, whereby buses have to move in their lanes with the result being realized in terms of fewer road accidents. Furthermore, although the city administration has tried to streamline the vehicular flow of traffic over the years, mainly through the construction of flyovers, much more needs to be done in terms of traffic management. This chapter deals with the problems of traffic in the city, and the efforts made till now by the civic and police administration to alleviate these problems.

The conditions of roads, their width and linkage to various parts of the city determine the time with reference to distance. In a country like the USA the distance is referred to through time. If one wishes to go from place x to place y instead of distance he/she will express the distance in terms of the time taken to travel it. Over the years with the liberalization of economic policies Delhi's car-owning population has increased considerably. (There are currently 56 lakh vehicles in the city.) With the increase of traffic pressure on roads in the city now even Delhiites have started using a similar terminology to express distance. Thus, instead of saying that the distance of Connaught Place from Mehrauli is 15 kms., a person will say that the two places are at a distance of 30 to 40 minutes.

Go anywhere in the city and you will invariably be trapped in a bad traffic jam. Be it East Delhi, West Delhi, North Delhi or South Delhi — for kilometers together traffic remains stuck and roads stay jam-packed. With the excess traffic on roads travelling time has increased to almost one and a half times the normal duration. The situation is worst during the monsoon season when roads are full of potholes everywhere. And yet, every year 70,000 more vehicles are added to Delhi's Roads. In fact, during 2007 on the eve of Dhan Teras and Diwali 28,000 new vehicles were purchased in Delhi.

In 1990 the population of Delhi was 89 lakhs. Today it is about 1 crore 70 lakhs. The increase in number of vehicles during this period is alarming. In 1990 there were 17 lakhs 64 thousand vehicles in Delhi, whereas now the number has gone upto more than 56 lakhs. The increase in population was two times but the increase number of vehicles was an alarming three times during the same period. The result is that our roads are totally jammed.

64 per cent of vehicles in Delhi are two wheelers, which shows that people in Delhi prefer their own conveyance because of mobiiity in job, convenience and a sense of ownership. Delhiites seem to be more possessive in general than citizens of other metros since in Bombay and Calcutta people prefer to commute on public transport. However the situation in Delhi has considerably improved after introduction of Metro. A large number of motorcycles and cars are seen parked in the parking lots of Metro stations which shows that many people are now parking their vehicles and travelling by Metro to their workplaces. If we Delhi gets increasingly connected by public transport systems like the Metro, most of the people who do not have travelling jobs will prefer to reach their workplace by using these services rather than their own transport which cause social and physical tension while driving on Delhi's roads.

A major reason for such a large number of private vehicles in Delhi is that there is no dependable public transport system except the Delhi Metro, which is catering to limited areas. The

Delhi Metro was introduced in 2002 with limited routes. Within the short period of 6 years since there has been an increase of 16,80,000 vehicles in Delhi. This is the condition when about 7-8 lakh commuters travel daily in the Metro. If there was no Metro then probably 150000 vehicles would have been added to Delhi's roads during this time span.

On an average 4 lakh driving licenses are issued in Delhi every year. Out of these about 12 per cent of the licenses are for commercial vehicles. Details of the progressive increase of driving license issued during last few years are given in Table 12.1.

Table 12.1 : Driving License Issued during last few years

Sl. No.	*Year*	*Driving Licenses Issued*
1.	2001 – 2002	329867
2.	2002 – 2003	354455
3.	2003 – 2004	362906
4.	2004 – 2005	387738
5.	2005 –2006	404616
6.	April 06 – December 06	304858

77 per cent of the total vehicles are cars and two wheelers and 3.1 per cent are Buses. 1 car on an average carries 2.2 persons whereas one bus carries 31 persons. 17 per cent of the total traffic is slow moving. The average speed of vehicles in Delhi is 14-15 km. per hour and if conditions don't improve the average speed is going to be as low as 5-7 kms. per hour by 2010.

As mentioned earlier, the growth of vehicles in Delhi has been more than the growth of the population itself. As on date the average growth of vehicles is more than 8.33 per cent. That means that for every 1000 persons in Delhi there are 317 vehicles. The number of registered vehicles in Delhi is increasing rapidly as well. In 2002 there were 39,25,771 registered vehicles. This number went upto over 56 lakhs by March 2008. Of course, the majority of the vehicles are two wheelers, their number being more than 35 lakhs. In addition there are more than 16 lakhs cars. Since the size of most roads cannot expand further the additional vehicles are only going to create more congestion and traffic jams. A side benefit of the slow traffic is that even if travelling in buses is cheaper, many people will now prefer the Delhi Metro, if available.

The vehicle holding capacity of Delhi's roads has reached a saturation point. For example, from 6.00 a.m. to 10.00 a.m. 1.44 lakhs vehicles pass through Naraina at Ring Road. These days it takes 30-45 minutes to travel a small distance of little over 1 km. from the Maya Puri flyover to Naraina Village. This speaks in itself of the ground realities present on the supposedly traffic signal-free Ring Road, as claimed by the authorities. Lakhs of vehicles pass from 6.00 a.m. to 10.00 a.m. in some areas such as those given in Table 12.2.

Tabel 12. 2 : Vehicles Passing through Busy Roads

Sl. No.	*Area*	*Vehicles in Lakhs*
1.	Ring Road Naraina	1.44
2.	Nizamuddin Bridge	1.43
3.	ITO Crossing	1.23
4.	NH – 8	1.19
5.	Tilak Marg	1.17
6.	Patel Road	1.17
7.	Ring Road	1.06 – 1.39

As per a study conducted in 1997, the average speed of vehicles in Delhi was 20-27 km. per hour. By 2002, it came down to 14-15 km. per hour. The speed has slowed down inspite of the fact that a number of flyovers have been constructed at various locations in the city. Many more flyovers are in the process of being erected. Coming back to the earlier example of travelling from the Mayapuri flyover to Naraina, there is again a Traffic Jam after crossing Brar Square on Ring Road. While land for the Naraina flyover was acquired after vacation of stay order from the Court, the Chief Engineer of the PWD stated that though the width of the Ring Road is 200 metres at present the PWD had acquired land width of 100 meters only. The statement made it seem that if required the authorities could easily obtain a 200 meter width. The Chief Engineer, I hope was aware of the fact that it took them years to get this land alone. The question then arises that if they required 200 meters width then why was it not taken over at that point of time itself? Everyone knows that Naraina was a major bottleneck on the Ring Road and has always affected smooth flow of traffic. Now while the flyover is under construction, it is an exceedingly arduous job to cross that patch of land at the risk of accidents to people and vehicles. Additionally, if more road width was not possible then an additional alternative alignment from Mayapuri flyover to a point prior to Brar Square should have been explored parallel to Riwari Railway line and cutting across some defence land. This would have not caused much dislocation while gaining an additional alternative road.

As per the norms of the Indian Road Congress if it takes more than 180 seconds or 3 minutes to cross an intersection then that intersection needs engineering intervention. Either a flyover or an underpass is required over there. At present there are a large number of intersections in Delhi, especially in congested areas, where commuters have to wait for more than 3 minutes. Some immediate traffic discipline and traffic management is required in these intersections to save time and fuel.

Inspite of the construction of a large number of flyovers there is no relief to road users because of the ever larger number of vehicles added to Delhi's roads every month. With economic development private vehicle owning population is increasing rapidly. Since rhere is no scope of further widening of the roads it remains to be seen what arrangements the Government is going to make through innovative traffic management policy and other mechanisms to ease the traffic flow on roads in 2010 when we hold the Commonwealth Games. The city will be flooded with vehicles then, leading to a truly testing time for Delhiites.

As compared to the increase in the vehicles, the development and widening of roads has been rather slow. In 1990 the length of roads in Delhi was 21,654 km. Thereafter 9,424 km. roads have been added till date. This is so because as per geography of the city further expansion of roads is not possible.

The officials, whether in the Delhi Secretariat or other Departments and Agencies, know it well that because of the non-availability of an integrated transportation system they cannot find any solution to the traffic jams on Delhi's roads. The Planning Commission in its 11th Five-Year Plan had constituted a group for urban transportation system in the country. The group has suggested in its report that people in metropolitan cities like Delhi preferred private vehicles due to the absence of public transportation system.

It is a fact that most of the commuters in Delhi have no road sense. However, when the Lt. Governor made a reference to this issue there was lot of hue and cry even though this was a true statement and a correct reflection on Delhi's road users. But the reaction only demonstrated a low sense of tolerance among Delhiites. People in Delhi do not believe in lane driving. Be it from the right or from the left, everyone tries to over take one another. We should not expect a sole constable on traffic duty to be able to check each and every road user. The users themselves must have road sense and exhibit a sense of responsibility while driving on Delhi's roads, both for their own safety and for the safety of others. Most of the deaths on Delhi roads and instances of road rage are the result of this behaviour by road users. This needs to be checked by self-discipline by the road users themselves.

The construction of flyovers by various agencies like Delhi Development Authority, PWD, Delhi Government and Municipal Corporation of Delhi has certainly helped improve the traffic flow to some extent. It was Shri Tejender Khanna, the then Lt. Governor of Delhi, who dwelled on the problem and initiated the process of identification of sites and planning of flyovers in 1998- 99. In his weekly meetings with the officers of the Delhi Development Authority, he regularly reviewed the subject of flyovers to be constructed. He had the foresight to see the role that flyovers would play in easing traffic congestion in the years to come. At his initiative some sites were identified and the planning process was started.

His successor, Shri Vijay Kapoor the then Lt. Governor of Delhi, gave even more emphasis to the flyover projects. By then the process had progressed from planning to the construction stage for certain flyovers. Shri Kapoor also worked out a list of flyovers to be constructed by Delhi Development Authority and other Departments so that more agencies could focus on this endeavour and the flyovers could be built faster. Besides his regular weekly review meetings with the officers of the Delhi Development Authority he used to visit these flyover sites for spot reviews and to motivate the site staff. Shri Kapoor is without doubt an urban visionary and has very clear views. When the planners of the Delhi Development Authority were reluctant to agree to a flyover at Mehrauli-Mahipal Pur Road at Nelson Mandella road T-point, on the plea that there was not enough traffic flow to justify construction of flyover, it was the Lt. Governor Shri Vijay Kapoor who thought of the years ahead and realized that the volume of traffic the road would have in the years to come because of its connectivity to the International and Domestic Airport as well as to Dwarka necessitated that a flyover be built there. Thus, on his emphasis the flyover was built and it has really helped to avoid congestion at that T- point. I only wish that the planners had also thought of the next 100 years and not just the next 10 -20 years.

In San Francisco, in the United States, the Golden Gate Bridge was constructed in 1934 with four lanes even though back then only very few cars passed through during the day. That is the type of vision planners should have. Planning should not be driven only by compulsion or compromise. It should also be based on reality. Though we have now constructed a number of flyovers in Delhi our scales are very conservative. For example, the flyovers constructed at the All-India Institute of Medical Sciences, Moti Bagh and Dhaula Kuan could have been planned for one or two more lanes. If one vehicle goes out of order on these flyovers we see a long queue of vehicles piling up behind it. Even though there was sufficient space available at these sites and no dearth of funds the flyovers weren't constructed on a larger scale. The result is that commuters have to waste lot of time daily in traffic jams on these flyovers if one lane is blocked by even one stranded vehicle. No specific study seems to have been made on the man hours lost in these traffic jams. The social tension caused by Traffic Jams also causes tremendous damage to an individual in terms of his peace of mind.

The excessive traffic on Delhi roads is a major source of social tension. Driving on Delhi roads is not safe. On a road of three lanes we can always see five rows of vehicles touching rear view mirror to rear view mirror and also moving bumper to bumper. Under these conditions if vehicles, especially the heavy vehicles, run beyond the prescribed speed limit they cause havoc by accidents. During 2006, 2009 people lost their lives in road accidents, out of which 264 people were killed by heavy vehicles. Similarly in 2007, 2050 people died, out of which 251 were killed by heavy vehicles. Other types of vehicles, which have caused major accidents and deaths, are given in Table 12.3.

Table 12.3 : Deaths Caused by Road Accidents — 2006 and 2007

Sl. No.	*Type of Vehicle*	*2006*	*2007*
1.	Heavy Vehicles	264	251
2.	Blue Line Buses	118	118
3.	Tempo	173	137
4.	DTC Buses	58	49
5.	School Buses	03	03
6.	Inter-state Buses	17	14
7.	Other Buses	73	64
8.	Tanker	20	14
9.	Trailer and Container	19	13
10.	Tractor	30	28
11.	Taxi	11	10
12.	Three Wheeler	45	30

Thus, life on the city's roads is so unsafe that on an average 5.6 persons die on the road every day. It is not only a statistical count of deaths but also an indicator of increased social tension and economic loss to the effected families suffered. The city has to be more sensitive to these deaths. There is currently no programme run by the Government or any other institution to impart civic education specific to this issue. Challans issued by the Police Department help only to a limited extent. What we need are stricter measures – for example, any one causing a fatal accident should not be allowed to drive for atleast 6 months. Some innovative ways to improve the traffic flow on the roads have to be evolved. The earlier we take these steps the better it will be for the safety of the public.

As mentioned earlier, the Metro has played a major partner's role in solving traffic congestion problem. There is tremendous relief in transportation on routes where the Metro is operating through Yellow and Blue Lines upon completion of its first phase. Work on the second phase is progressing very fast as well. In the second phase the Metro will connect places like Qutub Minar, All-India Institute of Medical Sciences and Airport. The areas likely to be connected by September 2010 are given in Table 12.4

Table 12.4 : Metro Lines to be Completed and Connected by 2010

Sl. No.	*Metro Corridor*	*Kilometers*	*Completion Date*
1.	New Delhi Raiiway Station-IGIA	19.2	August 2010
2.	Central Secretariat-Badarpur	19.55	September 2010
3.	Delhi University-Jahangirpuri	6.36	October 2009
4.	Central Secretariat-Gurgaon	26.80	June 2010
5.	Indraprastha –New Ashok Ngr	15.10	June 2009
6.	Yamuna River-Anand Vihar	6.16	October 2009
7.	Indraparstha-Kirti Ngr.-Mundka	18.50	March 2010
8.	Dwarka Sector-9-21	5.0	December 2009
	Complete Length	120.57	Approx. Expenditure Rs. 16887 Crore.

Delhi Metro's first phase covers a length of 65.10 km: - 4.5 km. is at ground level, 47.43 km is elevated and 13.17 km. is under-ground. The entire span covers 59 stations. Phase II line of Metro will another 83 stations. It will run for 94.13 km. at elevated level; 19.83 km. under-ground and the rest at ground level. Delhi Metro has played very important role in reducing road traffic congestion as about 7 lakhs passengers commute daily on the Metro. Metro's average daily income is about Rs. 70 lakhs through its 1100 trips. It is a clean, comfortable, punctual and fast mode of city transport. Many Delhiites now wish that the Metro had come to the city much earlier.

The increased number of vehicles in Delhi is not only a creating problems on the roads but also stressing parking in the city. Unfortunately, there is no concept of a garage in India. People park their vehicles on public land without caring for convenience of others. Lanes and bye-lanes in residential areas are generally full of parked vehicles. Just like we paid an emphasis on parks in the Second Master Plan we need to resolve the parking crisis in the Third Master Plan.

The problem of parking is worst during day time at business centers, shopping centers and workplaces. One can readily see the chaos created by unplanned and unauthorized parking at busy business and shopping centers. At many places like Karol Bagh, nearly half of the road width is used just for parking vehicles. It is an excruciating task to park a vehicle and later take it out of the parking spot since by the time you return to your vehicle you might often be stuck again as somebody else would have parked his/her car in front of yours. Atleast in regular parking areas, parking attendants help you in taking out your vehicle; there is no such luck in public parking areas.

The parking space available in the city can accommodate barely 50,000 vehicles. In a recent survey conducted by the RITES it has been reveal that University Metro Station, Old Delhi Railway Station, Karol Bagh and Bahadur Shah Zafar Marg had the most congested parking lots in Delhi. The survey also brought out that the existing parking lots are bursting at their seams. At all the places where the survey was conducted, including Connaught Place, where parking rates are very high, the demand for parking space is much more than the space available. Thankfully, the Government is planning for about 100 new parking sites and 25-multi-level parkings to cope up with the parking space shortage.

With the large number of vehicles being added to Delhi's Roads everyday the parking problem is going to become even acute in the days to come. The Government is therefore planning to hike parking charges. At some places hourly parking rates have been fixed. The following are some of the congested parking lots where there is lot of pressure:

Table 12.5 : Congested Paking Lots

Sl. No.	*Location*	*Parking Index*
1.	Old Delhi Railway Station	11.5
2.	Vishva Vidhyalaya Metro Station	11.4
3.	Karol Bagh (Guffar Market)	9.6
4.	Janak Puri District Center	9.4
5.	Karol Bagh (Gurudwara Road)	7.3
6.	Kanhaiya Ngr. Metro Station	6.3
7.	Lajpatrai Market	6.2
8.	Nehru Place	6.1
9.	Karol Bagh (Arya Samaj Road)	5.8
10.	Inderlok Metro Station	5.2
11.	Bahadur Shah Zafar Marg	4.9
12.	Welcome Metro Station	4.8
13.	Town Hall	4.8
14.	Cannaught Place (Outer Circle)	4.2

* Parking Index is the ratio of peak hours parking accommodation to parking supply.

* *Source* Times of India, July 1st 2008.

There is no immediate solution in sight to the issue of parking shortage in the city. As per an estimate about 5 lakh car owners pass through the terrible experience of not finding parking in a proper parking site. The Municipal Corporation of Delhi has just 187 parking sites, the DDA has only 55 sites and NDMC has 100 sites. Only 51000 cars can be parked in these sites. On an average out of 15 lakh cars only 60 per cent come on the roads everyday but even this smaller number of vehicles cannot find parking in authorized sites, where the parked cars are often spilling out the designated areas, thus having to resort to unauthorized sites. As per the MCD, there are about 1,000 unauthorized parking areas in different parts of the city. Even though the entrepreneurial private parking attendants at these sites park vehicles ingeniously in order to maximize the space, the security and safety of the vehicles in these unauthorized parking areas is at the mercy of the contractor, local leader and local police who are aware of such unauthorized parking. The MCD has initiated a plan to provide 36 new parking areas, which are expected to be ready by December 2009. In these new parking areas another 30,000 cars will be accomodated. If the increase in the number of vehicles continues in Delhi at the present pace where about 15000-20000 vehicles are purchased every month, it will be a real challenge to the Urban Authorities and Planners to find a more long-term solution to this problem since this is not a simple problem. On a deeper level, the problem is not just one of numbers – it is one of temperament, possessiveness, an increasingly status-conscious society and of various types of compulsions.

Traffic problem and parking are really a source of strain. Some study needs to be conducted on the social dimensions of Traffic Jams and parking problem in urban settings. This will be a very valuable work in the field of urban social harmony.

The problem of traffic needs to be handled from various angles. The first step is to make arrangements to provide metro connectivity in all the areas. The Delhi Metro has been one of the most remarkable landmarks in urban development since Independence. When more and more areas are connected to the Metro, the pressure on roads will decrease. The number of accidents will come down. Driving on Delhi's roads will become a more pleasant and hassle-free experience on Delhi's Roads. Another important area that will aid in the smooth flow of traffic is enforcing the use of roads only to carry commuting vehicles, not for the parking of stationary vehicles, Rehriwalas and other illegal encroachments. Shopkeepers should not be allowed to display their goods on footpaths so that pedestrians can move freely without risking life and limb. The traffic also needs to be regulated in terms of lane driving and speed. There should be an increased focus on civic education and the creation of Teaching Centers to educate road users and the pedestrians. This kind of education should also be provided through the media. For example, each TV channel should devote a fixed amount of time for this educational purpose as part of their social responsibility. Our education and management should be such that each citizen is be made to realize his/her responsibility towards others. Thus, civic education for the road users is the prime necessity of our times.

13 INSTITUTIONAL PARTNERSHIP FOR URBAN INFRASTRUCTURE

Everyday, thousands of people migrate to cities from villages and townships in search of employment and better prospects. These people need much more than mere shelter. A structure becomes a house and eventually a home only when it is supported with the required infrastructure in the neighbourhood as well at city level, but it is not limited to basic utilities such as water, electricity, sewerage and roads etc. For proper mobility and connectivity of places, a regulated road network and street pattern is required and needs proper maintenance to sustain and survive massive urban population pressure. Similarly, social infrastructure in the form of schools, hospitals, community centers, police stations, milk booths and other cultural areas are essential in city life. Parks, playfields and sport facilities are also essentially required for healthy living environment. An attempt has been made to reflect on the infrastructure required and infrastructure available and also to suggest a model whereby private and corporate institutions can be integrated to the urban institutional framework by making them partners for infrastructural development.

A proper balance is to be maintained between population pressure and the extent of services which a city can provide efficiently. In a city like Delhi, we all know that because of population pressure, besides emergence of *jhuggi-jhompri* clusters and development of unauthorized colonies, we experience shortage of water and electricity if not throughout the year, at least during critical summer season.

Life in general is affected by shortage of these services as well as inadequacy in urban infrastructure. In reality a large population of the city has to manage without sewerage. Unauthorized colonies expect their regularization, and such moves are particularly more forceful around election time. Similarly, squatters in the *jhuggi-jhompri* clusters also demonstrate their voting power during the election period. Their need, therefore, cannot be ignored. At the same time, one has also to see as to how much population load a city can afford. The population of Delhi has already touched 1.6 crores. It is going to cross 2.3 crores by 2021 as per "Master Plan" 2021. All these problems and issues which are very important and affect everybody's life are being discussed in this chapter. Efforts have been made to analyze the problem from a wider perspective keeping in view the ground realities.

Water Problem in Delhi

Delhi has always faced problem of acute water shortage. Although over the years it has augumented its water availability but the population pressure in the city is so strong that inspite of best efforts of the Government it has not been able to reach the satistfaction level. Water is the basic necessity. The day starts with water. The health and happiness of the family depends on water. Over the years Government has also supplemented its effort of supply by providing water through tankers but the problem still remains. It is worst during summer season when for a handful bucket of water people que up in the early morning hours and also run after the water tankers.

Even since 1951 we have noticed shortage of water in Delhi. In 1951 as aginst supply of 60 MGD there was shortage of 92 MGD. Again in 1981 against supply of 337 MGD shortage was of 178 MGD. However, the supply position improved considerably Suring 1991, 2001 and 2007. During these years inspite of population pressure the position of water improved though there was still shortage. As against 2001 when the supply and shortage of water was 650 and 211 respectively, the position improved in 2007 when the supply was up-graded upto 790

MGD and the shortage came down to 140 MGD. It is expected that by 2010 the supply will improve upto 930 MGD and city will have shortage of only 80 MGD. Similarly it is expected that by 2021 the supply will be to the tune of 1205 MGD and the shortage will be only 175 MGD. Thus inspite of the fact that the supply position has improved and will improve but the shortage remained and will remain. The water supply position and shortage from 1951 to 2021 (Projected) is reflected in Table: 13.1.

Table 13.1 : Water Supply Position from 1951-2021

Sl. No.	*Year*	*Population in MGD*	*Water Available in MGD*	*Shortage*
1.	1951	21.66 lakh	60	92
2.	1961	32.88 lakh	130	100
3.	1971	46.19 lakh	175	148
4.	1981	73.64 lakh	337	178
5.	1991	97.56 lakh	472	211
6.	2001	1.40 crore	650	211
7.	2007	1.50 crore	790	140
8.	2010	1.65 crore	930	80
9.	2021	2.2 crore	1205	175

Note: Data upto 2001 about water quantity in MGD is on the basis of economic survey of Delhi. Data for the subsequent period is as per Delhi Jal Board.

As on date population of Delhi is 1 crore 70 lakhs. There are 17 lakhs water connections and only 6 laboratories for testing the water. These 17 lakhs connections are against 34 lakhs houses. In addition there are 3000 tube-wells to meet the water requirement. Total water supply in the city is about 770 MGD. As the population of Delhi is growing fast the demand for water is also increasing. For the present population of the city, the water requirement is of 1050 MGD. Delhi Jal Board is working on two new plants: One at Dwarka and the other at Okhla expecting that these will be operational by 2010. Similarly Government is also planning to get more water for optimum utilization of Bawana Plant, which was constructed 5 years back, and is working to half of its capacity. As per Master Plan 2021 when Delhi's population is likely to be 2.3 crore the city will need 1500 MGD water.

When Dwarkawater treatment plant gets ready by 2010 Common wealth Games it will give additional 50 MGD water. During next 2 years a number of flyovers, hotels, shopping malls and convention centers are to come up. Indira Gandhi International Airport is also being expanded and up-graded. All this will need additional water therefore the capacity of Dwarka water treatment plant is proposed to be enhanced from 40 to 50 MGD. DDA has already given 32-acre land to Delhi Jal Board for construction of water treatment plant.

It is planned to set-up 20 MGD water treatment plant at Okhla. 3 lakh people will benefit with this plant, which will take about 3 years to complete. Delhi Jal Board is planning to lay down 20 km. long pipes from Wazirabad to Okhla Plant. At present 12 MGD plant exists at Okhla, but because of non-availability of water the plant is generating only 3 MGD drinking water. Okhla Plant when made operational to its full capacity will cater to the water requirement for Okhla, Kalkaji, Nehru Place, Chitranjan Park, Ashram, Maharani Bagh, Sukhdev Vihar, New Friends Colony, Jamia Milia Islamia University, Batala House, East of Kailash and some villages around.

The distribution of water is not uniform. In some areas water is available all 24 hours whereas in some areas it is available hardly for 1-2 hours in a day. The minimum water supply should be ensured for domestic use. For projected population of 2.3 crore by 2021 the Delhi Development Authority has worked out the water requirement of 1150 million gallon per day (MGD). As per the Delhi Jal Board's augmentation plan 2021 per day capacity can be increased to a maximum of 919 MGD as given in Table 13.2.

Out of about 1.4 million water connections upto 2003, only about 44 per cent subscribers were paying on the basis of actual consumption. This is because of the fact that 77 per cent Delhi Jal Board connections were metered and of them 43 per cent meters were not working. With meters not working, people

Table 13. 2 : Water Augmentation Plan of Delhi Jal Board

Sl. No.	*Water Treatment Plants*	*Capacity 2001 (in MGD)*	*Capacity 2021 (in MGD)*
1.	Chandrawal I and II	90	100
2.	Wazirabad	120	130
3.	Haiderpur I and II	200	216
4.	Bhagirathi	100	110
5.	Dwarka	—	40
6.	Sonia Vihar	—	140
7.	Nangloi	40	40
8.	Bawana	—	20
9.	Okhla	—	20
10.	Rainy Wells at Okhla	100	12
11.	Palla and Other Ground Water Sources	—	91
	Total	650	919

Source : Capacity 2021 is as proposed by DJB.

were either paying the minimum charges or average charges. The minimum charges were Rs.30/- for domestic connection, Rs.155/- for commercial and Rs.450/- for industrial consumption. Over the years people have also moved Consumer Forums for sending bills when there was no sufficient water supply. This is an awareness which is required to make the authorities realize that they can raise the bill only if they supply the water. It is likely that this awareness will become a public force and the people will question paying the bill to the electricity authority if they do not supply uninterepted power.

Suitable mandatory provisions should be made to implement rainwater as roof water harvesting schemes. Efforts should be made to improve the quality of river water and to secure its continuous flow. Surplus water during the monsoon should be retaining in the ponds alongwith river-bed area. Efforts should be made to reduce the water losses by surveillance and timely action.

With the efforts of the Government and promises that there won't be any problem of water and electricity shortage in Delhi by 2010 Commonwealth Games. We hope things will improve.

Let us see and hope for the best. We should also plan through Non-Government Organizations and educate the people about urban civic sense. They should be told not to waste water. They should open the tap only when water is required. Water seepage should be checked by the site engineers and workers. We should save water not by slogans but through actual demonstration.

Sewerage

Like water the city also faces problem with regard to other infrastructure like sewerage, drainage, power and solid waste. There are hundreds of unauthorized colonies and slum clusters where there is no sewerage facility. In addition to city level inadequacies there are imbalances in the Municipal Sewerage System. More than Urban Physical Infrastructure, this needs to be looked into and taken care of as a Public Health Issue.

Drainage

Similarly, we have drainage problem. Waste flowing through large drains is also a major source to health hazard. There are 18 drains which have direct outfall in river Yamuna. In the absence of adequate sewerage and sewage treatment facilities, a large flow of untreated waste water goes in the River Yamuna through these drains. Studies gave revealed that 7 of these 18 major drains contribute almost 95 per cent of the untreated waste water reaching the Yamuna River.

Solid Waste

So is the problem with dumping of solid waste as we are finding it difficult to identify landfill sites for future solid waste dumping. Some innovative scientific approach needs to be thought of for disposal of solid waste including recycling of some material.

Power

So is the problem about shortage of power. It's a common

feature that during summer months there are regular power cuts. Neither we have been able to generate sufficient power to meet the city requirement nor have we been able to regulate it properly. It affects industrial production, working effciency in offices and also flow of life in the city. When the traffic signals become unoperational due to power cuts, the chaos created at the road intersections is the worst form of urban chaos leading to disorder. Even the banking system which is now on internet also comes to halt. This shows the loss of business, manpower and inconvenience to the banking industry and the customers. The most important is the insecurity caused by power cuts during night.

I have just made a reference to the Physical Infrastructure because the main objective of the book is to dwell on the Unplanned Growth in terms of residential, commercial and institutional activities and improper utilization of urban land.

Partnership Approach

Besides the Delhi Development Authority, which is the major agency for city development, there are other organizations, which are directly connected with road, safety, fuel conservation and health. It is high time we decide to actively involve organizations, which are associated with the problem. If we save fuel by constructing flyovers and increase the traffic speed, the oil companies must welcome and voluntarily offer to share the cost of flyovers and road improvement. Fuel saving will help the oil companies. The major oil companies like Indian Oil Corporation, Bharat Petroleum and Hindustan Petroleum can thus be involved in the process of flyover construction and should be invited to involve themselves in contributing to the construction cost.

Similarly, a great amount is paid as compensation by the insurance companies *i.e.* General Insurance Companies as well as by the Life Insurance Corporation of India wherever there are accidents, deaths and injuries. By improving the road conditions and providing flyovers the number of accidents will come down drastically. Thus the insurance companies will have to pay less claims for accidents and deaths. These are directly connected with the road conditions and flow of traffic. If we are ensuring safety and speedy movement of vehicular traffic through construction of new roads and flyovers the insurance companies will make gains. Therefore, the Life Insurance Corporation and General Insurance Companies should be involved as partners and they should pay for the construction of flyovers in the city.

Similarly, the Delhi Government and the Municipal Corporation of Delhi should also participate equally in sharing the burden for the construction of flyovers. The Municipal Corporation of Delhi acting as an agency for the collection of house-tax should make contributions. The tax-payers in Delhi should be asked atleast for one year to pay the double house tax. This will be their one time contribution for improving roads and construction of flyovers and their assistance in city building through the MCD. It will be a nominal amount for the house owners but a substantial amount for the local body to give assistance in improving urban infrastructure. Similarly, the Delhi Government, through its road tax system should try to provide funds for the construction of flyovers. Here again, for one year the road users should be able to pay double road tax *i.e.* one year's additional tax for improving road conditions and building flyovers. In return for getting the facility of fast movement of their vehicles thus saving their time, energy and petrol, the road users should be willing to pay one year's extra road tax to the state, which can be utilized for the construction of flyovers. They should feel happy and privileged being partners in the improvement of the urban infrastructure of their city.

I am sure no organization or association should take such matters to Court because this is the process of city building through joint efforts. In the past, it has been noticed that the Courts have played a very positive role in helping city administration for improving environment and clearing encroached land sites. Here also the civic administration is sure to get all assistance from the Courts.

We have noticed that there are a number of private companies, which have maintained green areas in the city either in the form of parks or plantations on the islands and the central verge of roads. These organizations are willing to participate further in the development of the city. Therefore, major companies can also be associated for their involvement in the construction of flyovers in the city. For instance as a form of free publicity the name of the flyover being constructed and maintained by public/private company should be changed to the name of that organization for a period of ten years and so during that period of time the flyover will have two names, an original name as well as the name of the builder company.

Most of the organizations and companies should feel happy to contribute towards the development and progress of the city. At the same time, they will get recognition as partners in city growth. Wide publicity can be given to their involvement in the construction of flyovers and the citizens will be well-aware that their flyovers are financed by the insurance companies, oil companies and other organizations.

To start with a certain percentage can be worked out and the Government should invite these private corporations to become actively involved in such developmental projects. The financial involvement pattern of such organizations can be as follows :

> The LIC contributes 10 per cent of the cost of the flyover, three General Insurance Companies can contribute 5 per cent each, three oil companies can contribute 5 per cent each, DDA and MCD/Delhi Government. can contribute 10 per cent each and major industrial groups can contribute 5 per cent. Remaining 20 per cent can be generated by creating paid parking space around these and near these flyover.

An effective solution thus would be the construction of an Urban Infrastructure Facilitates Board, whose Chairman should be the Lt. Governor of Delhi and the Chairpersons of all these organization should be the members of the Board.

Thus if we have a programme for the construction of flyovers worth 1000 crores of rupees, a proportionate sharing as suggested above can be made by these organizations. Alternatively, the oil companies and insurance companies can be asked to adopt the construction and maintenance of one flyover each in the city. This will give them enough publicity and also help them in meeting their social commitment by providing the city with the much required urban infrastructure.

Serious thinking needs to be given to this kind of participation. Privatization does not mean only involving private organizations but this kind of public participation through institutional network is indeed the need of the hour. More so because these organizations are directly connected with issues of health, road safety, fuel conservation and time efficient traffic management etc.

The above mentioned ratio can be worked-out for new fly-over projects in such a way that some commercial space and paid parking space is created. This will result in generating revenue. If we ultimately involve oil agencies, insurance companies and other industries working in the field of automobile rubber technology construction, and health care, they can be active partners in the crucial process of urban growth. Similarly, dumping grounds should also be adopted by the corporate bodies to be developed as large green recreational areas for environmental and health projects. Large corporate bodies and public institutions should also be associated in clean Yamuna Project. The best way would be to encourage the corporate bodies to come out with their own projects for preserving the sanctity of the river. Besides roads, flyovers, parks and land fill sites River Yamuna is a major area which needs development through public–private partnership. Let DDA take lead and involve the corporate houses for these projects.

Thus this partnership between public and private efforts at city improvement will be a good beginning of involving various organizations which even otherwise also want to contribute towards city development as part of their social commitment and their attempt to gain publicity. This investment made today will play a strategic role in bringing huge returns later on thus ensuring that our tomorrow will be free of pollution, congestion and traffic hassles and provide a safer and healthier life for the citizens of this capital city of Delhi.

14 REMEDIAL APPROACH

A lot of work has been done during last two decades in terms of improving the physical and social infrastructure but still much remains to be done in the capital city. The capital has to acquire an international image. With economic development and increase in priced jobs there is a sea change in the business and service sphere but so far as the real need of shelter is concerned much needs to be done. The problem of unauthorized activity in the form of encroachments on right of ways, encroachment on public land, unauthorized colonization, sprawling unauthorized misuse of residential areas need to be addressed properly. Serious thinking is required by the administrators, planners, policy-makers and resident welfare associations, voluntary groups and media to evolve consensus and build a strong public opinion to suggest ways and means to improve the city and its image, so that living condition of a common man improves. In this chapter some remedial measures have been suggested to make a beginning and to take up as guidelines for improving the city and city life and also in helping to project and build Delhi a city of international character in this new millenium.

The metropolis of Delhi is growing at a very fast pace as the city is getting more crowded day by day. One notices on-going construction to accomodate the growing need for both residential accommodation and commercial space. Roadsides are blocked with traffic, pavements are jam-packed with pedestrians, pollution and unhygienic living conditions increasingly mark the city.

The population of Delhi is growing at an incredible rate. A city, which was relatively small at the beginning of the century with a small population of only about 17 lakhs at the time of the Partition of the country in 1947, currently has a population of more than 1.7 crores.

During peak hours, long queues of traffic are seen at check points and traffic signals. Even on the Ring Road which was conceived with the idea of facilitating a fast flow of traffic, one experiences long waits and sluggish movement of vehicles. From Ashram to Moolchand and from thereon to the Safdarjung Hospital it takes about half an hour to cover a distance of about 7 k.m. This entire stretch of road is characterized by bumper to bumper traffic during morning and evening hours.

The large number of vehicles and their poor state of maintenance was the major cause of pollution in Delhi till a few years back *i.e.* before the introduction of CNG. It was difficult even to stand for a few minutes in areas like the ITO intersection and the Raja Garden Ring Road Crossing, as one found it difficult to breathe in these heavily traffic-ridden and polluted areas of the city. It was felt at that time that unless a system is created for continuous, uninterrupted and smooth flow of traffic, it is going to affect the health of the citizens. With the increase in population and the expansion of the city, the movement of people travelling from one place to another is also increasing. The combined length of all the roads in Delhi in 1988-89 was 21175 k.m. With the expansion of the city the road length increased to 25948 k.m. by 1995-96.

Where there were just about 2 lakh vehicles in Delhi, back in 1971, now the number has gone upto about 56 lakhs. The number of vehicles in Delhi is more than the total number of vehicles in the three other metropolitan cities of Mumbai, Kolkata and Chennai put together. Since there is no proper rail transportation system in Delhi, people are forced to travel by road thus adding to the traffic congestion all around. In Delhi wherever possible, roads should be provided for slow moving vehicles because there are about 45,000 men and animal driven vehicles such as rickshaws and tongas in the city.

It is interesting to note that Delhi is one city where the number of vehicles exceeds the number of families. As mentioned earlier, over the years, the number of vehicles has gone up steadily. As on date there are about 56 lakh registered vehicles in Delhi whereas in 1992 there were about 20 lakh vehicles. Thus in 16 years we have added about 36 lakh new vehicles. City roadways have failed to keep pace with such steep rise in the number of vehicles. The largest number of vehicles consists of two wheelers followed by private cars. Amongst the heavy vehicles besides goods vehicles for carrying public goods, there are nearly 30,000 buses for public transport. In addition, vehicles from the neighbouring states pass through Delhi, thus adding to traffic congestion and pollution. Inspite of the check of heavy traffic vehicles in the city, vehicles continue to come into Delhi from satellite towns like Ghaziabad, Faridabad, Gurgaon, Bahadurgarh, Sonepat etc. It is imperative that an expressway should be constructed immediately so that trucks from U.P. can go to Haryana and Rajasthan without entering Delhi. Fortunately, the construction of such an expressway is already underway and will cover the towns of NCR and the vehicles will be able to go from one state to another without entering Delhi if not required. Work on this project is a priority area of the Government of NCR.

Apart from the huge number of vehicles, lack of discipline on Delhi roads is also a major factor behind bad traffic and driving experience. This is a phenomenon, which everybody talks about, but nobody in fact does much about. Drivers refuse to stick to their respective lanes, and resort to over-taking from the wrong side. It is apparent that simply making laws and attempting to enforce them, will not solve the problem. The road-users themselves must develop a temperament whereby they begin to observe the road rules so that driving is safe, smooth, tension and accident-free. Road rage is growing at an alarming rate. Thus driving on roads is not only unsafe because of more vehicles but also because of the road-users' temperament. This phenomenon is creating a lot of social tension and needs to be looked into. It cannot be ignored or allowed to grow to bigger, more disastrous proportions. Even educated people like doctors and professors and elderly car owners become victims of the violent behaviour of the road-users and road-ragers.

Besides pollution the fast increasing number of registered vehicles in Delhi is also causing physical illness and injury often resulting in emotional trauma to the citizens of Delhi. The number of accidents and deaths on Delhi roads is much more than other cities. Thus from the city health point of view and from the perspective of environmental improvement, it is necessary that a system should be evolved whereby a smooth flow of traffic is ensured. This will in turn help to check pollution. Speedy movement of traffic also helps in conserving petrol and time. Slow movement of traffic and traffic jams are costing Delhiites heavily and these need to be evaluated through proper studies.

Mostly, whenever we talk of traffic congestion, we only refer to pollution. Saving petrol and human resource are generally not thought of, whereas, these are important savings in the larger interest of the society.

During 1995, 10138 road accidents took place as against only 8070 during the year 1991. 10141 vehicles were involved, 2070 persons died and 9805 were injured in road accidents during 1995. This shows that there is a gradual increase in the number of accidents as well as in the number of deaths on roads. This results in social tension and disequilibrium in the society.

For quite some time now, there have been talks of traffic management and improvement in urban infrastructure. However, no concrete steps have been taken because we have introduced privatization with a limited scope. The need of the hour is to utilise the services of the agencies which can otherwise be associated for construction of roads and more flyovers.

Although the Ring Road was constructed to ensure the smooth flow of traffic a few decades ago, however, since the city has grown all-around the Ring Road, it has lost its status as an express passage for fast movement of vehicles. At points it appears that either we should go for another level road or there should be multi-level flyovers. It is difficult at this stage to check the number of vehicles registered in the city but it is possible to take advantage of the experiences of other cities. Even a city like Bangkok had tried to give more pace to its vehicular traffic by adding parallel roads, additional level roads and flyovers. This has really reduced the travel time and pollution besides giving the added advantage of fuel conservation.

In Delhi a number of flyovers have already been constructed at almost all the strategic locations. Few mores are under construction. These flyovers have not fully solved the traffic problem. But what they have really done to ensure that the traffic keeps moving and that there is no wastage of fuel as was noticed a few years ago at every red light. This has helped to save energy and time. Of course the problem still persists, however it is not because authorities have failed, but because of number of vehicles increasing manyfold. Delhiites have the number of vehicles on the road is increasing at a superfast speed, thanks to economic prosperity which has made car owners out of most families.

Although there are many new roads and some new flyovers have also been constructed, there is some improvement in the flow of traffic on the Ring Road. In some VIP areas and routes by which foreign dignitaries arrive, the roads are maintained better. However, for the general public, travelling time is increasing daily because of the bad conditions of the roads, over traffic and non-provision of flyovers where they are essentially required.

Major Reasons for Unauthorized Growth of the City are :

I. Population Pressure on the City: - Population is growing almost at a pace of 50 per cent increase every decade.
II. Industrial Employment is another reason. As against about 2.15 lakhs employees in the industrial sector in 1951 there were 11.36 lakhs industrial employees by 1996 and the number has further increased by now. Thus about one-third of the city population earns its source of livelihood from industrial employment.

III. Migration to the city is to the tune of about 4 to 5 lakhs persons per year. Of the total migration about 75 per cent is on account of families and employment (40 per cent by families and 35 per cent for employment)

IV. Encroachment of land is another reason for unplanned growth. Inspite of the fact that more than 3 lakhs *jhuggies* dwellers have been re-settled in the planned Re-settlement Colonies, the slum population keeps on increasing. In 1994 there were 4,80,929 *jhuggies* whereas in 1990 the number was only 2,59,344. Thus the number of *jhuggies* almost doubled within a period of nearly 4 years.

V. Slum population is also growing at a rapid pace because the authorities have not planned for low cost housing. Slum population which was only 15 lakhs in 1981 grew to 24 lakhs by 1994 and went upto 32 lakhs in 2001. It is expected that by 2011 the slum population will be 45 lakhs.

VI. Public in general has no respect for law and they are not scared of carrying out unauthorized construction.

VII. Allotment of alternative plots to *jhuggi-jhompri* dwellers has also encouraged to a considerable level in setting up more *jhuggi* clusters.

VIII. By not extending the Lal Dora of village *abadi's* which was last fixed in 1908, the villagers were forced to have settlements outside the original village boundary because their families have grown manifold during last hundred years.

IX. After the village was urbanized, the Gaon Sabha land was taken-over by the Government. Proper plan should have been drawn to utilize this land for extended *Village Abadi.*

X. When the trend of population increase was offering clear signals of requirement of housing and commercial space, the Government and specially the DDA should have planned mass housing for them. This was not done and the end result was emergence of Uauthorized Colonies.

XI. When the Government cannot provide jobs it must appreciate the effort of entrepreneurs. Non-establishment of Industrial Areas required to meet the production need led to emergence of unauthorized industrial areas.

XII. Government effort did not match with the requirement of commercial space as a result of which large-scale commercial activity came up in the residential areas leading to unplanned activity and traffic congestions. Vast chunks of lands acquired all-over Delhi were not timely and properly utilized as a result of which these got encroached. DDA has been able to provide only about 16 per cent of the targeted built up area for commercial purpose. This has also led to unauthorized commercialization of residential areas.

XIII. Enough places were not planned and developed for public functions like weddings etc. as a result of which farm houses and unauthorizedly built banquet halls are being used for weddings and other public functions.

XIV. Failure on the part of the DDA to allot plots and flats to its registrants under various schemes within reasonable time also lead to unauthorized colonization.

XV. Weak enforcement of the machinery has also contributed to the unauthorized growth.

XVI. Multiplicity of authority in Delhi and lack of responsibility on the part of the officials has also contributed to unplanned growth.

XVII. Non-determination of priority areas is also a reason for unregulated development.

XVIII. Each Development Agency like DDA, MCD, NDMC or Delhi Government work in isolation. There is no coordinated and jointly planned effort.

XIX. Lack of coordination between the Departments within the same organization is also a reason for unorderly growth.

XX. Non-review of the Master Plan as mid-term appraisal is a reason for non-direction.

XXI. Non-preparation of Delhi Master Plan in time leads to vacuum and confusion.

XXII. Master Plan – 2021 was prepared and approved in 2007 when one-third of the plan period was already over.

XXIII. Attitude of the officials for passing the responsibility on others Departments delays the matter and leads to unauthorized construction and encroachment.

XXIV. Non-implementation and slow implementation of projects is also a reason for unauthorized construction.

XXV. Provision for informal sector to earmark some land was not done as a result of which right of ways at many places gets encroached.

XXVI. Promises to regularize unauthorized colonies without proper survey and knowing the extent of effected population, leads to more unauthorized colonization.

XXVII. Non-receptiveness on the part of the Government is also a reason for unauthorized construction and violation of building bye-laws. Where simple changes are needed in the DDA flats or flats constructed by the Cooperative Group Housing Society, the DDA should give a list of permissible additions and alterations in the flats along-with the allotment letter itself. This is not done and allottees are forced to make minor changes.

XXVIII. Non-preparation and delay in preparation of zonal development plans.

XXIX. Making unrealistic plans without relating to the site realities.

XXX. DDA has increased the rates of residential and commercial property through its purely financially motivated auction scheme instead of giving priority to its social objective. Instead of releasing the plots in bulk, it releases the plots in small number so that it can fetch higher amount. This also leads to unauthorized construction and misuse of residential areas because the prices fixed by the DDA are beyond the reach of the common man.

XXXI. DDA has acted more like a commercial organization rather than a public service agency and has deviated from its social objective.

Our approach should be innovative. We know the reasons for unauthorized construction and encroachment, disorderly growth of the city, emergence of unplanned colonies, development of unapproved industrial areas, conversion of residential premises for commercial use and encroachment of land by *jhuggi-jhmpri* clusters. Unfortunately we have not thought seriously enough about avoiding these situations. Each official sitting in the Government at whatever position must feel concerned and own the city. Each of them must see at his level that the city belongs to him and he must not allow any unauthorized activity.

The magnitude of the problem of unauthorized construction and unplanned growth is reflected in the fact that as per status report submitted by the Municipal Corporation of Delhi to Sh. Tejender Khanna Committee which was constituted by the Ministry of Urban Development on 14th February 2006, it stated that as against 438 regular and approved colonies as on 1st January 1994 there were as many as 1641 unauthorized colonies awaiting regularization. As per MCD these colonies account for 35 lakhs people. In addition 30 lakhs people are estimated to be living in 6 lakh *jhuggies* spread over 1200 *jhuggi-jhompri* clusters. Besides these, 15 lakhs people are living in re-settlement colonies. Total population in these three kinds of settlements accounts for 55 per cent of Delhi's population. As per Municipal Corporation of Delhi, out of the 20080 cases booked for unauthorized construction, from 1st January 2001 to 31st December 2005, 10.29 per cent were for unauthorized construction addition and alteration in DDA flats and 15 per cent cases where extra floors beyond permissible limit were constructed. In 60 per cent cases deviations were found from the sanctioned plan. Similarly about 1 lakh shops have been provided by the DDA as against 4 lakhs operating in the city. Thus about 80 per cent shops are in violation of

Government rules and norms. Similarly as against about 96.13 lac sq. meter area which DDA was supposed to provide in 22 District Centres, it has been able to construct only 15.34 lac sq. meter which is just 16 per cent of the required commercial space.

Remedial Measures

The Government has been talking of making Delhi a World Class City. To achieve this goal, a dual approach is needed: – First to create infrastructure and second to change the thinking and attitude of the general public. The Government and also its various agencies like DDA, MCD and Revenue Department of Delhi Government have to be more responsive and serious.

Planning has to be realistic when we know the housing requirement of the city with reference to affordability. DDA as a model agency must plan accordingly.

I. Planning norms have to be flexible. If we know that large segments of the population cannot afford the housing provided by the DDA, it must come out with norms of a little lower level and develop areas, so that instead of taking a plot in an unauthorized colony, these people should come to DDA. If instead of buying a plot at the rate of Rs. 1 lakh per sq. meter they can purchase at the rate of Rs. 10,000-15,000 per sq. meter, they will certainly go to some unauthorized colony.

II. Land should be properly planned and utilized. Vast chunks of land can still be seen unutilized. Land earmarked for a freight complex in Madan Pur Khadar is getting encroached. A vast chunk of land near Badarpur Border is unauthorizedly under the use of building material suppliers. District Centre land in Dilshad Garden and Shastri Park has got encroached. A large chunk of land behind a petrol pump at Club Road in Punjabi Bagh has been lying unutilized for years together. So is the case with many such sites in North,

East, South, West Delhi which pose a real temptation to the land encroachers.

III. Widening of the Mehrauli-Mahipalpur Road is being talked of since long. Even available and acquired land has been encroached or is in the process of getting encroached. There have to be priorities for utilization of land and execution of projects.

IV. Inventory of all such vacant lands should be prepared within a suitable and efficient time-frame and utilization plans should also be drawn.

V. It must be ensured that such vacant lands should be utilized immediately and if required its use should also be changed keeping in view the community requirement.

VI. Protection of land for years together is neither possible nor required. Accountability for non-utilization of land should be fixed. Departments should not pass on the buck to others. They should all be concerned with the end purpose that is utilization of land for the purpose for which it is earmarked.

VII. When more than 11 lakh persons are working in indusrial areas we should have planned to create more industrial areas. Employment is a basic necessity. If industrial areas are not created these are certainly going to come up unauthorizedly. We should not be satisfied by regularizing the industrial areas. We must plan and create regular industrial areas as and when required.

VIII. Only 16 per cent of required commercial space has been created by the DDA. This has led to large scale misuse of residential area. Commercial area norms should have been revised in view of the purchasing power of the public and economic reforms. If no commercial area is created, residential premises are likely to be misused. Massive programmes must be drawn up by the DDA to meet the deficiency of the commercial area at district, community, local and convenient shopping centre level.

IX. In the unauthorized colonies still large area of vacant

land is available which the colonizers intend to sell. Such lands must be taken over by the Government for physical and social infrastructure, before it gets too late. By simply constructing boundary walls or a small room, fake occupancy is shown. A thorough survey needs to be done in these unauthorized colonies to know the exact position and to identify the land for institutional framework.

X. No encroachment of any sort should be allowed on right of way, irrespective of the ownership of land by various land-owning agencies. These roads should be under police patrol to ensure that complete right of way is available to the public. No unauthorized parking, squatting, temporary use of land by vendors etc. should be allowed.

XI. As citadels of natural beauty and bounty with the capital city, the River Yamuna and the wooded area of the Ridge have special sanction. These should be declared as **zero tolerance areas** so far as misuse of land or encroachment are concerned. No activity of any sort contrary to the plan provision should be allowed. Besides the land owning agencies, the police should play a more active role.

XII. If required a special Yamuna River Protection Development Authority should be created to see that the city drains carrying the waste of the city does not flow into the river. A time bound programme to check the wasteful flow in the river needs to be drawn. The river should be made a part of our life and pride and its sanctity must be restored.

XIII. City borders should be made attractive. A re-development plan should be drawn to beautify the city borders specially Shahdara and Badarpur where lot of unauthorized activities have come up. Visitors should have a feel of friendliness when they enter the city.

XIV. Delhi is full of historical monuments. These should be

protected and land around them should not be allowed to be encroached. Land status report with a photograph of such monuments should also be given to the local police for its protection and care.

XV. We all talk of Delhi as proud citizens. Slogans like – **MERI DELHI MERI SHAAN,** do create a sense of pride. We must activate the citizens to **own the city** and not to allow anything which destroys its character, its shape and its beauty. The Government must organize campaigns by involving the media to create a sense of pride among Delhiites. Media can play a more active role by highlighting activities which are against the law in terms of encroachment of Government land and demolition of historical monuments etc. It is a fact that more than 50 per cent of Delhi's population is living in unauthorizedly developed areas but with the Commonwealth Games scheduled in 2010 an atmosphere can be created for a really world class city. Let the **MERI DELHI** slogan be converted into reality. Let it be the feel of every citizen. And let everybody think and participate in a campaign to own the city, to have the city and to respect the city which in turn has given everything to us.

To conclude, I would just say that we all talk of making Delhi a World Class City, we have made sincere efforts to improve the physical infrastructure in terms of roads specially in the central part of the city, Ring Road and Outer Ring Road, flyovers and street lighting on the major city roads. We have also been to some extent successful in reducing pollution and also creating an environment congenial to healthy living conditions. We have also been able to develop green areas and bio-diversity parks in North and South Delhi, besides, sports facilities through Delhi Development Authority. But the fact remains that a large population in the city still remains in the unauthorized colonies and *jhuggi-jhompri* clusters. It is also a fact that a number of unauthorized industrial areas have come up because we have not provided for enough planned industrial estates. There is no denying the fact that unauthorized commercial activity in the residential areas is at a much larger scale than the commercial areas actually provided for under the plan provision. When the Supreme Court had to interfere and large scale sealing operations were carried out under Supreme Court orders, the whole city faced turmoil. We all saw agitations and agitated moods.

It's a reality that even in view of the ensuing Commonwealth Games of 2010 when we seem determined to improve the physical infrastructure and try to ensure that the city will certainly look different, unless the people change and there is change in their thinking to own the city we cannot expect Delhi to be a World Class City. Simply by creating improved road network or construction of flyovers, Delhi cannot claim to be a progressive city unless the road-users move in lanes, do not throw garbage on the roads and respect the rights of bicyclists and pedestrians. It is the attitude of the people that needs to be changed, so that they do not encroach the public land and resort to unauthorized construction. A strong public opinion for a clean, hassle-free and a comfortable city has to be created. If required Youth, NCC Volunteers and dedicated citizens should be involved. Unless alongwith physical and social infrastructure we change the mindset and thinking of the people to generate a sense of pride in their city, we will only be making a marginal dent in the city perception. It is high time that we involve even media for a healthy and happy city campaign. Through these efforts we should make Delhi a city of hope, a city of pride, a city of future and a city that smiles.

ANNEXURE–6 /1

JHUGGI-JHOMPRI CLUSTERS REMOVED FROM 1ST APRIL 1990 ONWARDS TILL MARCH 2008

Sl. No.	*Name of Cluster Removed*	*No. of Squatter Families Re-located*	*Area Where Re-located*	*Land-Owning Agency*
1.	Sanjay Gandhi Camp (Nigerian Embassy Site)	900	Sahyog Vihar	DDA
2.	Tilak Vihar (Riot Victims)	670	Rohini, Sec-XVI	Commr. Delhi
3.	Mansrover Garden	300	Sahyog Vihar Sec–I, Pappan Kalan	MCD
4.	G.B. Pant Hospital	56		PWD
5.	Sanjay Gandhi Camp (Iraq Embassy Site)	588	Bindarpur Pkt–1	DDA
6.	Andaman and Nicobar Guest House	12	Bindarpur Pkt–1	NDMC
7.	Civic Center Minto Road	179	Bindarpur Pkt–1	CPWD
8.	Nehru Camp, Chanakya Puri	115	Bindarpur Pkt–1	DDA
9.	Wazirpur Indl. Area (Rub)	164	Bindarpur	DDA
10.	Pandit Pant Marg	51	Sec–1 Pappan Kalan	NDMC
11.	Firoz Shah Road	51	Sec–1 Pappan Kalan	NDMC
12.	Harish Chander, Mathur Lane	114	Sec–1 Pappan Kalan	NDMC
13.	Dhobi Ghat No. Talkatora Road	141	Sec-1 Pappan Kalan	NDMC
14.	Dhobi Ghat No. 5 Talkatora Road	303	Sec–1 Pappan Kalan	NDMC
15.	R.U.B. Okhla	49	Sec–1	DDA
16.	Tikona Park Nizamuddin	62	Sec–1 Pappan Kalan	DDA
17.	N.P. Boys Sr. Sec. School	21	Sec–1 Pappan Kalan	Forest Dept.

Sl. No.	Name of Cluster Removed	No. of Squatter Families Re-located	Area Where Re-located	Land-Owning Agency
18.	Mata Ka Mandir Jhandewalan	29	Sec–1 Pappan Kalan	MCD
19.	A-1/70 to 72 Janakpuri	68	Sec–1 Pappan Kalan	DDA
20.	(A) Rani Jhansi Road Jhandewalan	27	Sec–1 Pappan Kalan	MCD
21.	Shri Ram Basti	125	Sec–VII Pappan Kalan	DDA
22.	Metcalf House	18	Sec–VII Pappan Kalan	Defence
23.	Mahadev Road Dhobi Ghat No.6	47	Sec–VII Pappan Kalan	NDMC
24.	Mayur Vihar Ph–1	29	Sec–VII Pappan Kalan	DDA
25.	Maya Puri Indl. Area E-174	34	Sec–VII Pappan Kalan	DDA
26.	Pankha Road	16	Sec–VII Pappan Kalan	DDA
27.	Nand Lal Camp Near Gopal Pur Village	124	Sec–VII Pappan Kalan	Irri. and Flood Control Deptt.
28.	Bara Pulla Nizamuddin	165	Sec–VII Pappan Kalan	DDA
29.	Kautilya Lane, Samrat Hotel	91	Sec–VII Pappan Kalan	NDMC
30.	Plot No. A-187, Okhla Indl. Area	47	Samai Pur Badli	DDA
31.	ITO Bridge and Slip Road	1108	Sec–III, Ph-III Pappan Kalan	DDA
32.	URI Enclave, Delhi Cantt.	115	Sec – I, III and VII Pappan Kalan	Cantonment Board
33.	Amar Jyoti Camp, Okhla Indl. Area	255	Samai Pur Badli	DDA
34.	JJ Cluster Ridge Area Indira Colony, Amar Colony, Shiv Basti Mandir Marg., near Ganga Ram Hospital, N.P. Sr. Sec. School Mandir Marg	301	Tikri Khurd	Forest Deptt.
35.	Katwaria Sarai Instt. Area	3	Tikri Khurd	DDA
36.	Sangli Mess, Mandi House	108	Sec–VIII Pappan Kalan	NDMC
37.	Niti Bagh	11	Bindarpur Pkt–IV	DDA
38.	Devli Pahari	124	Sec–VII Pappan Kalan	Forest Deptt.
39.	Mandir Marg.	41	Sec–VII Pappan Kalan	Forest Deptt.

Sl. No.	Name of Cluster Removed	No. of Squatter Families Re-located	Area Where Re-located	Land-Owning Agency
40.	Gyaspur Near Bridge Nizamuddin	49	Tikri Khurd	PWD
41.	Copernicus Marg	10	Tikri Khurd	CAT
42.	Old Police Line near Tis Hazari Court	15	Tikri Khurd	Police Deptt.
43.	Sanjay Camp, Kadambari	32	Rohini Sec–25	DDA
44.	Plot No. A-188,189, A-197, Okhla Indl. Area, Ph-I	178	Rohini Sec–25	DDA
45.	Shah Alam Bagh	127	Tikri Khurd	Irri. and Food Control Deptt.
46.	Kabir Nagar	10	Samai Pur Badli	DDA
47.	Inder Puri Naraina	8	Rohini Sec–25	Slum and JJ Deptt.
48.	Arunanchal Bhawan Chanakya Puri	192	Rohini Sec–25	PWD
49.	Teen Murti Police Compound	17	Rohini Sec–25	Police Deptt.
50.	Katwaria Sarai	49	Bindapur	Bharti Gyan Peeth
51.	Atul Grove Road	49	Tikri Khurd	NDMC
52.	Plot No.T-14, Ph-II B-44, B-148, B-48, B-96 Okhla Indl. Area, Ph-I	63	Rohini Sec–25	DDA
53.	Cooli Camp Nelson Mandela Marg.	32	Tikri Khurd	NDMC
54.	Road No. 62 Shahdara	79	Rohini Sec–25	PWD
55.	S.Q.T.B. Khalsa College	45	Rohini Sec–25	Delhi University
56.	R-Blk Jangpura Extn.	20	Rohini Sec–25	DDA
57.	C-II-B Janak Puri	1375	Pappan Kalan (Partially Cleard)	DDA
58.	Indira Camp, Kishan Kunj, Laxmi Nagar	177	Rohini Sec–25	PWD
59.	JJ Cluster Adjoining Chungi Lalita Park	20	Rohini Sec–25	PWD
60.	Thokar No. 16, Shamshan Ghat, Geeta Colony	219	Rohini Sec–25	PWD
61.	Thokar No. 15, Geeta Colony	56	Rohini Sec–25	PWD
62.	Shamshan Ghat, Geeta Colony	11	Rohini Sec–25	PWD
63.	Road No.70, New Seema Puri	279	Narela Sec–24 Rohini	PWD
64.	Vasant Kunj	67	Rohini Sec–25	DDA
65.	Jakhira	11	Samai Pur Badli	PWD
66.	Pull Mithai	13	Rohini Sec–24	MCD
67.	Diz Area, Gole Market	2220	Narela	MTNL

Sl. No.	Name of Cluster Removed	No. of Squatter Families Re-located	Area Where Re-located	Land-Owning Agency
68.	Rajiv Gandhi Camp, CGO Complex	207	Narela	MTNL
69.	B-Blk, Greater Kailash-I	83	Narela	DDA
70.	Nakki Sarai (MRTS)	271	Narela	DMRC
71.	Shahdara Rly. Station (MRTS)	21	Narela	DMRC
72.	Shastri Park (MRTS)	120	Narela	DMRC
73.	Vivekanand Camp Chanakya Puri	547	Narela	L and DO
74.	Balmiki Basti Mandir Marg	12	Narela	L and DO
75.	Step by Step Panchsheel	33	Narela	DDA
76.	Taj Colony (MRTS)	65	Narela	DMRC
77.	Hari Har Ashram Asaf Ali Road	5	Rohini	MCD
78.	Bapu Park, Kotla Mubarak Pur	293	Narela	DDA
79.	Tikona Park Vikram Hotel	94	Narela	MCD
80.	Andrews Ganj	146	Narela	PWD
81.	Rajiv Gandhi Camp Sadiq Nagar	419	Narela	PWD
82.	Gautam Nagar behind AIIMS	1604	Molar Bandh	AIIMS
83.	Ashok Vihar I-Block	126	Narela	DDA
84.	Rajiv Gandhi Camp CGO Complex	95	Narela	L and DO
85.	Mansrover Garden Blk-BandC	35	Narela	MCD
86.	Maya Puri Crossing	25	Narela	PWD
87.	Sadbhavana Raj Ghat	17	Narela	MCD
88.	Rajiv Gandhi Camp CGO Complex	3263	Narela	L and DO
89.	Gautam Nagar behind AIIMS	2390	Molar Bandh	AIIMS
90.	JJ Cluster Man Singh Road	200	Narela	NDMC
91.	Metcalf House	53	Narela	PWD
92.	Shaheed Bhagat Singh Park	89	Narela	MCD
93.	Posangi Pur Village Janak Puri	34	Narela	MCD
94.	Rouse Avenue, DDU Marg. Hathi Park	1817	Narela	L and DO

Sl. No.	*Name of Cluster Removed*	*No. of Squatter Families Re-located*	*Area Where Re-located*	*Land-Owning Agency*
95.	JJ Cluster on the banks of Nallah alongside Lodhi Road	122	Narela	L and DO
96.	JJ Cluster Vinoba Puri Lajpat Nagar	15	Narela	L and DO
97.	Indira Gandhi Camp Tikona Park Okhla	92	Narela	PWD
98.	JJ Cluster Pul Bangash (MRTS)	71	Tikri Khurd	DMRC
99.	JJ Cluster Sawarn Park near Railway Crossing	55	Tikri Khurd	DMRC
100.	Jhuggies opp. Samata Sathal Raj Ghat	4	——	MCD
101.	Player Building (Gautam Puri)	530	Bhalswa	PWD
102.	East of Kailash (Ekta Mazdoor and Balmiki Camp)	161	Bhalswa	MCD
103.	Tyag Raj Marg	66	Bhalswa	NDMC
104.	Jahangir Puri (Lak I, II Park)	979	Bhalswa	MCD
105.	Gopal Pur	176	Bhalswa	Irri. and Food Control Deptt.
106.	Seelam Pur	14	Bhalswa	DMRC
107.	G-Blk, Dakshin Puri	60	Bhalswa	Delhi Jal Board
108.	Labour Camp Hauz Khas	525	Bakkarwala	I.I.I
109.	JJ Cluster Thomson Road (MRTS)	15	Narela	DMRC
110.	Jaina Complex Preet Vihar	64	Bhalswa	DDA
111.	Press Road, M.S. Road Area	52	Narela	CPWD
112.	JJ Cluster (Amba Bagh) (MRTS)	10	Bhalswa	DMRC
113.	JJ Cluster Ward No.23 Rajouri Garden	16	Rohini	MCD
114.	JJ Cluster Plot No.C-149 Rewari Line Maya Puri Ph – II	66	Narela	DDA
115.	C and D Blk, Ashok Vihar	106	Bhalswa	DDA
116.	Sanjay Camp and Durga Camp, Sec-9 and 13 Rohini	970	Bhalswa	DDA
117.	Posangir Pur Janak Puri	65	Narela	MCD
118.	A-2, Paschim Vihar	56	Narela	DDA

Sl. No.	Name of Cluster Removed	No. of Squatter Families Re-located	Area Where Re-located	Land-Owning Agency
119.	Andrews Ganj Flyover	2	Narela	PWD
120.	Pandara Road	1	Tikri Khurd	CPWD
121.	JJ Cluster Bal Bhavan Awan-E-Galib, opp. Hindi Bhavan	133	Narela	CPWD
122.	Jhuggies near Kothi No.238 210 & Kotla Road Kothi No. 1, 3, 7, 10,12,13, 14,16	141	Narela	CPWD
123.	JJ Cluster behind Mata Sundri Gurudwara	129	Narela	CPWD
124.	Gandhi Market	75	Narela	CPWD
125.	Mahabat Khan Road	49	Narela	CPWD
126.	Blk-4, Rouse Aveneue	180	Holambi Kalan	CPWD
127.	Blk-1, 3 Press I and DDU Marg and near Dhobi Ghat No. 28	1077	Holambi Kalan	CPWD
128.	On Road and Barron Road	220	Narela	CPWD
129.	Durga Basti (MRTS)	1700	Holambi Kalan	MRTS
130.	Shankar Vihar	163	Holambi Kalan	DDA
131.	Rani Garden	103	Holambi Kalan	DDA
132.	Jahaz Cooperative Society	269	Holambi Kalan	MCD
133.	JJ Cluster NPL	260	Holambi Kalan	MCD
134.	C-Blk, Mansrover Garden	22	Holambi Kalan	MCD
135.	Addl. Jhuggies at Maya Puri Crossing	110	Holambi kalan	PWD
136.	Badli Indl. Estate	86	Holambi Kalan	Comr. (Ind.)
137.	Sodia Lohar Raja Garden			
138.	JJ Cluster Bela Road	11	Holambi Kalan	MCD
139.	East of Kailash	179	Molar Bandh	MCD/DDA
140.	A-5/A Posangi Pur Janak Puri	372	Holambi Kalan	MCD
141.	JJ Cluster Sec–9 Rohini	1073	DO	DDA (Rohini)
142.	JJ Cluster opp. Guru Gobind Singh Hospital Raghubir Nagar	2979	Bakarwala	S and JJ Deptt.
143.	JJ Cluster Acharya Narender Niketan behind IIPA	114	Narela	Sales Tax Deptt.
144.	Bapu Dham Patel Marg.	1602	Holambi Kalan-II	Delhi Police
145.	Bara Pulla East Nizamuddin	836	Bhalswa	DDA

Sl. No.	*Name of Cluster Removed*	*No. of Squatter Families Re-located*	*Area Where Re-located*	*Land-Owning Agency*
146.	Sudershan Park and Rajouri Garden	15	Rohini	MCD
147.	AP and AE Blk Shalimar Bagh	706	Holambi Kalan	DDA
148.	Shaheed Arjun Das Camp West Kidwai Nagar	1258	Madan Pur Khadar	NDMC
149.	Mazdoor Camp, Laxmi Bai Nagar	136	Madan Pur Khadar	NDMC
150.	A-4 Paschim Vihar	291	Holambi Kalan-II	DDA
151.	Apna Bazar, Nehru Nagar	25	Madan Pur Khadar	S and JJ Deptt.
152.	JJ Cluster Marginal Bund Road from Noida mod Vikas Marg Chungi, Pushta Road	1328	Holambi Kalan	PWD
153.	Pushp Vihar	73	Madan Pur Khadar	PWD
154.	AG Blk, Shalimar Bagh	60	Holambi Kalan – II	DDA
155.	Calcutta Bridge	5	Holambi Kalan – II	MCD
156.	MP Blk, Pitam Pura	441	Bakarwala	DDA
157.	FU Blk, near Income Tax Colony, Pitam Pura	284	Bakarwala	DDA
158.	V.P. Singh Camp Tughlaqabad	849	Madan Pur Khadar	CCL
159.	JJ Cluster (near Kurzon Road)	226	Holambi Kalan – II	L and DO
160.	Gali No. 14, near Zonal Office Seelam Pur	30	Narela	MCD
161.	Subhash Nagar Mod	352		MCD
162.	Left Bank of NG Drain near Manohar Park East Punjabi Bagh	27	Bakarwala	I and F
163.	Maharishi Dayanand Camp Chanakya Puri behind PMS House	299	Holambi Kalan-II	NDMC
164.	Jawahar Camp Raj Nagar Crossing	59	Bakarwala	PWD
165.	Cooli Camp, Nelson Mandela Road, Munirka Vihar	59	Bakarwala	PWD
166.	Gymkhana Club	174	Molar Bandh	Gymkhana Club
167.	Rajeev Basti Khalsa College	278	Narela	Univ. of Delhi
168.	Ambedkar Camp Sec– 9 R.K. Puram	24	Narela	L and DO Ministry of UD
169.	Neela Gumbad Survey of India	164	MadanPur Khadar & Molar Bandh	Archeological

Sl. No.	Name of Cluster Removed	No. of Squatter Families Re-located	Area Where Re-located	Land-Owning Agency
170.	Captain Gaur Marg	154	Madan Pur Khadar	PWD
171.	Indira Camp Naraina	389	Holambi kalan Ph-I	DDA
172.	Samru Place opp. Birla Mandir Gole Market	45	Holambi Khurd	NDMC
173.	Samru Place behind CNG Station, Gole Market	29	Holambi Khurd	NDMC
174.	Sawan Park, Ashok Vihar Ph – III	46	Holambi Kalan	MCD
175.	Reids Line Delhi University	85	Narela	Delhi Univ.
176.	Bara Bagh G.T. Karnal Road	615	Holambi Kalan Ph-II	DDA
177.	Bhai Veer Singh Marg, Gole Market	82	Holambi Kalan Ph-II	MRTS
178.	Raja Bazar (C – 35)	416	Bakarwala	CPWD
179.	Raja Bazar (C – 37)	244	Holambi Kalan-I	CPWD
180.	Birbal Road, Pant Nagar	33	Holambi Kalan-II	MCD
181.	Gautam Puri-II	367	Holambi Kalan-II	(L and DO)
182.	Gautam Puri-I	228	Holambi Kalan	(L and DO)
183.	Gate No.2, Rajghat Power House	92	Holambi Kalan	(L and DO)
184.	Kanchan Puri/New Kanchan Puri	809	Bawana	(L and DO)
185.	Sangam Park, Rly. Crossing	13	Holambi Kalan	
186.	Indira Colony Rajghat	530	Bawana	(L and DO)
187.	Dhapa Colony	468	Madanpur Khadar and Bawana	(L and DO)
188.	Petty Market, Red Fort	35		
189.	Jahangir Puri Blk.	126	Bawana	Deptt. of Education
190.	Jhilmil A Blk	23	Bawana	Slum and JJ Deptt.
191.	Factory Road Chhatlisgarh State Deptt. of Telecom. MCD (GW)	100	Bawana	Resident Com.
192.	Lawrence Road	64	Rohini Sec – 26 and Holambi Kalan	
193.	Civic Centre Minto Road	112	Holambi Kalan	
194.	Gadia Lohar Maya Puri	38	Narela	PWD
195.	Thokar No.8 Laxmi Nagar	236	Narela	PWD
196.	Road No.89 Naraina T-Junction Ring Road	21	Narela	PWD
197.	Chirya Colony	99		PWD

Sl. No.	Name of Cluster Removed	No. of Squatter Families Re-located	Area Where Re-located	Land-Owning Agency
198.	Anna Nagar	32	Narela	DMRC
199.	Cement Siding Shakur Basti	217	Narela, Bawana	Northern Rly.
200.	Jawahar Camp	266	Narela, Bakarwala	MCD
201.	N-13, Satyawati Colony	671	Narela, Bawana Sahyong Vihar Holambi Kalan	MCD
202.	Mansrover Garden	126	Rohini Sec–16	MCD
203.	Jwala Ghat !SBT	84	Bhalswa	DDA
204.	Indira Nagar (Bhati Mines)	524	Holambi and Bawana	RMB
205.	Balbir Nagar (Bhati Mines)	592	Holambi and Bawana	RMB
206.	Nagla Machi	1145	Savda Ghevra	IGPCL
207.	Thokar No.8, Yamuna Pusta	1370	Savda Ghevra	PWD
208.	Thokar No.16, Yamuna Pusta	1487	Savda Ghevra	PWD
209.	Thokar No.17, Yamuna Pusta	98	Savda Ghevra	PWD
210.	Thokar No.8, Yamuna Pusta	1456	Savda Ghevra	PWD
211.	Rany Wall 7 and 5	508	Savda Ghevra	PWD
212.	Thokar No. 79	84	Savda Ghevra	PWD
213.	Thokar No. 20	27	Savda Ghevra	PWD
214.	Thokar No. 21	177	Savda Ghevra	PWD
215.	Lal Bagh and Indira Camp	358	Savda Ghevra	DMRC
216.	Timar Pur	74	Savda Ghevra	Delhi Police
217.	Nagla Devat Village	1994	Savda Ghevra	Delhi Airport
218.	D – Blk, Tagore Garden Slum	235	Savda Ghevra	
219.	Bara Pulla, Sarai Kale Khan Karkardooma	90	Savda Ghevra	MCD
	Total	64832		

ANNEXURE 9/1

AGREEMENT BETWEEN THE GOVERNMENT AND THE DELHI IMPROVEMENT TRUST IN REGARD TO THE ADMINISTRATION OF CERTAIN GOVERNMENT PROPERTY

This Agreement made on thirty first day of March 1937 between The Secretary of State for India in Council [Herein after called "Government" which expression shall include his successor in Office and assigns] of the one part and The Delhi Improvement Trust [constituted under the United Provinces Town Improvement Act, 1919, as extended to the Province of Delhi] [hereinafter called "The Trust" which expression shall include its successors and permitted assigns] of the other part.

Witnesseth as follows

1. With a view to the orderly expansion of Delhi under the supervision of a single authority, Government agree that they will with effect from the 1st April 1937 and subject to the conditions hereinafter contained place at the disposal of the Trust the Nazul Estate described in schedule I to this agreement excluding any property in the occupation of any department of the Government of India or any local authority on that date until surrendered by Government or such authority when they will similarly be placed at the disposal of the Trust and hereinafter referred to as "The said Nazul Estate".
2. The Trust shall hold and manage the said Nazul Estate on behalf of Government and shall realize all dues in

respect thereof which may be outstanding on the 1st April 1937 or may arise on or after that date.

3. The Trust shall use its best endeavours for the improvement and development of the said Nazul Estate with special reference to the requirements and improvements of Delhi, and may incur expenditure upon the said Nazul Estate in accordance with the provisions of the United Provinces Town Improvement Act, 1919 as extended to the Province of Delhi [hereinafter referred to as "the said Act"]; Provided that no expenditure shall be incurred upon the purchase of land to be added to be said Nazul Estate unless—

   (a) The proposal to make the purchase has been specifically included in an Improvement Scheme sanctioned under Section 42 of the said Act; or
   b. If the value of the land to be purchased does not exceed Rs. 50,000/- the previous sanction in writing of the Chief Commissioner of Delhi Province [hereinafter referred to as "the Chief Commissioner"] has been obtained.
   (c) If the value of the land to be purchased exceed Rs. 50,000/- the previous sanction in writing of Government has been obtained.

4. The Trust may sell or lease any land included in the said Nazul Estate in pursuance of the provision of an Improvement Scheme sanctioned under Section 42 of the said Act.
5. The Trust may on its own authority and otherwise than in pursuance of a sanctioned Improvement Scheme, lease at full market rate any land included in the said Nazul Estate and may determine whether the consideration for any lease shall be paid wholly in the form of a recurring ground rent, or partly in the form of premium and partly in the form of ground rent. If it is proposed

to lease any land included in the said Nazul Estate at a rent less than the full market rate the Trust shall obtain:

(a) When the full market value of the land does not exceed Rs. 25000/- the previous sanction in writing of the Chief Commissioner; and
(b) When the full market value of the land exceeds Rs. 25000/- the previous sanction in writing of Government.

6. The Trust may, otherwise than in pursuance of an improvement scheme sanctioned under Section 42 of the said Act, sell any land included in the said Nazul Estate :

(a) On its own authority, for full market value where the full market value does not exceed Rs. 25000/-;
(b) With the previous sanction in writing of the Chief Commissioner, for full market value where the full market value exceeds Rs. 25000/- but does not exceed Rs. 50,000/-;
(c) With the previous sanction in writing of Government for full market value where the full market value exceeds Rs. 50,000/-;
(d) With the previous sanction in writing of the Chief Commissioner, for less than the full market value, where the full market value does not exceed Rs. 25000/- and the price proposed is not less than half of the full market value;
(e) With the previous sanction in writing of Government, for less than the full market value, where,

I. The full market value does not exceed Rs. 25000/- and the price proposed is less than half of the full market value, or

II. The full market value exceeds Rs. 25000/-.

7. The forms of conveyances and leases to be used by the Trust shall be as approved by Government.
8. The Trust shall assume full liability for all expenditure which has been or remains to be incurred upon the works described in Schedule II to this Agreement and shall arrange for the completion of the said works to the satisfaction of Government and shall indemnify Government on account of any claim arising on account thereof including any claims under the Workmen's Compensation Act, 1923.
9. The Trust shall maintain in accordance with rules to be made under Section 72 of the said Act separate accounts of all revenue realized from and all expenditure incurred upon the said Nazul Estate and shall pay to Government at the end of each financial year a sum of Rs. 2 lakhs, being a sum equivalent to the net income of the said Nazul Estate for the financial year1935-36. Provided that in any year in which the income from the said Nazul Estate has been permanently reduced by any sum exceeding Rs. 1,000/- (i) in consequence of the transfer of immovable property of the Chief Commissioner under Section 54A (2) of the said act, or (ii) from any other cause beyond the control of the trust [*e.g.* anti-malarial restrictions], the said amount payable to the Government shall be reduced by such sum.

   Any surplus funds in the Nazul Development Account remaining at the end of each financial year when the said sum has been paid shall be put at the disposal of Government and shall be applied until further orders of Government to the further improvement and development of the said Nazul Estate and/or to the repayment of loans made to the Trust as Government may direct.

10. In consideration of the liability hereby assumed by the

Trust for the management of the said Nazul Estate and the execution of the works described in Schedule II to this Agreement, Government shall pay to the Trust:

(a) A grant of Rs. 21.40 lakhs, being a sum approximately equivalent to one half of the estimated cost of the Sewage Disposal Scheme described in Schedule II to this Agreement;

(b) Loan of such amount as may be required to enable the Trust to complete;

   (i) The Sewage Disposal Scheme; and
   (ii) The programme of anti-malaria works described in Schedule II to this Agreement

At the interest equal to Government's rates for the time being for loans of Local Authorities.

(c) Such further loans as Government may sanction for the improvement and development of the said Nazul Estate; and

(d) By charge against the Nazul Development Account such equitable proportion of the Administrative costs of the Trust as may be agreed upon between Government and the Trust; and the service of one half of the loans referred to in sub-clause (i) of clause [b] and the service of the whole of the loans referred to in sub-clause (ii) of clause [b] and in clause [c] shall be a charge on the income arising from the development of the said Nazul Estate.

11. The Trust shall submit in accordance with rules to be made under Section 72 of the said Act separate estimates of income and expenditure in respect of the said Nazul Estate for each financial year.

12. Government may at any time on giving six months notice terminate this Agreement.

Schedule I

Properties of Government placed .at the disposal of Delhi Improvement Trust under Section 54-A of the United Provinces Town Improvement Act, 1919 as extended to the Privince of Delhi.

The following Nazul Revenue Estates :

List of 23 Nazul I Revenue Estates

1. Naiwala
2. Basti Rehgar
3. Karol Bagh
4. Bagh Raoji
5. Shidipura
6. Jhandewalan
7. Qadam Sharif
8. Paharganj
9. Burn Bastion Road
10. Garstin Bastion Road
11. Daryaganj South
12. Chiragh North
13. Chiragh South
14. Jhilmila Tahirpur
15. Inderpat
16. Arakpur Bagh Mochi
17. Aliganj
18. Southern Ridge
19. Sadar Bazar North
20. Sadar Bazar South
21. Inside City Walls
22. Daryaganj North.......
23. The Bela Road

Less those portions of these estates which fall within the limits of the Fort Notified Area Committee.

Properties as Described below Placed at the Disposal of Delhi Improvement Trust after Execution of the Agreement of 31-3-1937 under different notifications mentioned against each :

24. 9.13 acres comprised in Khasra Nos. 281 to 294 and 305 in the revenue estate of Sadhora Kalan [*vide* Govt. of India, Department of Education, Health and Land's letter No. F.101-18/37-L and O dated the 11th August, 1937].
25. 33.03 acres comprised in Khasra Nos. 52, 54 to 76, 78, 82 to 84, 423/98, 425/100, 101 to 103, 104/2, 105, 106/1, 106/2, 106/3 and 107 in the revenue estate of Sadhora Khurd [*vide* Govt. of India, Department of Education, Health and Land's letter No. F101-18/37-L and O, dated the 29th September 1937.]
26. 1.35 acres comprised in Khasra No. 242 in the revenue estate of Sadhora Kalan [*vide* Govt. if India, Department of Education, Health and Land's letter No. F.115-4/38-L and O dated the 28th February 1938.]
27. 108 bighas and 11 biswas of land outside the Delhi Gate formerly used as a dumping ground and recorded in the revenue records as Government property in the possession of the Municipal Committee, Delhi *vide* [Chief Commissioner's letter 5274-L.S.G. dated the 4th May 1938].
28. 10.47 acres comprised in Khasra No. 261 Part I the revenue estate of Civil Station [*vide* Government of India, Department of Education, Health and Land's letter No. F.29-35/39, dated the 4th August 1939.]
29. 1 bigha 10 biswas of land in the revenue estate of Aliganj formerly occupied by the Delhi Joint Water and Sewage Board [*vide* Chief Commissioner's letter No. F.1 [68] 40-LSG., dated 6th April 1940.]

Schedule II

A. Delhi Sewage Extension Scheme List of Works

(1) In New Delhi

(a) See page Recorders at places yet to be fixed.
(b) Storm over at point "Q" with control Penstocks.
(c) 66″ dia out-fall sewer from point 'A' to Kilokari.

(2) At Kilokari

(a) Penstock chamber and 66″ Penstocks.
(b) Detritus and screening plant with necessary Civil Engineering Works, pipeline etc.
(c) New pumping station building which also contains workshop, office and store-rooms and suction pumps connecting with existing work.
(d) Pumping plant comprising :

(i) Three electric pumping units of 12 MGD capacity.
(ii) Two electrically operated exhausters.
(iii) Two electrically operated bilge pumps.
(iv) Two electrically operated gland sealing pumps.
(v) Necessary penstocks valves, suction and delivery piping for items [i] to [iv].

(e) Overhead travelling crane.
(f) Low tension switchgear.
(g) Two transformers.
(h) High tension switchgear.
(i) Two overhead travelling cranes in workshop.
(j) Workshop equipment. Details as yet not fixed.
(k) Electric lighting and fans for building.
(l) One 44″ venturi meter and recorder.

(m) Roads and pathways.

(n) Rising main 44" dia 800' long with control valves and outlet chamber.

(3) From Kilokari to Disposal works gravity duct in masonry approximately 16500' long.

(4) At disposal works.

(a) Bio-Aeration plant consisting of 12 preliminary settling tanks, 108 Aeration pockets and 48 final settling tanks, the whole with necessary valves, piping, motors, shafting and other operating gear.

(b) Sludge pump house and 4 electrically operated sludge pumps and accessories.

(c) Two portable electrically operated dewatering pumps and accessories.

(d) Transformer House containing high-tension switchgear, transformers, low tension switchgear, overhead crane and other accessories.

(e) Electric cables supplying power and lighting circuits.

(f) Office building containing assistant superintendent's office, laboratory and equipment, clerk-rooms, store and lavatories and furniture.

(g) Assistant superintendent's Bungalow with 4 rooms.

(h) Five drivers quarter each with two rooms.

(i) Fifteen single room quarters.

(j) Necessary water supply, sanitary and electrical services for items [f] to [i].

(k) Roads and pathways inside disposal works compound, boundary fence and gates, trees and lawns.

(l) Electric lighting for whole installation

(m) Sludge drying bed with return sludge pumping plant with necessary flow and return piping to main plant.

(n) Three venturi flumes with electrical recording gear.

(5) Disposal work to River;
Effluent Channel with pitched bend and sides including aqueduct crossing over the Agra Canal.

(6) New Delhi Power House to New Works.
6600 volt transmission line to the disposal works with branch to new pumping station including railway and road crossings.

(7) Any acquisitions of land necessitated by this scheme.

Schedule II

B. Anti-malaria Works

(a) Filling depressions in Jamuna Village.

(b) Raising depressions in Storm water drains

  (i) Wall Road
  (ii) Upper Bela Road
  (iii) Kudsia Creck
  (iv) Metcalfe Nala

(c) Filling depressions near Metcalfe House

(d) Filling and draining block 169 [between Hardinge Avenue and Muttra Road] to R.L. 669, 5-668.

(e) Filling and draining area east in Muttra Road, from Hardinge Bridge to Nizamuddin and Borrow pits west of line.

(f) Filling excavations between Lytton Road, Hardinge Aveneu and Bhagwan Dass Road.

(g) Filling and draining disused part of D. Pt. Outfall Nala.

(h) Canalization and connecting of Q.Pt. outfall drain from Lodi Bridge Road to Railway Bridge south of Nizamuddin and below this for a short distance and filling borrow pits alongside this.
Additional of stone-pitching.

(i) Diversion of City Ditch.
(j) Filling and draining pits west of Paharganj.
(k) Filling and draining pits along Lower Bela and Power House Roads.
(l) Filling borrow pits along road east of Ferozshah Kotla. Petty works in Fort Area.
(m) Demolition of Power House Irrigation Canal.
(n) Modification of Road Syphons.
(o) Mosquito proofing cisterns on latrines and pail shutes outside compounds.
(p) Closure of Western Jamuna Canal at Najafgarh Cut, filling bed from here to Pul Mithai, lining certain minor branches.

As witness the hands of the parties the day and year first before written.

Signed by Sir Girja Shankar Bajpai,
Secretary to the Government of India
in the Department of Education,
Health and Land's by order and Sd/- G.S. BAJPAI
Direction of the Governor-General of
India in Council acting in the premises
for and on behalf of the Secretary of
State for India in Council in the
Presence of

Sd/-
Deputy Secretary to the Government of India,
New Delhi.

Signed by Andrew Park Hume on behalf
of the Delhi Improvement Trust in the Sd/- A.P. HUME
Presence of

Sd/-
Deputy Secretary to the Government of India,
New Delhi.

ANNEXURE 9/2

No. 4 (19) / 78-SS. II (Vol. II)
Government of India
Ministry of Supply and Rehabilitation
(Department of Rehabilitaton)

Jaisalmer House, Man Singh Road,
New Delhi, dated 2nd September, 1982.

To,

The Vice-Chairman,
Delhi Development Authority,
Vikas Minar,
Indraprastha Road,
New Delhi – 110002.

Sub: - Transfer of utilized lands within the urban/urbanisable limits of Delhi/New Delhi under the charge of the Department of Rehabilitation to the Delhi Development Authority.

Sir,

I am directed to say that in 1967, the Cabinet approved the proposal of he Ministry of Works and Housing in regard to large-scale acquisition and development and disposal of land in Delhi (*vide* case No. 14/2/67, dated the 17th January, 1967) that *inter-alia* provided that unutilized lands with the Department of Rehabilitation within the urbanisable limits of Delhi should be transferred to the Delhi Administration at market value on negotiated basis to be fixed by the Department of Rehabilitation. It was considered that since the Delhi Administration itself was transferring all its lands to the Delhi Development Authority, the lands in question should be transferred direct to the Delhi Development Authority in constitution with the Ministry of Works and Health.

2. Negotiations were held with the Ministry of Works and Housing and the Delhi Development Authority to arrive area mutually agreed cost formula. The Delhi Development Authority has agreed to take-over these lands on 'as-is-where-is' basis on payment of Rs. 30/- crores.
3. I am accordingly to convey the sanction of the President to the transfer of unutilized lands (both developed and undeveloped) measuring approximately 1020 acres to the Delhi Development Authority on payment of Rs. 30/- crores, subject to the conditions laid down in paras 4 to 7 below. The broad details of the surveyed and un-surveyed lands are given in Annexure 'A' and Annexure 'B' respectively. The particulars of lands not being transferred to Delhi Development Authority and retained by the Department of Rehabilitation are given in Annexure 'C'. The details shows in these Annexure are based on the result of the joint survey carried out by this Department and the Delhi Development Authority from 1978 onwards in respect of the surveyed colonies and on the basis of this Department's Record in respect of unsurveyed colonies. There are likely to be some omissions/variations in the areas shown against different colonies. The exact area transferable to the Delhi Development Authority under this sanction will be as per physical handling over/taking over the lands. Rs 30/- crores has been agreed as a package deal and this amount shall not be changed if the variations are found in the actual area of the land either on plus or minus side.
4. Where the Department of Rehabilitation is required to allot/transfer some land in pursuance of the existing or future judgments of the Courts, Arbitrators, Tribunals etc. such cases/judgments will be fully honoured/ implemented by the Delhi Development Authority.
5. If any case of commitments made by the Department

of Rehabilitation comes to the notice later on such cases will be examined on merits and decided in consultation with the Delhi Development Authority.

6. The Delhi Development Authority shall pay to this Department a sum of Rs. 30/- crores (Rupees Thirty crores) only by three equal installments. The first installment of Rs. 10/- crores will be paid by the Delhi Development Authority by 31st October 1982 and the subsequent installments will be paid by 31st October 1983 and 31st October 1984. In default the Delhi Development Authority will be liable to pay interest for the unpaid amount at he rate fixed by he Central Government from time-to-time.
7. Full particulars of the land, the broad details of which are given in annexures 'A' and 'B' together with sketch plans etc. will be furnished by the Deputy Chief Settlement Commissioner (M) to the Delhi Development Authority within a period of two months from the date of issue of this sanction. The Delhi development Authority shall render all assistance to ensure speedily process of handing-over/taking-over the lands and for preparing the sketch plan.
8. The transfer of the lands I question shall take effect on the payment of first installment of Rs. 10/- crores. The Delhi Development Authority shall maintain, develop and dispose of these lands under the provisions of the Delhi Development Act.
9. The payment to be made by the Delhi Development Authority under this package deal will be made to the Department by way of a Demand Draft drawn in favour of "Deputy Controller of Accounts (Rehabilitation), New Delhi" for being credited under the following head: "088-Social Security and Welfare Relief and Rehabilitation of Displaced Persons – Displaced Persons from former West Pakistan – Receipts forming part of the Compensation Pool – Receipts on account of

Acquired Evacuee Properties adjustable by the Deputy Controller of Accounts (Rehabilitation), New Delhi.

10. The sanction issues with the concurrence of the Finance Branch *vide* their U.O. No. 2510/Fin./82, dated 2.9.1982.

Yours faithfully,

SJ/-
(M.L. KANSAL)
Under Secretary to the
Govt. of India
Tel : - 381540.

ANNEXURE 'A'

DETAILS OF LANDS IN VARIOUS REHABILITATION COLONIES ALREADY SURVEYED

DEVELOPED LANDS

Sl. No.	*Name of Colony*	*Total No. of Plots/Pockets*	*Total Area in Square yds.*
1.	Jangpura A, B, and Ext.	29 plots, 17/46 pocket	37274
2.	Defence Colony	13 plots, 11/24 pockets	52205
3.	Nizamuddin (East and West)	8 plots, 6/14 pockets	30345
4.	Lajpat Nagar I and II	12 plots, 1/13 pockets	3182
5.	Vinoba Puri	21 plots	14445
6.	Lajpat Nagar IV	8 plots, 10/18 pockets	100733
7.	Lajpat Nagar V	2 pockets	29739
8.	Khanna Market	2 pockets	6388
9.	Aliganj	14 pockets	5499
10.	Kalkaji	88 plots, 10/98 pockets	162427
11.	Ramesh Nagar	36 plots, 11/47 pockets	38776
12.	Tilak Nagar	1 plot, 9/10 pockets	120772
13.	Tihar – I	19 pockets	24801
14.	Tihar – II	2 plots, 15/17 pockets	18125
15.	Moti Nagar	9 pockets	51800
16.	Industrial Area Kirti Nagar	2 pockets	4908
17.	Patel Nagar (East South and West)	4 plots, 21/25 pockets	32457
18.	Old Rajinder Nagar	6 pockets	9633
19.	New Rajinder Nagar	16 plots, 12/28 pockets	81325
20.	Malka Ganj	4 pockets	9856
21.	Vijay Nagar (single storey)	4 pockets	8608
22.	Vijay Nagar (double storey)	6 pockets	2633
23.	Hakikat Nagar	7 pockets	4146
24.	Shahdara (Kasturba Nagar)	8 pockets	39031
25.	Andha Mughal	9 pockets	7263
26.	Gulabi Bagh	1 pocket	1179
27.	Mall Road	1 pocket	764
28.	Motia Khan	3 pockets	164
29.	Bharat Nagar	8 pockets	8897
30.	Indira Nagar	5 pockets	5891
31.	Malviya Nagar	18 plots	12280
	Total	256 plots, 233/489 pockets	9,25,552 or 191.23 acres

UNDEVELOPED LANDS

Sl. No.	*Name of Locality*	*Total land area in Acres*
1.	Jangpura A, B and Ext.	13.58
2.	Defence Colony	3.48
3.	Lajpat Nagar I and II	17.10
4.	Lajpat Nagr V	19.85
5.	Tihar – I	5.82
6.	Tihar – II	10.40
7.	Industrial Area Kirti Nagar	51.05
8.	Patel Nagar (East, West and South)	10.40
9.	Kalkaji	84.32
10.	Malviya Nagar	216.21
	Total	432.21 acres

ANNEXURE 'B'

DETAILS OF LANDS IN REHABILITATION COLONIES NOT YET SURVEYED

DEVELOPED LANDS

Sl. No.	*Name of Colony*	*Total No. of Plots/pockets*	*Total Area in sq. yds*
1.	Gandhi Nagar	366 plots	37100
2.	Gur Ki Mandi	4 plots, 1/5 pockets	2117
3.	Narela	14 plots	7567
4.	Sarai Rohilla	4 plots	673
5.	Chitranjan Park	6 pockets	75020
	Total	388 plots 7 pockets 395	1,22,477

UNDEVELOPED LANDS

Sl. No.	*Name of the Colony*	*Total Land Area in Acres*
1.	Gandhi Nagar (Jhil Khuranja)	97.60
2.	Gur ki Mandi	4.00
3.	Sarai Rohilla	6.96
4.	Narela	44.75
		153.31

URBAN VILLAGES

Sl. No.	*Name of the Villages within Urban Or Urbanized limit in Delhi*	*Approximate in Acres*
I.	Lado Sarai (Pulpehlad)	45

II. Trans-Jamuna Area Villages

Sl. No.	*Name of Village*	*Approximate Area*		*No. of Kh.*
		Bighas	*Biswas*	
1.	Chadrawali *alias*-Shahdara	392	02	18
2.	Seelampur	12	04	05
3.	Khureji-Khas	228	02	98
4.	Uldhanpur	40	03	35
5.	Saqdarpur	173	12	66
		816	23	222

OR: - 176 Acres.
The above figures are subject to physical verification.

ANNEXURE 'C'

DETAILS OF LAND RETAINED BY THE DEPARTMENT OF REHABILITATION BEING COMMITTED CASES

1. Malviya Nagar Colony — **Lands transferred to Rehabilitation Ministry Employees Co-operative House Building Society Limited.**

Name of the Village	*Khasra Numbers*
Sarai Sahji	220/74; 76-min; 80,81,82-min, 139/84; 88; 89; 90; 91; 92-min, 5, 96, 97-min, 98-min, 173/99-min, 174/99, 176/100, 177/100, 101/min; 154/102-min; 141/84, 140/84, 155/102-min, 103-min, 93.
Begumpur	361/171, 362/171-172/1; 362/171/2; 360/170-171; 359/170/1; 359/170/2, 165, 168, 169, 167, 174, 179/1, 179/2, 180, 182, 352/181, 351/181, 185, 186, 187, 188, 189, 453/192, 452/192, 191, 190, 193, 442/348/178/1, 443/348/178/1, 443/348/179-min; 196-min, 194; 302/287/209, 303/287/209; 207, 205, 297/208, 298/208, 288/209, 347/148, 363/172/1, 166, 312/210, 313/210, 314/210, 211, 334/206, 336/206, 364/172, 154-min, 156-min, 163, 164, 183, 371 to 374/2127, 216, 215, 220, 214, 408/213, 409/213, 308/212 and 225.
Village Patti Hamid Sarai	182 to 187/2-min, 1, 12, 15, 13-min, 11-min, 10, 29-min, 61; 128-129/62, 67, 68, 69, 64, 71, 72, 73, 74, 126/70-min, 27/70-min; 75-min; 76, 7-min, 78, 79, 80, 81, 14, 5, 82, 65, 143/134/66, 163/135/66, 180/137/3, 4/27, 165/6-7, 167/22-25 and 166/16-21.
	Total Land Area: 60 Acres
Kalkaji Colony	Land opposite to Delhi Administration Flats near Cycle Equipment Company.
	Area 10.25 acres.

Basai Darapur (Najafgarh Road)	Urban land Khasra No. 3148/2039/981 under litigation……. Area 2.5 acres.
Malviya Nagar (Khirki Village)	About 78 acres (under litigation) – appeal filed by Deptt. of Rehabilitation is pending in High Court.

ANNEXURE 9/3

GAZETTE NOTIFICATON NO. S.O.1810 DATED 20.7.74 REGARDING PLACING OF CERTAIN NAZUL LANDS AT THE DISPOSAL OF DDA

GOVERNMENT OF INDIA
MISINTRY OF WORKS and HOUSING
(NIRMAN AUR NIWAS MANTRALAYA)

NEW DELHI, THE 12th JULY 1974

NOTIFICATION

Whereas terms and conditions upon which Nazul Lands specified in the Table below will be taken-over by the Delhi Development Authority have been agreed upon between the Central Government and that Authority.

Now therefore, in exercise of the powers conferred by sub section (1) of Section 22 of the Delhi Development Act, 1957 (61 of 1957)the Central Government hereby please with immediate effect, the Nazul Lands specified in the Table below at the disposal of the Delhi Development Authority for the purpose of development and maintenance of the said lands as green and for taking such steps as may be required to serve the said purpose subject to the condition that the Delhi Development Authority shall not make or cause or permit to be made any construction on the said lands and shall when required by the Central Government so to do, replace the said lands or any portion thereof as may be so required at disposal of the Central Government.

THE TABLE

Sl. No.	Location	Area	Schedule of Boundary
1.	Original Road and Faiz Road	0.655 acre (Approx)	North by allotted to Director of Education Delhi Admn. Youth Center and Library South by allotted for Maratha Mitra Mandal, East by Jhandewalan Reservoirs West by Parking.
2.	Jagan Nath Temple Site Opp. Shanti Van	0.54 acre (Approx)	North by city wall South by Bela Road. East by Delhi Admn. Playgrounds West by Elgin Road.
3.	Triangular Plot on Todar Mal Road.	0.05 acre (Approx)	North by Service Road. South by Todar Mal Road. East by Road. West by Plot No. 85.
4.	At the junction of Todar Mal Road and Bazaar	0.44 acre (Approx)	North by plot No. 69-A. West by Bazaar Road East by Todar Mal Road.South by Todar Mal Road
5.	At the junction of Jan Path and Ashoka Road	4.9 acres (Approx)	North by Service Road, South by Ashoka Road, East by Janpath Road, West by Service Road .
6.	Vacant Area (Graveyard) Behind 4 and 6 Curzon Road and 2 and 4 Hailey Road	0.4396 acres (Approx)	East by Service Road. South by Plot No. 19 North West by Plot No. 19 and 20.
7.	Vacant Area Extn. ex of Dip. Enclave	127.406 acres	North by British Road and South by New Railway Boundary East by Chandra Gupta Marg, West by Road.
8.	Vacant area between Rly. and Philippine Embassy	0.344 acre	North by Chandra Guprta Marg, South by New Railway Boundary, East by Chandra Gupta Marg, West by Road.
9.	Vacant area between Bapu Dham and Def. Officer Flats	7.983 acres	North-East by Sweeper Quarters and 1 B's Training School and Staff Quarters. West by Defence Officers Flats. East by Road South by Defence Officers Flats,
10.	Vacant area at the Junction of Sardar Patel Road and Ring Road	13.0 acres	North-East by Railway land North-West by Sardar Patel Road, South-East by Land allotted to Ministry of Defence for Play Ground South West by Ring Road.
11.	Vacant Area between Moti Bagh-I and Military T.P.T	11.4 acres	North by Government Land South by Road

Sl. No.	Location	Area	Schedule of Boundary
	Company		North-east by Govt., Land North-West by Road.
12.	Vacant area of Nanakpura	18.00 acres	North by Service Road, South by Govt. Qrs. Madarasi Higher School and Middle School East by Road and Water Tank West by Road.
13.	Vacant area in University Enclave Dhaula Kuan	35.00 acres	North by Govt. Land, South by Road and DMC Park & Spring Dales School, East by College, West by Govt. Land and Ram Lal Anand College.
14.	Vacant area between Chanakyapuri I Railway Line towards Safdurjung Aerodrome	1.00 acre	North by Road, South by Railway Land, East by Road. West by Railway Quarters
15.	Pillanji Village (Sarojini Nagar)	5.92 acres	North by Government Qrs, South by Edge of Qushak Nallah, East by Road. West by Govt. Qrs.
16.	Area of Service Road Behind Press plots Mathura road	0.42 acre (1) 1880 sq. ft	North by Service Road, South by Service Road, East by Mohdn. Cemetry, West by Service Road.
		(2) 8440 sq. ft.	North by Service Road, South by Service Road, East by Mohdn. Cemetry, West by Service Road.
		(3) 2488 sq. ft.	North by Service Road, South by Service Road, East by Service Road, West by Pearey Bhawan (Plot No. 1 and 2)
		(4) 300 sq. ft.	North by Pearey Bhawan (Plot No. 1 and 2) South by Service Road, East by Service Road, West by Service Road.
		(5) 1232 sq. ft.	North by Service Road, South by Pratap (Plot No. 5), East by Service Road, West by Approach Road.
		(6) 1280 sq. ft.	North by Service Road, South by Milap (Plot No. 8-A), East by Service Road. West by Approach Road
17.	Area between Nallah and	10.00 acres	North by Government Land,

Sl. No.	*Location*	*Area*	*Schedule of Boundary*
	Laxmibai Nagar		South by Nallah, East by Government Land West by Nallah.
18.	Area between Nallah and West Kidwai Nagar	5.00 acres	North by Storm Water Drain, South by Government Land, East by Road, West by Government Land,
19.	Vacant area opp. Defence Colony and Kasturba Nagar	0.35 acre	North by Road, South by Government Land, East by Road, West by Government Land
20.	Vacant area in P.K. Puram Sector-XIII near UP Samaj	2.666 acres	North by Road, South by Road, East by Road, West by Road.
21.	Vacant area at the South Periphery Road Sector-VI R.K. Puram	3.7 acres	North by Service Road, South by Road, East by Primary School, West by Road,
22.	Rocky area between Sector-III and IV R.K. Puram	21.00 acres	North Govt. Land South by Southern Periphery Road, East by Government Land, Children Park and West by Govt. Land and Nallah and Horticulture Nursery.
23.	Vacant area in Sector-V R.K. Puram	1.492 acres	North by Road, South by Road, East by Road, West by Road,
24.	Vacant area in Sector-III R.K. Puram along Nallah	0.5 acres	North East by Road, Northwest by Tot Lot, South East by Play-round South-west by Nallah.
25.	Vacant area in Sector-III R.K. Puram, along Nallah	0.90 acre	North by Nallah, South by Service Road, East by Service Road, West by Service Road.
26.	Area at the crossing of Link Road and towards Ring Road Defence Colony	2.864 acres	North by Road, South by Road, East by Road, North West by Road.
27.	Vacant land near Pumping Station at Najafgarh Nallah	14.287 acres	North by Military Parade and Pumping Station, South by Private Land. East by Najafgarh Drain, West by Private Land,
28.	Along Najafgarh Nallah and	2.00 acres	North by Poultry Farm,

Sl. No.	*Location*	*Area*	*Schedule of Boundary*
	Hakikat Nagar		South by Mall Road, East by Najafgarh Nallah, West by DMC School and Quarters.
29.	At the crossing of Princess Road and Karnal Road	2.3 acres	North by Nallah 16' Wide South by Karnal Road East by C.Wall of T.B. Hospital, West by Princess Road
30.	Near Model Town at Karnal Road	3.044 acres	North East by Model Town, North west by Model Town, South East by Area Occupied by M/s EDW Keventers. Sout- west by Karnal Road.
31.	Near Burma Sheall Petrol Pump at Alipur Road	0.2 acre	North by Metcalfe Road. South by u/a DDA Shops, East by Road. West by Land Allotted to Delhi Admn. for Taxi Stand.
32.	At the back of Bal Bharti School and D.A.V. School Lodi Road	2.00 acres	North by I.A.F. barracks, South by Road, East by Institutional Area West by Gujranwala Arya H.S. School
33.	Between Nallah Link Road and Nizamuddin West	9.00 acres	North East by Nallah, South eats by Nallah, West by Link Road.
34.	Between C. Power Station and Jamuna Bridge	3.903 acres	North by Barrage , South by D.E.S.U, East by Railway Boundary West by Ring Road and proposed for Police Post.
35.	Between C. Power and Nallah	3.18 acres	North by Security Police South by Nallah East by Railway Line West by National High Way.
36.	Between Oberoi Hotel and Blind Institute	2.762 acres	North by Oberoi Hotel, South by Blind Institute, East by Kitchloo Marg, West by Golf Links Area
37.	At the back of Police Station Andrews Ganj	1.652 acres	North by Police Station, South by Road, East by 150 Wide Road West by Nallah.
38.	Behind Lodi Hotel	1.10 acres	North by Road, South by Nallah, East by allotted site for Hostel,

Sl. No.	*Location*	*Area*	*Schedule of Boundary*
			West by crossing of Nallah and Road.
39.	Between Housing Factory and Railway Crossing	7.818 acres	**Schedule of 1.548 acres** North by Railway Land South by Crossing of Road and Railway Land East by Railway Land, West by Road. **Schedule of 6.27 Acres** North by Railway Land, South by Crossing of Railway Land and Prefabricating Housing Factory Area, East by Road, West by Prefabricating Housing Factory.
40.	In Nehru Nagar	10.325 acres	**Schedule of Site No. A** North East by Road, North-West by Dev. Samaj, School-South East by Road, South-west by T.B. Clinic, **Schedule of Site No. B** North-east by Joint Water Sewage Board, North-west by Govt. Land and Sewer Line, South-east by Road and DDA Land, South-west by Land for H.H. Factory.
41.	Bhoori Bhatyari Area	7.00 acres	North-east by Road, North-west by Road, South-east by Road, South-west by Road.
42.	Kitchner Road in Diplomatic Enclave	3.5 acres	North by Road, South by Nallah; East by Road, West by Ashoka Hotel.
43.	Near Ashoka Hotel	3.195 acres	North by Kautalaya Marg, South by Panchsheel Marg, East by Road. West by Ashoka Hotel.
44.	Between Railway Line and Laxmibai Nagar	8.166 acres	North by Railway Boundary, South by Bridgadier Hoshiar, Singh Road, East by Qutab Road, West by Nallah.
45.	Along NDMC Market Chanakyapuri	18.0 acres	North by NDMC Shopping Centre, South by Railway Boundary,

Sl. No.	*Location*	*Area*	*Schedule of Boundary*
			East by Vinay Marg, West by Road.
46.	Along Nallah between Aerodrome and Vinay Marg	18.0 acres	North by Govt. Land, South by Govt. Land, East by Kautalaya Marg, West by Central Sect. Staff Playground.
47.	At the back of INA Colony and Market	55.259 acres	North by Road, South by Road, East by Round-about, West by Mehrauli Road.
48.	In Golf Links Colony	0.674 acre	Plot No. 67 North by NDMC ESS Staff Quarters, South by NDMC CW Center Site, East by Road, Plot No. 69 North by Road, South by Plot No.70 and Service Road, East by Road, West by Road.
49.	Between Staff Plots and Security Quarters at Kautalaya Marg.	1.147 acres	North by Temple, South-east by Proposed Service Road, South-West by Kautalaya Marg.
50.	By the side of India International Center on Circular Road at Diplomatic Enclave.	1.651 acres	North by Govt. Land South by Road, East by World Assembly for Youth West by Government Bungalows
51.	Pinjra Pole Society at the back of Andrews Ganj.	75.494 acres	North-east by Andrews Ganj, North-west by Road 100' Wide South-east by Nallah, South-west by Govt. Land
52.	Along DTC Building at Ring Road	946 acres	North by DTC Building, South by Railway Line, East by National Highway, West by Railway Land.
53.	Near Munirka	27.2 acres	**Schedule of Portion (A)** North by Govt. Land, South by Govt. Land, East by Govt. Land, West by Govt. Land, **Schedule of Portion (B)** North by Road, South by Govt. Land, East by Road, West by Govt. Land,
54.	Near Rajghat	7.866 acres	North by a Power House South by Proposed Road

Sl. No.	*Location*	*Area*	*Schedule of Boundary*
			East by Jamuna River West by Gandhi Samarak.
55.	Behind P and T on Ring Road	4.00 acres	North by Govt. Land South by Matcalfe Nallah Road East Govt. Land West by Service Road
56.	At the Junction of Rajpur Road near Alipur	0.30 acre and 0.44 acre	**No. 1** North by Road. South by Govt. Land. East by Alipur Road. West by Road. **No. 2** North by Junction of Alipur, Road and Rajpur Road, South by MCC Health Laboratory, East by Alipur Road, West by Rajpur Road.
57.	Behind Khyber Pass	2.00 acres	North by Govt. Land, South Service Road, East by Govt. Land, West by Govt. Land,
58.	Near Grid Station	4.48 acre	**Schedule of (A)** North by Kacha Path 17' Wide, South by Grid Station, East by Kacha Path 17', West by Khyber Pass Market and Delhi Admn. Bungalows. **Schedule of (B)** North by Quarters, South by Kacha Path 17' wide, East by Chandrawal Water Works West by Kacha Path17' wide
59.	Between Magazine Road, Timarpur	128 acres	North by Govt. Land, South by Khyber Pass Market, East by Yamuna River, West by Timarpur.
60.	On Lucknow Road	4.828 acres	North by Defence Land, South by Govt. Land, West by Govt. Land. East by Lucknow Road
61.	Near DTC Shed Coronation Road	15.737 acres	North by Private Land, South by DTC Workshop, East by Najafgarh Drain, West by Coronation Road.
62.	Near Gora Cemetery	0.75 acres	North by Road, South by Cemetery, East by Post-graduate Student

Sl. No.	Location	Area	Schedule of Boundary
			Hostel West by Govt. Land
63.	Near T.B. Hospital	0.9 acres	North by Vacant Land under Cultivation, South by Nallah 16-0' Wide East by Govt. Land, West by Princess Road.
64.	Site Lying near NAC Hospital	3.00 acres	Northy NAC Store and Cooperative Society Land, South by Delhi Admn. Quarters East by MCD Qrs. and IOC Petrol Pump and Mall Road West by NAC Store and Delhi Admn. Qrs.
65.	Between Hill Road and Ludlow Castle Road	17.00 acres	North by under Hill Road South by Ludlow Castle Road East by Private Bungalows West by Private Bungalows.
66.	Malkaganj Graveyard	6.00 acres	North by Service Road, South by Mohamdan Graveyard, East by Government Land, West by Road,
67.	Near ESSO Petrol Pump At Alipur Road	0.5 acres	North by Govt. Land and Shop South by Road, East by Road, West by Nicholson Cemetery
68.	Near School Old Police Line	0.27 acres	North by Police Line, South by Road, East by Road, West by Petrol Pump.
69.	Behind Gokhle Market	7.395 acres	North by Road, South by Road, East by Road and Residential Area. West by Road
70.	Hotel site near Railway Crossing at Kitcher Road	6.00 acres	North-east by Road, North-west by Kircher Road, South-east by Defence Land, South-west by Railway Line.

(Sd/-)
(S. CHOUDHARI)
Jt. Secretary to the Govt. of India

To be published in Part-II, Section-3
Sub-section (II) of the Gazette of India

GOVERNMENT OF INDIA MINISTRY OF WORKS AND HOUSING (NIRMAN AUR AWAS MANTRALAYA)

NEW DELHI, Dated the 21st August 1975

NOTIFICATION

No. S.O. 4719 whereas the terms and condition upon which Nazul Lands specified in the Table below will be taken-over by the DDA have been agreed upon between the Central Government and the Authority.

Now, therefore in exercise of the powers conferred by Sub-section (i) of Section 22 of the Delhi Development Act, 1957 (61 of 1957) the Central Government hereby places, with immediate affect, the Nazul Lands specified in the Table below at the disposal of the Delhi Development Authority for the purpose of development and maintenance of the said lands as green and for taking such steps as may be required to serve the said purpose subject to the condition that the D.D.A. shall not make, or clues of permit to be made, any construction on the said lands and shall when required by the Central Government. So to do replace the said lands or any portion thereof as may be so required at the disposal of the Central Government.

THE TABLE

Sl. No.	*Location*	*Area*	*Schedule of Boundary*
1.	Area near NDMC primary school and storm water drain, Kasturba Nagar	0.273 acre	North by Road, South by Road, East by Road, West by Road,
2.	Area near NDMC primary school and storm water drain, Kasturba Nagar	0.084 acre	North by Railway Land, South by Road, East by Road, West by Nallah,
3.	Area adjacent Ramjas College Society towards West at Junction of Poorvi Marg	2.941 acre	North by Pusa Road, South by Govt. Land, East by Ramjas College and Govt. Land. West by Poorvi Marg.
4.	Area around Humayun Tomb	20,981 acres	North by Sunder Nursery, South by Humayun Tomb, East by Railway Land, West by Mathura Road.
5.	Area back of Humayun Tomb near Gurudwara Dam Dama Sahib	3.528 acres	North by Gurudwara Dam Dama Sahib, South by Govt. Land, East by Railway Land, West by Humayun Tomb.
6.	Area of National Rifle Association	95.7 acres	North by Reserved Forest, South by Cantonment Land, East by Reserved Forest, West by Cantonment Land.
7.	Whole wide strip of land adjacent to 30 wide at to from back of Cambridge School to Arya Samaj Temple near L shape market (Sriniwaspuri)	3.68 acres	North by Cambridge School, South by Private Colony, East by 'H' Block, West by Nalah.
8.	Area 'L' shape market, JJ Colony, Sriniwaspuri	1.06 acres	North by Road, South by Road, East by Road, West by Nallah.
9.	Area opposite enquiry office Sriniwaspuri	0.444 acre	North by Road, South by Road, East by Road, West by Nallah.
10.	Area by the side of Child Welfare Centre, Sriniwaspuri	0.6 acre	North by Road, South by Child Welfare Centre, East by Road, West by D/S Quarters.

Sl. No.	Location	Area	Schedule of Boundary
11.	Area opp. S Quarters, Low Income Group originally proposed as Dhobi Ghat at Cattle Byre Site (Sriniwaspuri)	8.343 acres	North by Road, South by Nallah Land, West by Nallah, East by Govt. Land
12.	Area originally proposed for 3 fuel depots by side of Nallah, Sriniwaspuri (in two places)	A-19.0 sq.yds B-442.0 sq.yds 641.0 sq. yds	"A" – North by Road. South by Road, East by Road, West by Road, "B"- As 'A' same schedule.
13.	Triangular piece of land adjacent to Nallah at the back of Higher Sec. School, Sriniwaspuri	0.713 acre	North by S. Lane, South by S. Lane, East by Road, West by Nallah.
14.	Triangular piece of land adjacent to Nallah at the end of JJ Colony towards Rly. Line	0.7 acres	North by JJ Quarters, South by Private Colony, East by Railway Line, West by JJ Quarters
15.	Site as marked for memorial park at Circular Road (N.A.C. Area)	18.8 acres	North by Memorial Park, South by Road, East by Road, West by Road,
16.	Site between built up quarter along Bridgadier Hoshiar Singh Road and Rly. Land Boundary Sarojini Nagar	10.0 acres	North by Rly. Land, South by Govt. Quarters, East by Nallah, West by Road.
17.	Site by the side of Gwalior Pottery, Sarojini Nagar	95.0 sq. yds	North by Road, South by Gwalior Pottery, East by Primary School, West by Road.
18.	Area lying behind NDMC School in 'B' Block, Sarojini Nagar	0.325 sq. yds.	North by Road, South by Road, East by Road. West by Road,
19.	Site occupying by the Khalsa School near Children Welfare Center, Sarojini Nagar	0.75 acre	North by Road, South by Road, East by Road, West by Road.
20.	Area along Nallah and build up quarters 'B' Avenue to Pillanji Village.	5.00 acres	North by Pillanji Village, South by Nallah, East by Nallah, West by Govt. Land.
21.	Site at Ring Road along Nallah, Netaji Nagar	5.00 acres	North by Road, South by Ring Road and Petrol Pump,

Sl. No.	Location	Area	Schedule of Boundary
			East by Road, West by Govt. Land.
22.	Area allotted to Navyug School, NDMC but partly unauthorized occupied by Arya Samaj Temple in Netaji Nagar	2.413 acre	North by Boys Hr. Sec. School, South by Road, East by Road, West by Road.
23.	Site between Women's College and Cement godown wall occupied by Paramount School, Netaji Nagar	0.756 acre	North by CPWD Store, South by Girls Hr. Sec. School, East by Road, West by Govt. Land.
24.	Site Near C.G.H.S. Dispensary, Netaji Nagar	300 sq. yds.	North by Road, South by Road, East by Road, West by Road.
25.	Area behind NDMC School pilot project near Moti Bagh–I	10.00 acre	North by Railway Line, South by Staff Quarter, East by NDMC School and Personnel Quarters, West by District Park
26.	Area between Bidhan Chandra Vidyalaya and Ring Road, R.K. Puram Sector-XIII	0.40 acre	North by Bidhan Chandra Vidyalaya, South by Ring Road, East by Govt. Quarters, West by Road.
27.	Area allotted to CGHS Dispensary but u/a occupied by quarters, R.K. Puram Sector-XIII	0.685 acre	North by Govt. Land, South by Road, East by Road, West by CGHS and Playground
28.	Area near CGHS occupied by u/a Gurudwara and area allotted for 3 Tennis Courts and a Club in R.K. Puram	2.00 acres	North by Road, South by Road, East by Road, West by Road,
29.	Area allotted to U.P. Samaj for Primary School R.K. Puram	2.724 acres	North by Road. South by Road and U.P. Samaj Temple, East by Road, West by Road and U.P. Samaj Temple.
30.	Plot No. 34 in Diplomatic Enclave	4360 sq. yds.	North by Road, South by Road, East by Faridkot House, (plot No. 35), West by Pataudi House (plot No. 33).
31.	Plot No. 18 in Diplomatic Enclave	3430 sq. yds.	North by plot No. 17, South by S. Road, East by S. Road, West by Approach Road.

Sl. No.	Location	Area	Schedule of Boundary
32.	Nallah in side of Keventer Dairy, Diplomatic Enclave	41.45 acres	North by Nallah, South by Railway Land, East by Aerodrome, Race Course , Govt. Quarters, West by Keventer Dairy Kautliya Marg
33.	Open space in the side of Convent School, Diplomatic Enclave	1.25 acres	North by Road South by Road East by Road West by Road
34.	Site near Ghana Embassy, Diplomatic Enclave	3.5 acres	North by Road, South by Road, East by Road, West by Road.
35.	Site near Malaya Embassy, Diplomatic Enclave	3.5 acres	North by Road, South by Road, East by Road, West by Road.
36.	Area of Shah Kamal Mosque DIZ Area, Gole Market	1000 sq. yds.	North by Road, South by Road, East by Road, West by Road.
37.	Site on Mandir Marg adjoining Kali Bari DIZ Area	400 sq. yds.	North by Govt. Land, South by Road, East by Road, West by Quarter No. 1.
38.	Site on Mandir Marg adjoining Kali Bari DIZ Area	200 sq. yds.	North by Govt. Land, South by Govt. Land, East by Road. West by Govt. Land,
39.	Mandir Marg near Govt. Built Quarter	1500 sq. yds.	North by Govt. Land, South by Govt. Land, East by Road. West by Govt. Quarter,
40.	Site opposite Kali Bari	600 sq. yds.	North by Govt. Land, South by Road, East by Govt. Quarters, West by Mandir Marg.
41.	Area near Rocky Area Nanak Pura (Shashti Market)	6.0 acres	North by Ring Road, South by Land Transferred to DDA, East by Road, West by Road.
42.	Rocky Area, Nanakpura	3.5 acres	North by Govt. Land, South by Road,

Sl. No.	Location	Area	Schedule of Boundary
			East by Govt. Quarters, West by Govt. Quarters.
43.	DMC School site; Nanakpura	0.50 acre	North by Govt. Land, South by Govt. Land, East by Govt. Land, West by Govt. Land,
44.	Lawn in Nanakpura	0.75 acre	North by Road, South by Govt. Land, East by Govt. Quarters, West by Govt. Quarters.
45.	Lawn in Nanakpura	0.2 acre	North by Road, South by Govt. Land, East by Govt. Land, West by Govt. Land.
46.	Dispensary Site, Nauroji Nagar	0.34 acre	North by Road, South by Road, East by Road, West by Road.
47.	Unauthorized Gurudwara Site, Nauroji Nagar	0.2 acre	North by Road, South by Road, East by Road, West by Road.
48.	Gahi Mandu Area (Sherpur and Saudetpur)	1350 acre	North by Govt. Land, South by River Jamuna No. Govt. Land, East by Govt. Land, West by Govt. Land.
49.	Dhobi Ghat site on Ring Road, Nauroji Nagar	0.206 acre	North by Ring Road, South by Nallah, East by Nallah, West by Road.
50.	Vacant area near Primary School in Sector-I, R.K. Puram	1.518 acres	North by Road, South by Road, East by Road, West by Community Centre.
51.	Area near Central School R.K. Puram	0.5 acre	North by Road, South by Road, East by Church, West by Central School.
52.	Land south of Mohammed Pur	8.80 acre	North by Proposed , South by Road, East by Road, West by Road.
53.	Site adjoining Central School R.K. Puram	1.75 acres	North by Central School, South by Road,

Sl. No.	Location	Area	Schedule of Boundary
			East by Nallah, West by Road.
54.	Undeveloped land adjoining Nallah opp. Central School, R. K. Puram	1.5 acres	North by Nallah, South by Govt. Quarters, East by Govt. Quarters, West by Govt. Land.
55.	Site for K.C. School in R.K. Puram	1413 sq. yds.	North by Road, South by Road, East by Road, West by Road.
56.	Library Site, R.K. Puram Sector- II	1.355 acres	North by H.S. School, South by Road, East by Road and Govt. Quarters, West by Road.
57.	Land Near Govt. Offices Block-6, R.K.Puram	2.00 acres	North by Road, South by Road, East by Road, West by Road.
58.	Tot Lot in R.K.Puram, Sector-III	0.5 acre	North by Road, South by Road, East by Road, West by Road.
59.	Area around Monuments in Sector-III, R.K. Puram	1.42 acres	North by Road, South by Road, East by Road, West by Road.
60.	Area earmarked for Primary School, in Sector No. III R.K. Puram	2.25 acres	North by Nallah, South by Road, East by Road, West by Nallah.
61.	Park site, Sector-III, R.K. Puram	1.5 acres	North by Road, South by Road, East by Road, West by Nallah.
62.	Area earmarked for H.S. and Primary School in R.K. Puram	2.5 acres	North by Vanketeshwara Temple. South by Road, East by Road, West by Road.
63.	Rocky area and Vacant Land along Nallah	5.00 acres	North by Road, South by Road, East by land transferred to DDA, West by Road.

Sl. No.	*Location*	*Area*	*Schedule of Boundary*
64.	Site earmarked for CGHS Dispansary behind Police Station, R.K. Puram-IV	1.00 acre	North by Police Station, South by Govt. Quarter, East by Govt. Land, West by Road.
65.	Undeveloped Land earmarked for playground along Police Station, R.K.Puram-IV	2.00 acres	North by Road, South by School (Ramjas), East by Road, West by Police Station and Govt. Land.
66.	Site earmarked for NS-cum-R.C. in R.K. Puram	0.817 acre	North by Road, South by Road, East by Road, West by Road.
67.	Area around Monument in R. K. Puram	3.00 acres	North by Road, South by Road, East by Road, West by Road.
68.	N. School-cum-R.C. Behind Petrol Pump, R.K. Puram	0.853 acre	North by Road, South by Road, East by Road, West by Road.
69.	Site for community Centre in R.K. Puram	0.528 acre	North by Road, South by Road, East by Road, West by Road.
70.	CGHS Dispensary in Sector-VI, R.K.Puram	0.65 acre	North by Community Centre, South by Road, East by Road, West by Road.
71.	Four Religious sites in R.K. Puram-VII	1.5 acres	North by Road, South by Road, East by Road, West by Nallah.
72.	Unauthorized Temple site along Nallah in Sector-VI R.K. Puram	3.50 acres	North by Road, South by Road, East by H.S. School, West by Nallah.
73.	16.9 acres land allotted for sports centre	16.9 acres	North by Road, South by Road, East by Road, West by Road.
74.	Site for Playground in Sector-VIII R.K. Puram	1.5 acres	North by Road, South by Road, East by Road, West by Road.
75.	CGHS Dispensary and Maternity Center and Rocky	3.00 acres	North by Road, South by Post Office and H.S.

Sl. No.	Location	Area	Schedule of Boundary
	Area 2 acres (allotted for H.S.S. out of 5.316 acres area) R.K. Puram		School, East by Road, West by H.S. School.
76.	NUS-cum-R.C. School in R.K. Puram-VII	0.38 acres	North by Road, South by Road, East by Road, West by Road.
77.	NUS-cum-R.C. School in R.K. Puram-VII	2088 sq. yds	North by Road, South by Road, East by Road, West by Road.
78.	Site for Community Centre at R.K. Puram-VII	1.5 acres	North by Road, South by Road, East by Road, West by Road.
79.	Site for Park in R.K. Puram Sector-VII near Malai Temple	0.6 acres	North by Road, South by Road, East by Road, West by Road.
80.	Site for Park in R.K. Puram	0.6 acres	North by Road and Govt. Quarters, South by Road, East by Road, West by Road.
81.	Site for Play Ground in R.K. Puram	0.6 acres	North by Community Center, South by Road, East by Road, West by Road.
82.	Site for Community Center near Play Ground, R.K. Puram-VIII	2.00 acres	North by Road, South by Play Ground, East by Road, West by Road.
83.	Nursery School near Community Center at R.K. Puram-VIII	0.395 acres	North by Road, South by Road, East by Road, West y Road.
84.	Nursery School in R.K. Puram-VIII	0.3 acres	North by Road, South by Road, East by Road, West by Road.
85.	Park Opp. Hr. Sec. School at R.K. Puram-VIII	0.66 acres	North by Road, South by Road, East by Road, West by Road.
86.	Play Ground site in R.K. Puram-VIII	0.23 acre	North by Road, South by Road, East by Road, West by Road.

Sl. No.	Location	Area	Schedule of Boundary
87.	Park in R.K. Puram-VIII	0.118 acre	North by Road, South by Post Office, East by Road, West by Road.
88.	Play Ground site in R.K. Puram-VIII	0.35 acre	North by Road, South by Hr. Sec. School, East by Road, West by Road.
89.	Allotted Post Office site in R.K. Puram-IX	1787 sq. yds.	North by Road, South by Govt. Land, East by Road, West by Road.
90.	Institutional Area in R.K. Puram-IX	0.32 acre	North by Road, South by Road, East by Road, West by Community Centre.
91.	Community Centre Dispensary and Electric Sub-station at R.K. Puram-IX	1.5 acre	North by Road, South by Road, East by Institutional Area, West by Road.
92.	For Park and Taxi Stand at R.K. Puram	1.95 acre	North by Road, South by Road, East by Road, West by Road.
93.	Nursery School-cum-R. Center in R.K. Puram-IX	0.641 acre	North by Road, South by Road, East by Road, West by Road.
94.	Nursery School in R.K. Puram-IX	0.641 acre	North by Nallah, South by Govt. Quarters, East by Nallah, West by Road.
95.	Site for Play Ground in R.K. Puram-IX	1.3 acres	North by Road, South by Road, East by Road, West by Road.
96.	Park at R.K. Puram-IX	0.37 acre	North by Road, South by Road, East by Road, West by Road.
97.	C.V.T. Pool Housing for type-I quarters service personnels, Community Centers Primary School service personnel, by Roads 1.20 acres (approx.) in R.K. Puram-X	26.80 acres 1.20 acres 28.00 acres	North by Road, South by Play Ground and Dhobi Ghat, East by Road, West by Road.

Sl. No.	*Location*	*Area*	*Schedule of Boundary*
98.	Allotted Play-ground in R.K. Puram-X	26.25 acres	North by Road, South by Road, East by Govt. Offices, West by Dhobi Ghat and Govt. Land.
99.	Allotted Play-Ground near Police Station in R.K. Puram-XII	19.3 acres	North by Road, South by Road, East by Road, West by Road.
100.	Tot lot plot in R.K. Puram – XII	0.25 acre	North by Govt. Quarters, South by Govt. Quarters, East by Road, West by Rashtriya Bhashas. Parchar Samiti,
101.	Tot lot plot in R.K. Puram – XII	0.331 acre	North by Road, South by Road, East by Govt. Quarters, West by Govt. Quarters.
102.	Tot lot plot in R.K. Puram – XII near Nursery School	0.331 acre	North by Road, South by Road, East by Govt. Quarters, West by Govt. Quarters.
103.	Vacant land on Ring Road at R.K. Puram, New Delhi	0.35 acre	North by Road, South by Govt. Quarters, East by Ring Road, West by Road.
104.	Nursery School in R.K. Puram-XII	0.45 acre	North by Road, South by Road, East by Road, West by Road.
105.	Nursery School in R.K. Puram-XII	0.4 acre	North by Road, South by Road, East by Road, West by Road.
106.	Park and Library in R.K. Puram-XII	4.5 acres	North by Govt. Land, South by Road, East by Road, West by Road.
107.	Play Ground in R.K. Puram-XII	0.2 acre	North by Nursery School, South by Govt. Quarters, East by Road, West by Govt. Quarters.
108	Police Station and Staff Quarters in R.K. Puram-XII	3.526 acres	North by Road, South by Road, East by Govt. Quarters, West by Road.
109.	School site near Police	6.00 acres	North by St. Columbus School

Sl. No.	Location	Area	Schedule of Boundary
	Station, R.K. Puram-XII		and Delhi Public School, South by Road, East by Govt. Quarters, West by Road.
110.	Earmarked for Quarters on Ring Road, R.K. Puram-XII	3.00 acres	North by Road, South by Govt. Quarters, East by Road (Ring Road), West by Columbus School. earmarked for School,
111.	Site allotted to St. Columbus School at R.K. Puram-XII	6.749 acres	North by Road, South by land earmarked for School, East by Govt. Quarters, West in Delhi Public School and. CGHS Dispensary,
112.	Institutional Plots in R.K. Puram-XII	0.682 acre	North by Road, South by Road, East by Nagaland Guest House, West by Air India Guest House.
113.	Area was allotted for State Bank near Air India Guest House in R.K. Puram-XII	0.174 acre	North by Road, South by Road, East by Air India Guest House, West by Road.
114.	CGHS Dispensary and Taxi Stand, Sector-XII, R.K. Puram	0.801 acre 0.074 acre 0.875 acre	North by Road, South by St. Columbus,School, East by St. Columbus School, West by Road.
115.	Vacant area near Hr. Sec. School in R.K. Puram-IV	1.378 acres	North by Nallah, South by Road, East by Road, West by Govt. Hr. Sec. School.
116.	Budh Vihar Temple, R.K. Puram-III	14/3" X 11/-3" sq. yds.	North by Govt. Land, South by Govt. Land, East by Govt. Land, West by Govt. Land.
117.	Area behind Law Institute Tilak Marg	1.00 acre	North by Road, South by Road, East by Road, West by Road
118.	Plot behind (AGCR) Building	2000 sq. yds.	North by Road South by Road East by Road West by Road
119.	Piece of Land Bearing	58921 sq. yds.	*Part A*

Sl. No.	*Location*	*Area*	*Schedule of Boundary*
	Kahsra No. 1 to 6, 9, 277 to 279, 201, 202 measuring 50 bighas 10 biswas. Rajpur Village was leased out to one Sh. Radhey Sham and Sh. Sham Sunder (in two parts)		North by Govt. Land South by Govt. Land East by Govt. Land West by Govt. Land *Part-B* North by Road South by Govt. Land East by Road West by Govt. Land
120.	Taj Barracks at Janpath	2.599 acre	North by Kealing Road South by Telecommunication Building East by Service Land West by Janpath
121.	Area on Ring Road near Primary School pilot Project, New Moti Bagh-I	0.40 acres	North by Govt. Quarters South by Ring Road East by Road West by Primary School

Sd/-

(No. 1/21/68-LI) (Mir Nasrullah)

Joint Secretary to the Govt. of India

To,

The Manager
Govt. of India Press,
Ring Road, Maya Puri
Industrial Area,
New Delhi.

The Vice-Chairman, Delhi Development Authority (Sh. Jagmohan) New Delhi.

The terms and conditions as detailed in this Ministry's letter No. 1/21/68-LI) dated 17.8.1974, will apply to these lands as well.

Sd/-

(H.R. Nigam)

Under Secretary to the Govt. of India

ANNEXURE 9/5

Year-wise break up of land acquired and placed at the disposal of the DDA under Section 22 (i) of Delhi Development Act, 1957 by the Delhi Administration from April 1961 to March 2008 .

Sl. No.	Year	Area (in acres)	
1.	1961-62	258.45	
2.	1962-63	1748.64	
3.	1963-64	1619.84	
4.	1964-65	1740.90	
5.	1965-66	2406.72	
6.	1966-67	33.44	
7.	1967-68	6847.41	
8.	1968-69	349.45	
9.	1969-70	—	
10.	1970-71	—	
11.	1971-72	3040.66	
12.	1972-73	4574.12	
13.	1973-74	3802.15	
14.	1974-75	120.99	
15.	1975-76	1142.99	
16.	1976-77	465.71	
17.	1977-78	1459.32	
18.	1978-79	2220.90	
19.	1979-80	94.12	
20.	1980-81	8455.91	
21.	1981-82	4578.35	
22.	1982-83	1250.00	
23.	1983-84	1531.87	
24.	1984-85	636.59	
25.	1985-86	1161.05	
26.	1986-87	7342.07	
27.	1987-88	73.75	
28.	1988-89	104.88	
29.	1989-90	17.92	
30.	1990-91	8.68	
31.	1991-92	936.58	Including physical possession.
32.	1992-93	1468.68	-do-
33.	1993-94	31.44	+ 820.22 physical possession.
34.	1994-95	19.02	-do-
35.	1995-96	1127.57	Only physical possession.

Sl. No.	*Year*	*Area (in acres)*	
36.	1996-97	430.65	Only physical possession-
37.	1997-98	463.00	-do-
38.	1998-99	322.86	
39.	1999-2000	375.97	
40.	2000-2001	1683.80	
41.	2001-2002	473.25	
42.	2002-2003	2114.78	
43.	2003-2004	770.70	
45.	2004-2005	1781.92	
46.	2005-2006	3488.76	
47.	2006-2007	1932.58	
48.	2007-2008	1126.87	
	Total	75435.71	

ANNEXURE 9/6

GAZETTE NOTIFICATON No. S.O.2190 DATED 20.8.74 PUBLISHED ON 24.8.74 REGARDING TRANSFER OF GAON SABHA LANDS

PUBLISHED IN PART II, SECTION 3, SUB-SECTION (ii) OF THE GAZETTE OF INDIA OF SATURDAY, AUGUST, 24, 1974/BHADRA 2, 1896 ON PAGE 23334 (IN ENGLISH)

MINISTRY OF WORKS and HOUSING

New Delhi, the 20th
August, 1974.

S.O.2190— Whereas the terms and conditions upon which Nazul Lands specified in the Schedule annexed below will be taken over by the Delhi Development Authority have been agreed between the Central Government and the Authority.

Now, therefore, the exercise of the powers conferred by sub-section (i) of Section 22 of the Delhi Development Act, 1957 (61 of 1957), the Central Government hereby places, with immediate effect, the lands which had vested in the Central Government on the urbanization of the villages specified in the said schedule at the disposal of the Delhi Development Authority for the purpose of development and maintenance of the said lands as green and for taking such steps as may be required to serve the said purpose, subject to the conditions that the Delhi

Development Authority shall not make, or cause, of permit to be made any constructions on the said lands and shall when required by the Central Government so to do, replace the said lands or any portion hereof as may be so required, at the disposal of the Central Government.

Schedule

Sl. No.	*Name of the Village*	*Sl. No.*	*Name of the Village*
1.	Khureji Khas	25.	Ber Sarai
2.	Sadhora Kalan	26.	Katwaria Sarai
3.	Sadhora Khurd	27.	Madangir
4.	Chowkri Mobarkabad	28.	Badarpur
5.	Neemri	29.	Khan Pur
6.	Dhaka	30.	Tughlakabad
7.	Salim Pur Mazra Madipur	31.	Dhirpur
8.	Azadpur	32.	Bharola
9.	Shakurpur	33.	Peepal Thala
10.	Madipur	34.	Wazirpur
11.	Khiala	35.	Ghonda (4 parts)
12.	Keshopur	36.	Mouj Pur
13.	Basaidara Pur	37.	Karkardooma
14.	Najafgarh	38.	Seelampur
15.	Masudabad	39.	Ghondli
16.	Haibatpur	40.	Mandoli Fazalpur
17.	Mehrauli (Kishan Garh)	41.	Ghazipur
18.	Lado Sarai	42.	Khichri Pur
19.	Khirki	43.	Hasan Pur
20.	Budhela	44.	Shakarpur Khas
21.	Jasoala	45.	Saboli
22.	Madanpur Khadar	46.	Hastsal (Partly urbanized)
23.	Tehkhand	47.	Pitampura (Partly urbanized)
24.	Houz Rani	48.	Mangolpur Kalan (Partly urbanized)

GLOSSARY

1.	Shazra	:	Revenue Map of agricultural land.
2.	Khasra	:	Plot number in the revenue map.
3.	*Kaccha*	:	Stucture built with thatch etc.
4.	*Pucca*	:	Structure built with bricks and cement
5.	*Malba*	:	Waste Material.
6.	*Abadi*	:	Settlement.
7.	Chowkidar	:	Guard/Watchman.
8.	Masjid	:	Mosque.
9.	Kabristan	:	Muslim Burial Ground
10.	Gaon Sabha	:	Body constituted under the act to manage the village land.
11.	Khasra Girdawari	:	Statement of use of the agricultural land
12.	Goan Sabha Land	:	Common land of the village
13.	Jhuggi	:	Shelter generally made of thatch/ plastic roof or any very low cost material
14.	Jhuggi-Cluster	:	A cluster of very poor residential settlement
15.	Bund	:	Embankment
16.	Dharamshala	:	A common utility place for the community
17.	Samadhi	:	Hindu Graveyard

Index